PUTIN v. THE PEOPLE

SAMUEL A. GREENE AND GRAEME B. ROBERTSON

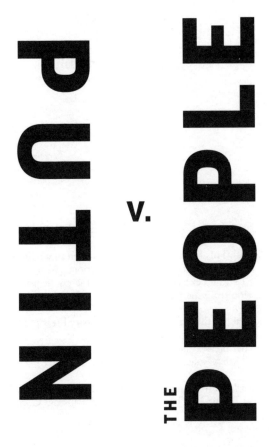

PUTIN

V.

THE PEOPLE

THE PERILOUS POLITICS OF A DIVIDED RUSSIA

YALE UNIVERSITY PRESS
NEW HAVEN AND LONDON

To Elyana and Anya
—SG

To Ceci, Tomás and Mili
—GR

For information about this and other Yale University Press publications, please contact:
U.S. Office: sales.press@yale.edu   yalebooks.com
Europe Office: sales@yaleup.co.uk   yalebooks.co.uk

Set in Adobe Caslon Pro Regular by IDSUK (DataConnection) Ltd
Printed in Great Britain by TJ International Ltd, Padstow, Cornwall

Library of Congress Control Number: 2019932772

ISBN 978-0-300-23839-6

A catalogue record for this book is available from the British Library.

10 9 8 7 6 5 4 3 2 1

CONTENTS

ACKNOWLEDGMENTS

We are grateful to the many people who have contributed to our thinking on the issues addressed in this book. Though too numerous to list individually, we greatly appreciate the insight and support of all of the colleagues, students and friends who continually challenge and shape our perspectives. We are particularly grateful to a number of people who gave selflessly of their time, reading and commenting in detail on this book as it took shape, including: Charles Clover, Maria Lipman, Cecilia Martinez-Gallardo, Peter McKellar, Silviya Nitsova, Sarah Oates, Roland Oliphant, Roberto Palacios, Gulnaz Sharafutdinova, Marat Shterin, Regina Smyth, Tim Walker, Jonathan Weiler and Ilya Yablokov. We are grateful to the Smith Richardson Foundation for financial support for the surveys on which much of this book is based. Special thanks go to Svetlana Koroleva and Alexei Levinson at the Levada Center, and to Elena Koneva, for helping to make our research possible. And a debt of gratitude is owed to the entire team at Yale University Press, for helping to turn an idea into a book. Much of what works in this volume is down to the generosity and goodwill of all these people and more. Whatever does not work, however, remains the exclusive responsibility of the authors.

ONE

THE PEOPLE AND VLADIMIR PUTIN

Vladimir Putin is a popular man. He is also a dictator. That is not a contradiction.

Putin has been the dominant figure in Russian politics since he first emerged on to the public stage twenty years ago. He has served fourteen years in his current job as president and another four as prime minister. He has survived economic booms and busts. He has led Russia through war and sanctions, through huge street protests and the horrors of terrorism. His power has rarely been challenged. Putin's presence has seemed inevitable, a fixed point in a changing world. As other political leaders have come and gone, Putin has remained.

How does he do it?

Being a dictator helps. The president of Russia sits at the top of a huge coercive machine dedicated to policing and controlling. Putin has used the vast power of the Russian state's repressive apparatus to intimidate would-be rivals and to expropriate, imprison or exile opponents. Other challengers have been even less fortunate. Some of those who were Putin's most vocal critics when we began this research did not survive to press day.

But focusing only on coercion and violence leaves us with an incomplete and misleading picture of Russian politics. Dictators, we generally assume, rule despite the masses, who, given the opportunity, would gladly kick them out of office. Although true in some places, this is hardly the case in Russia. Vladimir Putin's rule is not forced on an oppressed and unwilling public, but is jointly built—co-constructed—through a process of political struggle involving Putin, his opponents and tens of millions of supporters.

In this book, we chart Putin's rise from lowly KGB colonel to an extraordinary position in the politics of the country. He is not simply president: he is a rallying point for the nation and a synonym for the Russian state itself. Across the world, journalists and politicians ask themselves, not "what will the Russians do," but "what will Putin do?" In reality, however, it is impossible to answer these questions separately. Putin has been able to rise above the normal push and pull of politics not by force alone, but because he has been lifted up by millions of Russian people. They hold him aloft for a range of reasons, some personal, some material and some emotional. In this book, we explore those reasons, while also seeking to understand those who oppose Putin—and those who are indifferent. The result is a story of Russian politics that is quite different from the one you may be used to hearing.

The role of Russian society in building Putin's power— what we call the co-construction of Russian power—is most often overlooked in the shelves full of books about "Putin's Russia." But the focus on what Putin has done to Russia is misguided. We need to think not of Putin's

Russia, but of Russia's Putin. We need to understand that Putin is not above the country; he is *of* the country, of its politics, its society and its history. Instead of focusing on Putin himself, we need to think about Russia and its citizens, asking not only when the ruler might finally loosen his grip, but how and when the ruled might loosen theirs.

NATALYA AND MAXIM

Shortly before Putin was reelected in March 2018 we asked Natalya why she was planning to vote for him.[1]

Time after time in the interview, the 44-year-old receptionist in Yaroslavl—an ancient city of about half a million people, some 160 miles northeast of Moscow—prefaced her answers by claiming to be uninterested in politics, claiming not to know much, claiming to be a neophyte. "You should ask my husband," Natalya would say. "He knows about these things." But for all that, her political views were clear enough.

When we spoke, she recalled an incident just a couple of weeks earlier, waiting for an appointment at her local clinic.

"This woman was saying to her friend, 'How come everyone is voting for him?'" Natalya remembered. The "him," of course, was Putin. "And he [the friend] answered, 'Well, he increased their pensions by 30 rubles, and they all vote for him!'"

Natalya was aghast. To her, this was more than just cynicism: it was ingratitude. "Even if they're complaining about their pensions, they have children who are earning good money, who drive cars, and so on," Natalya explained.

"In my view, God forbid the opposition should come to power," she went on. "It would be chaos. . . . Let us continue developing, and let Putin be in power. We're developing. Gradually. And let there be less of all this democracy."

When we interviewed Maxim around the same time, one of the questions we asked him was whether he thought it was important for ordinary Russians—like the ones waiting in line at Natalya's clinic—to have the right to criticize those in power. In Russian, the word we used was *vlast*, most directly translated as "power" but often used loosely to refer to "the authorities." Like many Russians, Maxim—a 34-year-old product designer for a textile manu- facturer in St. Petersburg—associates the concept most closely with the president. And so, when we asked him whether he thought it was appropriate for people to criti- cize *vlast*, he was adamant.

"No, I think that's wrong," Maxim said. "No one should criticize *vlast*."

Why?

"Because, who are we?" he asked, rhetorically. "We don't have the kind of information that the people in power have. That's why we elect them, to manage everything."

Russians of all political stripes are fond of a particular adage—coined by the reactionary nineteenth-century French philosopher Joseph de Maistre—that "every people gets the government it deserves." When those Russians who would rather not live under Vladimir Putin bring up this quote, they have in mind people like Maxim and Natalya: people who not only support the president, but who seem to do so unquestioningly, as though Putin's power were part of the natural order of things and, as such, beyond criticism.

For Putin, Maxim and Natalya are in many ways ideal Russian citizens, not simply accepting his policies, but reinforcing his power by treating any criticism of him as illegitimate. By contrast, to many in the opposition Maxim and Natalya are walking caricatures of everything that is wrong with the country. But mockery in this case is misleading. In order to understand how Putin's power is built and how it is exercised, we need to know more about who holds these attitudes and why and how their attitudes affect others around them. When we do that, we start to understand the real relationship between the Russian people and their authoritarian state.

LISTENING TO THE PEOPLE

The idea that every nation gets the government it deserves is not one we would accept. In a single stroke, it reduces entire populations to a diagnosis, depriving individuals of the ability to make independent decisions or to see things in their own way. As social scientists, we prefer to start with the individual and then work our way up to an explanation of why both individuals and groups—whether communities or social movements, companies or nations—behave the way they do. From this perspective, the only fundamental difference between a Russian and an American is that one lives in Russia, and the other in the United States.

When it comes to studying countries like Russia, however, this approach—putting ordinary people at the center of our analysis—presents something of a challenge. Most discussion of Russian politics in the press focuses in one way or another on President Putin. Large looming photographs of the evil dictator and his latest machinations frequently adorn the front pages of newspapers like *The New York Times*, *The Economist* and *The Guardian*. If something sinister is afoot in Russia, or increasingly around the world, we should look for the hand of Vladimir Putin.

Interestingly, journalists' focus on Putin is often shared by social scientists. Much of the political science research on dictatorship (and there is quite a bit of it) focuses on elites and the environments they create. The emphasis is on how leaders manipulate politics and political institutions— parliaments, elections, courts, bureaucracies and the like— in order not just to marginalize the opposition, but to channel it in ways that are actually helpful to the regime. Academic bookshelves are full of examples of how autocrats have become increasingly sophisticated at coopting potential challengers and manipulating the information space, even as the internet has shattered their previous monopoly over the media. In short, the argument goes, dictatorship survives and even thrives because dictators themselves have become better at managing and shaping politics to stave off challenges.

There are problems with this account, however. In a world of imperfect information and ubiquitous unintended consequences, the picture of the cunning and indefatigable dictator asks a lot of the human beings who actually fill these posts. What's more, the conventional wisdom oversimplifies the relationship between the ruler and the ruled, supposing that it runs only in one direction: from the top down.

In this book, we look at authoritarian politics in Russia not only from the top down, but also from the bottom up—we explore Russia's Putin, rather than just Putin's Russia. We reject stereotypes and prejudice and present analysis based on solid evidence and proven social scientific methods. Our approach is systematic, drawing on the lessons of research conducted in Russia, but also elsewhere. Much of this research is groundbreaking, including the first systematic study of the role of personality psychology in Russian politics.

We listen to how ordinary Russians talk about themselves, their lives and their politics. We ask them about their political views and their economic welfare, as well as about their personalities and emotions. Do they like to blend in or stand out? Are they outgoing or anxious, detail-oriented or more interested in the big picture? Are they proud of Russia and its rulers, or ashamed and angry? Are they hopeful about the future? To this we add millions of lines of social-media data. What causes do they support, and how? What issues get them talking, and what leaves them cold? We take advantage of leaked internal documents to get a first-hand insight into how the Kremlin tries to manage the people and shape their views. The result is an entirely new perspective on Russian politics.

THE POLITICAL FOUNDATIONS OF PUTIN'S POWER

Vladimir Putin listens to the Russian people, too—and not only in the manner of the KGB. Rather, Putin takes his approval ratings very seriously and is an avid reader of opinion polls. Why would a man like Putin want to be popular, when he has the entire coercive apparatus at his disposal? For one thing, popularity is a crucial political resource, even for a dictator. After all, ruling by coercion is expensive and risky. In fact, many dictators fall precisely because they get the coercive calculus wrong, provoking a popular backlash so overwhelming that no amount of force will suffice to keep them in power. Putin knows that and so listens carefully—though perhaps not always carefully enough—to public opinion when making policy decisions. What's more, being the most popular politician in the country is critical for Putin in getting Russia's ruling class to follow his instructions and for discouraging potential challengers, whether from inside or outside the ruling elite. As a result, Putin finds it important not only to be popular, but to be the most popular man in the land.

Since it relies not just on top-down coercion but also on social support, Putin's power must be built through aggressive campaigning, both in public and behind the scenes. In this, the Kremlin is creative and adaptable, using different strategies at different times. Sometimes, the campaign is to mobilize wedge issues that galvanize millions of conservative Russians against a "modern," "globalized" world that threatens their values. At other times, the emphasis is on using institutions like the Russian Orthodox Church and the school system to normalize Putin's rule and to make this otherwise unremarkable man seem inevitable, indeed essential, for the survival of the Russian state. For much of the last four years, it has also meant turning Putin into the symbol of a political community of which—warts and all—most citizens are proud to be a part.

In the twenty-first century, winning a campaign—even in an authoritarian country—means dominating the media space. As we will see, expanding control over the media has been among Putin's top priorities since his very first days in the Kremlin, but achieving that domination has become increasingly difficult. Controlling television is easiest, but even there the Kremlin is forced to play a perpetual game of cat and mouse, as brilliant and brave journalists seek creative ways around the state to reach the masses. Much harder to control has been the internet, where the Kremlin was late to the game. Playing catch-up against the opposition, the authorities have worked a dual strategy of eliminating competition and enlisting supporters to monitor and shape online discussions. This strategy has had mixed success. Leaked internal documents paint much of the effort as bumbling and reactive, with officials being pulled along by a tide of events to which they are powerless to react. Nevertheless, in the process new and proud identities as guardians of Putin's Russia have emerged amongst pro-Kremlin and nationalist bloggers and activists.

Events have also sometimes played into Putin's hands, most notably the annexation of the Ukrainian province of Crimea. Before Crimea, most Russians—while generally supportive of Putin—were emotionally detached from politics and from their leader. In fact, if ordinary Russians had any emotions at all about politics, they were equally likely to be negative as positive. Crimea changed that. Collective euphoria over events in Ukraine, as portrayed on Russian state television, led to a huge outpouring of pride, hope and trust in Russia's leaders. This emotional wave led to soaring approval ratings for the president, but it also made Russians feel better about their lives in general. Many of the people we spoke to suddenly believed that the country had become less corrupt and its economic future brighter, despite the fact that the Crimean annexation and war in Ukraine led to ever tightening economic sanctions.

The case of Russians' reactions to Crimea and the ensuing war in eastern Ukraine teaches us about one other thing: the power that can be created when a dominant state and a willing public come together. The collective euphoria that sent Putin's support to record highs was built on shared myths—lies, really—that could only have been created by a monopolized media and an enthusiastic populace acting together. Fake news is only as powerful as the willingness of people to believe it. When we combine people who are open to national-patriotic stories with increasingly rabid news coverage, the result is a world of emotional politics largely disconnected from reality, and thus extremely resistant to change.

All of these facets of Russian power—the campaigns, the media dominance, the mythmaking—are intensely political. They are also often more uncertain than they seem from the outside. Behind the solid-looking façade, there are structural problems in the edifice of Putin's power that make its durability questionable. The success of all of these efforts depends not only on what Putin does, but on what the people do: hence the edifice is co-constructed. If they were to withdraw their support, Putin, too, would tumble. Fragility, rather than permanence, is the mark of Russian politics today.

THE SOCIAL FOUNDATIONS OF PUTIN'S POWER

When Natalya or Maxim or any other Russian citizen decides to support Putin—or to oppose him—they are making more than just a personal choice. Their choice is part of a social process, one that involves tens of millions of people interacting in schools, workplaces, churches, the media and elsewhere. For many ordinary Russians, their attachment to Putin is first and foremost about attachment to their community. The pride people feel in Russia's accomplishments, or the social pressure they feel to be politically in step with their compatriots, emerges not from Putin's *diktat*, but from their own relationships with their friends and family, neighbors and colleagues. For some years now, this sense of community has overwhelmingly been attached to support for President Putin. But this state of Russian society is not permanent. When the mood begins to shift, Russians' attachment to their community will likely remain, but the attachment to Putin may not. This is critical if we want to understand Russia today. And it's even more important if we want to think about Russia tomorrow. After all, even Putin is mortal and politics in Russia will continue after he is gone.

The whole edifice of Putin's power is reinforced day after day by the actions and beliefs of millions of Russians all across that vast country. This is what we mean when we say that power in Russia is co-constructed. The power generally ascribed to Putin himself actually stems from millions of private citizens willingly acting as unprompted enforcers of Putin's power in society. This happens in myriad ways. People take part in pro-government shows of strength on the streets and volunteer to fight in Ukraine. At the extreme, some seek to enforce Putin's will by beating or even murdering his critics. More often though, co-construction means reinforcing Putin's power in more mundane ways, through small-scale social pressure: the boss who insists his employees vote; the school teacher who inculcates uncritical acceptance of official stories of Putin's heroism; the friends who mistake support for Putin for patriotism. These are the real sources of Putin's power today.

And co-construction goes beyond agreeing with policies or political slogans. Instead, we show how support for Putin and his policies has become normalized as the socially appropriate set of attitudes to have. In a society like Russia, those who step outside of these norms risk real social and sometimes economic consequences. As a result, people who are concerned with fitting in, or who are attached to institutions like the Orthodox Church in particular, have internalized these norms of support and loyalty to the president.

To say that Putin's power is built with, and not over, Russian society is not to say that it is an inherently Russian trait to support autocrats. This charge, made by many over the years, is demonstrably false and strays into the territory of Russophobia. Many Russians are implacably opposed to President Putin and are willing to take extraordinary personal risks to challenge him. In fact, even beyond this brave minority, most Russians believe in the value of democratic elections and freedom of speech. Russian society is diverse and boisterous, fractious and exciting, riven by the same conflicts and contradictions—between progress and conservatism, ambition and anxiety—that rack most democratic countries. This is despite the state's tight grip on the media, on the economy and on most of the public spaces in which ideas are formed and debated.

Our argument may seem controversial. On the one hand, it could be seen as victim-blaming: ordinary Russians are clearly the injured party in their relationship with the state, so how could we argue that the state is, in fact, partly of their making? On the other hand, it might seem to imply complicity, perhaps even reminiscent of the complicity of some ordinary Germans in Hitler's crimes. In truth, we mean neither of these things.

What we mean is that dictators like Putin are best understood as competitors for power in their own state, striving to lead society but often forced to follow. As we will see, Putin's Kremlin goes to great lengths to analyze threats and opportunities, to develop strategies for achieving and maintaining political advantage, and it never seems to feel too sure of its own inevitability. In fact, often the view from the Kremlin is one of relative powerlessness in the face of events, whether on the ground in Ukraine or in the world's currency markets.

As a result, for all his vaunted strength and longevity, Putin's domination of Russian politics is contingent and fragile. Social support can disappear or erode over time. Often, such support disappears overnight. Citizens who can fall in love with their leaders can fall back out of love, too. Indeed, there were signs that this process was already under way as we went to press. Events out of control of the leadership still drive an enormous amount of politics, and missteps taken in response to these events can be very damaging. Being both popular and a dictator makes Putin strong. But Putin's reliance on popular support also makes him vulnerable.

RUSSIAN EYES

Vladimir Putin, of course, is not the world's only autocrat. In 2018, Hungary's nationalist prime minister Viktor Orbán—flush with victory in a gerrymandered parliamentary election—announced himself as the death knell of "liberal democracy." In Turkey, Recep Tayyip Erdoğan is broadly seen as having presided over the end of that country's democratic project. And it is not just in autocracies that nationalism, populism and strong-man rule are making a comeback. In Brazil, France, Italy, Israel, Poland, the Czech Republic, the UK and, perhaps most significantly of all, the United States people worry about the survival of liberal freedoms and democracy. Freedom House, an American advocacy group that tracks political and media freedom globally, has declared that "Democracy's basic tenets—including guarantees of free and fair elections, the rights of minorities, freedom of the press, and the rule of law—are under siege around the world."[2] Putin may have led the way in capturing the media and rallying millions of supporters around an emotionally charged nationalist agenda, but Orbán, Erdoğan and the others have demonstrated just how easy it is to replicate Putin's success.

It is not just the model that has been copied. The 2016 Brexit referendum to take the UK out of the European Union is a case in point. The links between various Russian nationalists and the European far right are extensive and well documented. The rejection of liberal universalism—of the idea that all human beings are fundamentally the same and endowed with the same rights—unites people like

Nigel Farage, who led the campaign in favor of Brexit, with Orbán in Hungary, Marine Le Pen in France, and, of course, Putin and Trump.

And so, in some ways, this book is about much more than Russia. In asking how Russia threw off Communism but fell back under the sway of a dictator, we can learn lessons about populist politics more broadly. The case of Russia underscores the importance of compliant media outlets and foreign adventures, but also the role of society, pride and emotion in constructing and maintaining understandings of the world that are both divorced from reality and yet widely believed. It also illustrates how democracy and free speech can be eroded even in a country where most people believe in both.

But we can learn, too, about the importance of struggle and resistance. In the focus on the rise of authoritarianism, we often lose sight of the millions who stand up and fight. As we will see in this book, for all Putin's apparent might, the group that rose to oppose his return to power in 2011 and 2012 began a public conversation about the purpose of the Russian state and the meaning of Russian citizenship— not an open and balanced one, but a conversation nonetheless. This opposition has not gone away. In fact, as the Kremlin has sought to consolidate its positions and push back hard against its opponents, the other side has become more galvanized in its response. The most important battle for Russia's future is being fought not in Ukraine, not in Syria, but inside Russia itself.

To understand where our world is headed, then, it may be instructive to view it through Russian eyes.

TWO

THE KREMLIN UNDER FIRE

It wasn't so long ago that Russia was hip. In Moscow and St. Petersburg, coders and freelancers and designers mingled with bankers and lawyers and commodities traders. They took to social media with abandon and aplomb. Suddenly, everyone was a blogger. Facebook and Twitter brought global trends and ideas into Russian circles instantaneously. Newly flush with cash, they would come back from holidays in Europe determined not to emigrate, as earlier generations might have, but to remake their own lives and neighborhoods on the models of London and Paris and Berlin. Russia wasn't just rich. Russia was buzzing.

Where there's a buzz, though, there's bound to be a buzzkill, and for Russia's emerging urban elite, the buzz-kill's name was Vladimir Putin.

MR. PUTIN

Vladimir Putin was born in an ordinary Leningrad communal apartment in 1952 to two ordinary parents. His father, also Vladimir, had served on submarines in the

Soviet Navy during the war and took a job at the Egorov train car factory after his discharge. Putin's mother, Maria, survived the brutal two-and-a-half-year Nazi siege of the city and later worked in the same factory. Only Putin's paternal grandfather—Spiridon Putin—had seen a lick of fame, as a chef for the highest-ranking Soviet officials, including both Lenin and Stalin. If the young Vladimir was impressed, it didn't show; after a moderately rambunctious youth involving a handful of backstreet brawls, he studied law and took a shine to the glamor of the KGB, which recruited him in 1975. Ten years later, the KGB stationed him in Dresden, where, evidently, he learned to appreciate the ability of beer to punctuate the boredom of sorting East German press clippings.[1] Four years later, he watched the Berlin Wall collapse. Two years after that, back in Leningrad, he watched his own country disappear. So did Maxim, who was 7 at the time, and Natalya, who was 17.

From that moment onward, Putin made a career of being in the right place at the right time. Resigning formally from the KGB, albeit with a tacit understanding that he might be called upon again one day, he took a job with his former law professor Anatoly Sobchak. Sobchak had just been elected mayor of the city soon to reclaim the name St. Petersburg. Among Putin's official responsibilities was attracting foreign investors, a task thought to have been made easier by his international experience and fluent German. Money—including German money—began to flow in his direction and through his office, and so too did potentially influential contacts. When Sobchak failed to win reelection in 1996, one of those contacts called Putin to Moscow, where he joined Boris Yeltsin's Presidential Administration as a deputy director, with responsibility for legal affairs and oversight of foreign property owned by the Russian state.

Supported by old friends from St. Petersburg—including other ex-KGB agents, but also liberal economists—Putin rapidly gained authority and trust in the eyes of Yeltsin. He was appointed head of the FSB, the successor to the KGB. Then, in August 1999, Yeltsin appointed Putin prime minister. At the time, few in Russia or abroad expected much of the man; few, indeed, had ever heard of him. But his decisive response to a string of terrorist bombings the next month, and the evident skill with which he prosecuted a renewed war in Chechnya, won him high marks from the public. In August 1999, Putin enjoyed the support of only 2 percent of Russian voters, according to opinion polls. By October, 21 percent of voters said they supported him for presidency. By November, 45 percent of voters were telling pollsters they intended to support Putin to succeed Yeltsin. Yeltsin's decision to resign at the turn of the new millennium, making Putin acting president, seemed almost natural. In March 2000, Putin won his own term as president with 54 percent of the vote.

The difference between Putin and Yeltsin—an athletic virtual teetotaler, versus an elderly alcoholic in failing health—could not have been starker, but Putin had one other thing that Yeltsin never did: high oil prices. Crude oil spent most of Yeltsin's presidency below $20 a barrel. Starting in 2000, however, oil began an upward trend that would continue almost uninterrupted, peaking first above $70 in 2006, and then above $130 in 2008. For an economy overwhelmingly dependent on oil and gas exports, it was a remarkable run, fueling unparalleled growth in ordinary Russians' incomes and standards of living. Russians were more prosperous than they had ever been in history, a fact that contrasted sharply with the penury millions had experienced under Yeltsin in the 1990s.

But that prosperity came at a cost—a dramatic reassertion of state control over the media. Three months after winning his first presidential election, Putin oversaw an investigation into a company, Media-Most, that controlled Russia's most successful independent media outlets. Its owner, a stage director turned banker, Vladimir Gusinsky, was arrested on charges of financial fraud. By the fall, Gusinsky had fled the country and relinquished control of his assets to Gazprom, the state-owned natural gas monopoly. In January of the following year, another so-called "oligarch," Boris Berezovsky, read the writing on the wall and handed over control of his television station, ORT. He fled the country shortly thereafter. Putin— whose election campaign had been partly financed by Berezovsky—called the decision "wise."

In fact, it took Putin less than a year in power to consolidate full control over the national airwaves. Public protest, however, was muted. To many, the journalists of NTV, ORT and other outlets were out-of-touch elites, earning in some cases hundreds of thousands of dollars a year at a time when ordinary Russians were struggling to bring home $100 a month. For such largesse, it was assumed, journalists served the interests of their paymasters, not the public. Gusinsky and Berezovsky themselves were seen as having profited from the corrupt, insider-dominated privatization schemes of the 1990s, and thus having bilked the country out of billions of dollars. Few tears were shed.

There was similarly little sympathy for another of Russia's most powerful businessmen, Mikhail Khodorkovsky, when the state came for him in October 2003, seizing his oil company, Yukos, and sentencing him to a decade in a Siberian labor camp on tax charges. Among Khodorkovsky's sins, it seems, had been an effort to support opposition parties in the State Duma—the lower house of parliament, where most legislation is done. Two months after Khodorkovsky's arrest, Putin's favored United Russia party consolidated control over the Duma, giving the Kremlin an outright majority of seats for the first time in post-Soviet history. The remaining parties were offered finance vetted and directed through the Presidential Administration; none refused. Three months after that, in March 2004, Putin cruised to reelection, winning 71 percent of the vote on a platform of "stability."

IN TANDEM

As his second term wore on, Putin was facing a problem: Russia's constitution. After eight years in power, he was legally barred from serving a third consecutive term. Speculation ran rampant: would he change the rules, as leaders in neighboring Belarus and Kazakhstan had? Probably not, the reasoning went. That would mark Putin as a despot and hurt his respectability on the global stage. Would he ride off into the sunset? Some thought he might. After all, he had once complained of working "like a galley slave." Perhaps he was tired.

In the end, and not for the first time in his career, Putin decided to have it both ways. He tapped Dmitry Medvedev, a long-time aide and graduate of the same law school as Putin, to run for the presidency. Medvedev had served as Putin's assistant back in St. Petersburg before running Putin's 2000 presidential campaign and joining the Presidential Administration. Putin would take the reins of the ruling United Russia party (although he didn't actually join the party). When Medvedev won 70 percent of the vote (conveniently, a single percentage point below the record result of his proud predecessor), he duly appointed Putin prime minister.

Between the two of them, they covered the waterfront. Medvedev was young, smiling and—happily to many— had none of Putin's background in the KGB. He traveled to Silicon Valley, marveled at an iPhone and, after Putin had fallen out with George W. Bush over Iraq, pursued a "reset" in relations with a freshly-minted President Barack Obama. At home, he declared that "freedom was better than non-freedom" and promised toleration. Putin, meanwhile, kept a watchful eye. In what became known as the "tandem," Putin's position was constitutionally inferior, but no one harbored any doubt where the real power lay. With this tandem in place, Russia emerged virtually unscathed from the financial collapse that sent the United States and Europe into years of recession. Even a five-day war with Georgia over the disputed territories of Abkhazia and South Ossetia couldn't dampen Russia's seemingly inexorable rise.

As it turned out, only Putin himself could do that. In September 2011, Medvedev announced to the United

Russia party convention that he would not, in fact, seek a second term in office. Instead, Putin would run again in elections scheduled for the following March. To be sure, few had any genuine love for Medvedev, but his election—and the respect for the constitution that had led to it—felt like a step forward. Putin's impending third term, by contrast, felt like a step back.

In parliamentary elections that December, many of those incensed by the reversal of the "tandem" decided to take out their frustrations by voting against United Russia. Some of those people also decided to become volunteer election observers, monitoring polling stations to prevent—or at least document—fraud. And document it they did: as voting progressed, smartphone videos began to circulate online of ballot stuffing, of people being herded from station to station to cast multiple votes, and of outright falsification. When the results came in, they showed a far better outcome for United Russia in the urban centers than any of these voters believed could be possible.

The result was six months of rolling protests, peaking at as many as 200,000 participants, which became known as the "For Fair Elections" or "Bolotnaya" movement, after the Moscow square on which some of the largest rallies were held. What was supposed to have been Putin's triumphant return to the Kremlin instead provoked the greatest political challenge he had ever faced. To make matters worse, the economy was no longer producing new wealth at anything like the clip it had enjoyed in his first decade or so in office, and all forecasts were for things to get worse. Putin had seemingly lost his political mojo, and nothing he could do was enough to stop the bleeding.

A DEAD END

The batons first flew on Dmitry Medvedev's last day in the Kremlin.

Even when Medvedev occupied the country's highest office, few people inside or outside Russia harbored any illusions about the nature of Vladimir Putin's political system. The state—directly or through proxies—controlled all four of the parties in the State Duma, all of the governorships, and most of the television stations. It kept civil society organizations under an increasingly suffocating blanket of regulation and harassment. The outcomes of elections were never uncertain. But for all its autocracy, Putin's Russia was not particularly coercive. Outside of the North Caucasus—where low-grade counter-insurgency wars imposed an almost permanent state of emergency, filling both prisons and cemeteries—the main risk Putin's opponents seemed to face was futility. The murders of critical journalists, lawyers and activists like Anna Politkovskaya, Natalia Estemirova, Paul Khlebnikov, Stanislav Markelov, Anastasia Baburova and others left little doubt that the state and its allies could kill, but it usually did not. Russia was not North Korea, not Uzbekistan, not even China.

True to form, the protests that had been roiling Russia ever since the December 2011 Duma election had, until Medvedev's final day, been peaceful. With the exception of an initial round of arrests after the first protest on December 5, the police had stood by as thousands, then tens and hundreds of thousands of protesters took to the streets in Moscow, St. Petersburg and a handful of other cities. The Kremlin, it seemed, was confident in its strength and unfazed by the challenge from the streets. Moreover, events had evidently turned in their favor: Putin had been reelected on March 4 with 63.6 percent of the vote, and opposition rallies that had once garnered more than 100,000 supporters by mid-spring struggled to top 10,000.

The opposition, however, had planned one last hurrah for May 6, 2012, the day before Putin's inauguration. Protesters declaring, "We're the power here!"[2] were to march north up Bolshaya Yakimanka Street, across Maly Kamenny Bridge and onto Bolotnaya Square—the square that had, almost half a year earlier, given the protest movement its name. But it wasn't to be.

Halfway up the bridge, in the shadow of the infamous "House on the Embankment," where so many Communist-era functionaries had lived before being dragged away in Stalin's terrors, three protest leaders, Alexei Navalny, Sergei Udaltsov and Boris Nemtsov, sat down on the asphalt and declared a "sitting protest."[3] Riot police were blocking the entry from the bridge onto Bolotnaya Square. As the police began to push the protesters back away from the square—back down the bridge, across the river, further from the Kremlin—scuffles broke out, and then a stampede. In all, after two hours of standoff and skirmish, some 400 were arrested and more than twenty protesters were hospitalized, as were a similar number of police officers.[4]

A day later, when Putin's motorcade descended toward the Kremlin on the opposite side of the river and he was reinaugurated into an office he never really left, all was quiet. There were no crowds to jeer, or even to cheer. Not a soul was in the street.

It was a false silence.

ANATOMY OF REPRESSION

The Kremlin's seeming nonchalance about the opposition that had emerged in late 2011 was deceptive. In fact, the Kremlin had been given a real shock, which ultimately led it to transform its political strategy. Up to that time, ideological ambiguity and peaceful coexistence with society had been the name of the game. Rather than driving a mobilizing political agenda, the goal for the most part was to keep politics away from the people and the people away from politics. The challenge from the streets in 2011 changed all that. Now, the Russian state would actively take politics to the people, first in the form of policemen and prison guards, then on television and online. The goal was to transform passive acceptance of Putin's rule into active participation in that rule, by using tried and tested political technologies to mobilize supporters and demonize opponents.

While the riot police had initially kept their batons sheathed, other actions betrayed the concern amidst the highest echelons of power. Navalny and Udaltsov had both been arrested on December 5, 2011, and held for fifteen days. In January 2012, a court reopened proceedings against Alexei Kozlov, the husband of Olga Romanova, a journalist turned human-rights campaigner who had emerged as a key organizer of the Bolotnaya protests, threatening him with reincarceration at any moment on trumped-up charges of embezzlement.[5] And on March 3—just a day before the presidential election—police arrested Nadezhda Tolokonnikova, Maria Alekhina and Ekaterina Samutsevich, three members of the Pussy Riot group that had protested against Putin in Christ the Savior Cathedral in February.[6]

If anyone had expected the coercion to cease once Putin was safely ensconced again in the Kremlin, they would have been sorely disappointed. In fact, what happened was a squall of repression unrivalled in post-Soviet Russian history, before or since. Within two weeks of the inauguration, Kozlov was handed a new sentence and returned to jail. In May 2012, investigators opened cases against lawyers and academics accused of sympathizing with jailed oligarch Mikhail Khodorkovsky, forcing some—including renowned economist Sergei Guriev, who had advised both Medvedev and Navalny—to flee the country.[7] Tolokonnikova, Alekhina and Samutsevich, of Pussy Riot, went on trial in July 2012 and were sentenced in August to two years in prison, though Samutsevich's sentence was later commuted.[8]

But nothing compared to the trials of those who joined in the May 6 protest. Immediately after the violence, the Kremlin launched a series of arrests, interrogations and hearings that lasted more than three years. In all, nineteen people received sentences of varying severity, most on charges of fomenting unrest. The way in which the state drew out the repression seemed almost calculated: the first "May 6" verdict was handed down in November 2012 and the last in December 2015—some forty-three months after the fact.[9] For those linked to the movement, the slow drip of arrests, trials and sentences created a pervasive sense of fear.

The longest sentence was reserved for Udaltsov. On October 5, 2012, the state-owned NTV television channel aired *The Anatomy of Protest 2*, a documentary that purported to show Udaltsov and two of his comrades colluding with a Georgian agent to foment revolution in Russia. Udaltsov was called in for interrogation five days later.[10] Leonid Razvozzhaev was effectively kidnapped in Ukraine by Russian law enforcement officers on October 19, 2012, and after an extended period of arrest, Udaltsov and Razvozzhaev were charged with incitement to violence and attempted revolt.[11] Both men were sentenced to four and a half years in prison.[12] Lebedev, the third comrade, was tried on other charges but turned state's evidence against Udaltsov and Razvozzhaev—although he claimed to have done so under duress and recanted his affidavit in court.[13]

And so, in the aftermath of the Bolotnaya protests and Putin's reelection, a Russian political system that had never been entirely "vegetarian"—to borrow a term current in the Russian opposition—became even more carnivorous. Putin was delivering on the threat he had made at his only presidential campaign rally, held on February 23, 2012, marking Defender of the Fatherland Day: those who sought to prevent his reelection, he told the crowd, were akin to the traitors who had cheered the invading armies of Hitler and Napoleon.[14]

DON'T EXCITE THE PEOPLE

For most of his time in office, Vladimir Putin's Kremlin stuck to a simple principle: "don't excite the people."[15] As Putin's political career progressed, he may have recalled one of the more indelible memories from his KGB days in Dresden. As the Berlin Wall was falling, a crowd of angry East Germans gathered outside the Soviet facility, where the young Putin was stationed. As the center of the Eastern

Bloc and the occupying power in East Germany, the Soviet Union had backed the deeply unpopular dictator Erich Honecker, whose brutal repressions had pushed the country to boiling point. It was inevitable that they, too, would come in for some of the revolutionary wrath.

As East Germans crashed the gates, Putin called headquarters in Moscow for instructions. Should the East German police be called to intervene? The Soviet military? Moscow was silent, and in the face of the crowd that silence was deafening. It was then, Putin told interviewers in 2001, that he realized the Soviet Union was through, two years before it would finally collapse. For the future Russian president, the lesson seemed obvious: keep the people calm and the message clear.

In October 2002, midway through Putin's first term in office, tragedy struck, and Putin may again have felt that the crowd was at the gates. The story of how Putin responded was most clearly told by Boris Nemtsov, the Yeltsin-era reformer who would later become an anti-Putin opposition leader. Nemtsov was among a handful of public figures called in to help negotiate the release of 916 hostages held by terrorists at a theater in Moscow. On his way to the theater, Nemtsov received a call from the Kremlin to stand down. Later that night, special forces stormed the theater. By the time the smoke cleared, 174 of the hostages were dead. Nemtsov helped launch an investigation, which determined that most of the deaths had been caused by the gas used by the special forces, compounded by the fact that the forces had refused to tell emergency responders and doctors exactly what was poisoning their patients.[16] Nemtsov pressed Putin to act on the findings, but Putin quashed them instead. "Don't excite the people," he told Nemtsov.[17]

That idea may have been at the back of Putin's mind when, six months after he was reelected to his second term in office, terrorists struck again, this time seizing a school in Beslan, North Ossetia, in Russia's North Caucasus—the region that includes Chechnya, which the Kremlin was still struggling to pacify after two scorched-earth wars. The attackers took more than 1,000 hostages, most of them children. A military raid on the school led to the death of more than 300, including at least 186 children.

While the country mourned, however, Putin pressed his political agenda still further: citing the attack, he declared that federalism had "gone awry" and decreed an end to the direct election of governors in the country's eighty-nine regions. From then on—until the "reform" was partially rolled back in 2012—governors would be appointed by the Kremlin. There was very little controversy, and even less debate. Television, all in the hands of the state, presented the "reform" as a fait accompli. The images of death and destruction were swiftly replaced by something different: the clear message that the state was strong, and that when the phone rang Putin would answer.

By the end of 2004, then, there were no longer any independent centers of power in Russia: television, the titans of industry, the political parties and regional leaders had all been brought to heel. All that remained outside of the Kremlin's direct control was the street—and Putin had reason to worry. In November 2003, street protests in neighboring Georgia removed President Eduard

Shevardnadze from power, in what became known as the "Rose Revolution." Almost exactly a year later, the "Orange Revolution" in Ukraine likewise saw the street thwart the ambitions of increasingly autocratic leaders there.

From Moscow's perspective, it did not help matters that the new presidents of both countries—Mikheil Saakashvili in Georgia and Viktor Yushchenko in Ukraine—sought to deepen their ties with the European Union, NATO and the West more broadly. In this, the Kremlin saw the hand of the US, accusing Washington of meddling and promoting "color revolutions." The fact that sitting presidents had also been overthrown by protests in Serbia and Kyrgyzstan added fuel to the fire. In response, Putin tasked one of his closest advisers, Vladislav Surkov, with mobilizing constituencies at home, to prevent the emergence of such a challenge in Russia itself.

It was almost too late, though. In January 2005, hundreds of thousands of protesters poured out into the streets of cities around the country to push back against a proposed welfare reform. Believing that control over the Duma and the airwaves meant they had an unassailable political position, officials admitted they had never really investigated how the public might react. Spooked, the government quickly backed down. Surkov, meanwhile, redoubled his efforts, launching an ever-escalating assault on Russian activists, civil society organizations, and foreign funders and non-governmental organizations operating in Russia, which continues to this day.

For Putin himself, though, the way to keep the people calm—that key lesson from Dresden—was to remain above politics. "Don't excite the people" became his mantra.

Although he supported United Russia, the ruling party, Putin never actually joined its ranks. He never debated his election opponents, never appeared in campaign ads. When he was interviewed, the questions were always reviewed beforehand, and his answers—always confident and detailed—were ready to go. But he largely avoided ideology, seeking instead to be all things to all people. Thus, in a sop to nostalgia he restored the Soviet-era national anthem and declared the fall of the USSR "the greatest geopolitical catastrophe of the twentieth century," but he pursued liberalizing economic reforms, free trade and a digitized economy. In his annual addresses to parliament he continually spoke of the value of freedom and democracy, while claiming the lineage of tsars and general secretaries alike. And oil prices, of course, continued to work their magic. As a result, throughout his first two terms in office, Putin's approval ratings rarely fell below 70 percent.

PUSSY RIOT

Putin and his advisers generally believed that ideological divisions among ordinary citizens were essentially artificial, created and manipulated by political elites to suit their own purposes.[18] According to Gleb Pavlovsky, who served as Putin's chief political adviser in his first term as president, the Kremlin tended to see its role as preventing these kinds of cleavages from emerging—avoiding "public excitement"—and thus maintaining the loyalty of all but the most marginal social groups.

By the end of 2011, however, the Kremlin recognized that this strategy was no longer working, and it soon set out to create and manipulate ideological cleavages to its own advantage. The goal was to find issues that could "weaponize" an existing but dormant social consensus and mobilize that consensus against the opposition to the advantage of the regime. This is an old political technique, commonly used in Western democracies, that political strategists refer to as mobilizing "wedge issues"—issues that are not central to the usual axes of political competition, but that can cleave off part of an opponent's potential support.[19] And in Russia, as elsewhere, wedge issues meant bringing up the previously unmentionable—religion and sexuality.

The first cause for public excitement was an unexpected gift for the Russian authorities. On February 19, 2012, five members of Pussy Riot—a punk protest band, loosely linked to a global feminist collective and the St. Petersburg radical art group Voina—performed a piece entitled "Blessed Virgin, rid us of Putin!" in the Yelokhovo Cathedral in the Baumanskaya neighborhood of northeast Moscow. Two days later, they repeated the stunt, but this time in Christ the Savior Cathedral, just down the embankment from the Kremlin, and the country's most prominent Russian Orthodox site.[20]

It took a few days for the authorities to realize the value of what had happened, but one week later an investigation was launched and arrest warrants were issued, even though the performers had been wearing masks and had not been publicly identified. On March 3, the day before Russians went to the polls to reelect Putin, three members of the band—Tolokonnikova, Alekhina and Samutsevich—were arrested. The investigation and trial were uncharacteristically swift—the trial and sentencing were completed by mid-August. The women were each sentenced to two years in prison. On appeal and after expressing remorse, Samutsevich had her sentence commuted. Tolokonnikova and Alekhina, however, served their time in remote prison camps, like Soviet-era dissidents before them.[21]

Jailing the women was only part of the plan, though. As journalist Andrei Melnikov wrote in Moscow's *Nezavisimaya gazeta*, "what matters most in this story isn't so much the fate of the girls, but the consequences this case will have for the relationship between the Church and society."[22] After an extended silence from the official Church, Archpriest Vsevolod Chaplin—then the Church's ultra-conservative spokesman—called for the state not just to punish Pussy Riot, but to enshrine in law the defense of religious sentiment.

The ensuing debate—both over what to do with Pussy Riot and what to do with the law—captured media attention, peaking in August 2012, when the three women were sentenced, but then spiking in January 2013 when a law "On defending the feelings of religious believers" was drafted, and again into the summer, as the law worked its way through the Duma.[23]

The tenor of the campaign was aimed less at attacking the opposition directly, and more at galvanizing public opinion around a position guaranteed to be offensive to the opposition—in other words, religion became a wedge issue. On May 14, 2013, Vladimir Legoida, a journalist, lay member of the Church hierarchy and one of the Church's most visible spokesmen, penned an op-ed in *Nezavisimaya gazeta*, the same newspaper Chaplin had used to launch the campaign a year earlier. Legoida wrote:

The saying that one shouldn't enter another's monastery with their own charter is, evidently, so deeply engrained in the consciousness of Russia's multinational population because it reflects the archetypal Russian. The notorious story of the blasphemous action in Christ the Savior Cathedral provoked debate only about the severity of the punishment; almost no one sympathized with the indecent dance before the altar.[24]

Clearly, the agenda was much wider than just trying three punk artists—the goal was to ensure that as many Russians as possible felt personally offended by what Pussy Riot had done.[25] The law on religious sentiment was a clarion call to conservatives of all stripes—what the liberal newspaper *Vedomosti* called "quasi-coercive groups formed of adult men with adolescent psyches, dreaming of wearing folk costumes and frightening their neighbors"—and it worked.[26] The spirit of public "excitement" remained long after the law on religious sentiment had been passed, after Tolokonnikova and Alekhina had served their time and been released.

Perhaps no one embodied that spirit better than Dmitry Tsorionov-Enteo, leader of a group calling itself "God's Will," best known for organizing riots at Moscow art exhibitions that Enteo felt to be sacrilegious. "There are apostles of the Antichrist among the liberals," Enteo told *The New Times* in 2015, after his group disrupted a major sculpture exhibition. "I know their names."[27] The opposition knew exactly who Enteo had in mind: them.

FAMILY VALUES

If the assist on the religious sentiment law came from Putin's opponents, the second big wedge issue of the post-Bolotnaya period came from a friend Putin probably never knew he had. Vitaly Milonov was elected to the St. Petersburg city council in 2007, at the age of 33, and soon made a name for himself promoting conservative causes: banning the teaching of evolution in schools, for example, or creating a "morality police" staffed by Cossacks to patrol the streets.[28] Most of these initiatives never got off the ground, but in February 2012—after months of trying, and about a week after Pussy Riot performed in Christ the Savior Cathedral—he pushed through the St. Petersburg city council a bill imposing fines for "propaganda of pedophilia and homosexuality."[29]

In fanning public hostility to the LGBT community and turning it into a political resource with which to beat the supposedly pro-Western opposition, the Kremlin was doing nothing more than plucking a page from an old Western playbook. Margaret Thatcher tried to weaponize public antipathy to gay rights in the 1987 British general election and after through the Clause 28 campaign against "positive images" of homosexuality in education. The similarity with the Russian legislation is not coincidental.

As divisive as the Pussy Riot affair had been, the emergent anti-LGBT crusade aroused passions rarely seen before in Russian public politics. The initial response to Milonov's efforts in St. Petersburg had been lukewarm, with very little discussion in the media. Milonov's most vocal support at the time came from the influential TV journalist Dmitry Kiselev, who called for gays to have "their hearts removed, burned and buried in the ground."[30] In the early going, however, Kiselev's view was the exception. For most people in Russia, LGBT issues simply weren't on the agenda.

Interest in the topic picked up, however, when the St. Petersburg bill was passed, and then spiked when a similar bill was introduced in the State Duma. The federal law was passed almost in the same breath as the law on religious sentiment. Again, the focus seemed to be on galvanizing majority opinion around a set of views that would isolate the opposition—in this case, an opposition that aspired to European values. As the law came up for a vote in Moscow, the Smolensk newspaper *Rabochy put'* opined in an editorial:

> A state that "forgets" that the union of a man and a woman is holy faces demographic catastrophe. Only a normal family—a small church—can be the foundation of a sustainable society. . . . There is only one way to prevent the tragedy that has afflicted Europe: to combat same-sex marriages with normal families.[31]

On cue, the Bolotnaya opposition took the other side of the argument—despite never having embraced LGBT issues before. On the night of May 10, 2013, a young gay man, Vlad Tornovoi, who lived in the Krasnoarmeiskii neighborhood of the city of Volgograd, was horrifically murdered by two men. The killers, who had been involved in previous attacks on gay men, claimed that Tornovoi's "provocative behavior" offended their patriotic feelings.[32]

Writing in *Vedomosti*, the Moscow-based journalist and activist Maria Eismont drew a parallel between Tornovoi's murder and the effects of an earlier government campaign against Georgian immigrants in 2006. Back then, central government criticisms of Georgians had led to spontaneous persecution in which local officials and even school teachers were spurred to root out Georgians in their midst. "Every self-respecting person in Russia today should become gay," Eismont wrote after Tornovoi's death. "Not literally, but in the same sense that in 2006 all self-respecting Russians became Georgian."[33]

And as with the law on religious sentiment, the debate became even more provocative after the law itself came into effect. In January 2014, Ivan Okhlobystin—a priest turned popular sitcom actor—penned an open letter to Putin, calling for the anti-LGBT law to be supplemented with the recriminalization of sodomy.[34] Predictably, the rhetoric of such high-profile people as Okhlobystin and Kiselev emboldened criminals. According to human-rights activists, Russian courts registered 33 hate crimes against LGBT individuals in 2012, 50 in 2013, 52 in 2014 and 65 in 2015; of those, 90 were murders.[35]

DRIVING THE WEDGE

The use of the religious sentiment and anti-LGBT laws as wedge issues did exactly what it was designed to do: it widened the ideological divide between the pro-Putin majority and the oppositional minority in the country. In October 2013, we surveyed a sample of online, educated urbanites—exactly the constituency that turned on Putin in 2011–12 and which the Kremlin hoped to win back. We asked them, among other things, about their opinions on the two laws, as well as about their voting history.[36] As expected, support for the two laws diverged along "party" lines. While a majority of Russians overall supported both pieces of legislation, opposition supporters were about three times more likely to oppose each piece of legislation than Putin supporters.[37]

These wedge issues did not achieve their aims magically, however: they had help from the media. Viewers of state-controlled television, which pushed for both the religious sentiment law and the anti-LGBT legislation, were much more supportive than those who used alternative media sources. While all of our respondents spent at least some time online, about half reported getting their news on the federal TV channels daily, while some 16 percent reported rarely or never turning on the TV news. The correlation between media use and attitudes is striking—and stronger than the correlation between attitudes and partisanship.[38]

Of course, correlation is not causation. It is hard to be certain whether people who were more supportive of the legislation simply like state TV news more and so watch more of it, or whether watching state TV made people more supportive. In reality—and judging by similar research on other countries—the process probably works both ways. People who are already supportive of gay rights probably do not spend much time on official news sources, for they would certainly find the coverage disagreeable. On the other hand, most watchers of state television news had probably spent little time thinking about either gay rights or the rights of Orthodox believers, and so when state news told them that one set of rights had to be abrogated and the other supported, they were probably quick to agree. Whatever direction the causation goes in, the whole point of wedge issues is to separate people, dividing them into unbridgeable camps, experiencing different realities in their different media spheres, and to firm up coalitions of a majority (whether silent or moral or what have you) against the minority. And in this sense, the data show that television clearly plays a role.

All of which, from Putin's point of view, is wonderful—as long as people are watching television.

LET IT RAIN

About halfway through Medvedev's presidency—sometime toward the end of 2009—Mikhail Zygar and his friends noted an odd trend.

"Everyone was bragging about how they never watched television, how they had thrown out their TV sets," Zygar recalled. "Now, of course, that wouldn't surprise anyone at all, but back then—back then that was a totally new phenomenon."

By "everyone," of course, Zygar meant everyone in his social circle—and it was, to be sure, not your typical Russian social circle. Born in Moscow, Zygar grew up in Angola, studied in Cairo and got his degree in journalism from the prestigious Moscow State Institute of International Relations. From there, he went on to become one of Russia's most adventurous foreign correspondents, covering wars in Iraq, Lebanon and Palestine, and revolutions in Ukraine and Kyrgyzstan. Writing for the daily newspaper *Kommersant* and the Russian-language edition of *Newsweek*, Zygar moved—and was read—in decidedly liberal circles. And it was these circles, Zygar and his friends noticed, that had stopped watching television.

The obvious thing to do, then, was to start a new television channel. In October 2010, Zygar—at the age of only 29—became the first editor-in-chief of Dozhd (meaning literally 'Rain'), a new cable and online channel that aimed to do what other Russian channels no longer would: to broadcast live, to cover everything and everyone, and to be fun to watch.

"It was just this kind of instinctive feeling, that it would be interesting to make something new, for ourselves, for our friends, for those who we might consider like-minded people," Zygar explained. "Something that would talk to people in a normal, human language, definitely not in the language of officials."

Slowly, gradually, the channel began to grow. With investment from Alexander Vinokurov—a highly successful banker, married to the channel's executive director, Natalia Sindeyeva, who also invested in the online media projects Slon.ru and Bolshoi Gorod—Dozhd occupied a studio in the hip warehouse district of Moscow's old Red October chocolate factory. They broadcast interviews with everyone from outspoken rock singer Yury Shevchuk to President Medvedev himself. It was the Bolotnaya movement of 2011–12, though, that put Dozhd on the map for good.

"Bolotnaya gave Dozhd the opportunity to play the role of the only normal television channel in Russia," Zygar said, recalling how coverage was organized on a shoestring. "Because when something like that is going on, any normal television channel is obliged to cover it. I mean, that's the point of the profession. If the protests on Bolotnaya Square, on Sakharov Avenue and all the others had been covered by the mainstream media—if NTV, Channel 1, REN-TV or even [music channel] Muz-TV had bothered to cover it—Dozhd would have ceased to exist. Our coverage of the really important events would never have had any viewers, if we had any competition."

THE KREMLIN LOGS IN

For most of Putin's time in office, the Presidential Administration had informal "curators" looking after television and print media, whose role was to help guide coverage of topics important to the Kremlin (and prevent coverage of less "convenient" issues) and, when necessary, to enforce "oversight." It wasn't until 2012, however, that it first appointed a "curator" to look after the internet.

As the Kremlin was rapidly learning, the fact of different communities living in different political realities—one on television, the other online—had a serious downside. The anti-Putin opposition had been incubating in cyberspace, and while television and other traditional media could help consolidate a rump pro-Putin electorate—and keep his approval ratings from falling below 60 percent—letting a digital opposition thrive was clearly a very risky strategy. Something had to be done.

True to form, part of the Kremlin's initial response to this challenge was coercive. In the spring and summer of 2012, the government threw its support behind a proposal—initially drafted by the conservative Duma deputy Elena Mizulina with the support of the "Safe Internet League," itself backed by the Russian Orthodox Church and the religiously minded businessman Konstantin Malofeev—to create an internet blacklist.[39] The law, which was ostensibly designed to protect children from homosexuality, pedophilia, extremism, narcotics and suicide, was passed only two months after Putin reentered the Kremlin.[40] The blacklist, however, was not only about protecting children. It was also used to block opposition-minded news and commentary on websites like Grani.ru, EJ.ru and Newsru.com, as well as the blogs of opposition leaders Alexei Navalny and Garri Kasparov.[41]

In 2014, a group of business interests close to Igor Sechin—the CEO of state-owned oil company Rosneft and a close associate of Putin—forced the ouster of Pavel Durov, CEO of VKontakte, Russia's largest online social network. Durov had refused to hand information on protest activity to the security services. Control over the network was transferred to Alisher Usmanov, owner of Arsenal soccer club and an oligarch with close relations with the Kremlin.[42] A few months earlier, in December 2013, Putin himself issued a decree firing Svetlana Mironiuk, the head of the state-owned news agency RIA Novosti. Mironiuk had a reputation for running a professional and objective news organization with a strong online presence. She was replaced by Dmitry Kiselev, the man who had called for gay people to have their hearts burned. The accompanying order folded the agency into a broader holding with Russia Today and the domestic television station Rossiia-1, placing the whole structure under

Kiselev's editorial command and ordering it explicitly to serve Russia's national interests.[43]

But even all of that was just the beginning. Three days after signs and banners at the largest of the December 2011 protests had ridiculed Putin's performance on his most recent "Direct Line" with the nation, the president fired Vladislav Surkov, his chief image-maker and head of the domestic politics division of the Presidential Administration. Surkov was replaced by Viacheslav Volodin, a long-time Duma deputy from the city of Saratov on the Volga River. Volodin had a reputation for bare-knuckles politics and little patience for the finesse Surkov had sought to bring to the job. He also, reportedly, had little regard for the internet: "The internet is nothing," he was reported as saying. "For our lifetime, newspapers will do."[44]

Enter Kristina Potupchik. As a press secretary for Nashi—a Kremlin-backed youth group that had been created by Surkov—Potupchik had coordinated a massive effort to pay bloggers and other social media "influencers" to produce content favorable to the Kremlin. Realizing she could make more money in the private sector, Potupchik eventually left Nashi and started selling her social-media services to the highest bidder. By mid-2012, that bidder was again the Kremlin. We know this because, in December 2014, a group of hackers going under the name Humpty Dumpty broke into the email of her boss, Timur Prokopenko, the Presidential Administration official in charge of "curating" political coverage on the internet. In among his vacation photos and grocery lists was a stack of emails from an account under the name of Anna Veduta.

The name belonged to the woman who was at the time Navalny's press secretary, but the account belonged to Potupchik.[45]

Among the emails from Potupchik to Prokopenko placed in the public domain by Humpty Dumpty were 157 documents, written over a seven-month period from June through December 2014, in which Potupchik provided almost daily reports from the online "front." She also reported on the advice she gave to a group of people she called the *okhraniteli*—"the guardians."[46] These emails and the reports they contain provide us with a unique glimpse into the inner workings of the Russian state, as it pressed its ideational campaign deeper into the heart of what evidently felt like enemy territory.

The strategy adopted by the Kremlin in this campaign was different from its approach to television. While the authorities could exercise substantial control over physical space in Russia and could completely dominate the airwaves, they had previously largely ceded the online space to the opposition. Rather than being in the dominant position to which it was accustomed, the Kremlin found itself in the role of an upstart. The challenge it faced was to try to create the same kind of consistency of message for online readers as was already provided for television viewers. The 2012 Mizulina internet-filtration law made it easier for the state to block viewers' access to oppositional content, and the state certainly had the ability to coerce internet companies (at least Russian ones) and the authors of critical material into changing their behavior. But Potupchik and Prokopenko wanted to do more. Their goal was for the *okhraniteli* to build an online following as powerful as that of the opposition, one capable of creating its own echo-chamber of opinion, of countering the opposition's appeal and even shaping the online agenda.

THE DEFENDERS

To really resonate, Potupchik and the *okhraniteli* would have to choose their words carefully and structure their arguments in ways that really connected to how people were thinking. Any group of people who want to achieve a political goal rely on a shared set of understandings—a sense of justice and injustice, of right and wrong, of purpose and strategy, and a sense of solidarity, community. Sociologists call this a "frame."[47] These shared understandings evolve over time as events challenge or reinforce earlier ideas, and as allies are added to or depart from the coalition. In the process, frames both build on and contribute to participants' sense of identity.[48] Potupchik's reports, then, can provide at least a partial record of how she and the *okhraniteli* understood what they were doing and the contours of the fight in which they were engaged— and how those understandings changed over time.

The trouble for the Kremlin, however, was that try as they might to generate clear, powerful frames that could drive the narrative, events kept getting in the way. Early efforts to frame the opposition and its foreign adversaries as "Gay-ropa" (a play on the Russian word for Europe, "Evropa") failed to gain much traction and were soon dropped. Instead, much of Potupchik's time was taken up playing defense rather than offense, with an agenda dictated by a combination of events and the opposition themselves.

The main adversary, in Potupchik's mind, was blogger
and opposition leader Alexei Navalny. In fact, Navalny's
name features in almost exactly the same number of
reports as Putin's does—as these records were also meant
for consumption higher up the bureaucratic chain, Putin
appeared almost every day.[49] Typically, the goal was to
discredit Navalny's narrative of events as promoted by his
blog and opposition supporters, or, at least, to reframe the
discussion in terms less favorable to the opposition.

One way to do this was to challenge the honesty of
non-Kremlin information sources. Potupchik, for example,
instructed the *okhraniteli* to question Dozhd's objectivity,
suggesting that they accuse it of "bought-and-paid-for"
reporting. Similarly, as Navalny went on trial for yet more
trumped-up fraud charges, she suggested that the *okhraniteli* turn their anger not only against the opposition leader,
but against his supporters as a whole, for having tethered
their political ambitions to what was so obviously a sinking
ship.

Soon, though, the sinking ship was again dictating the
agenda. In September 2014, Navalny published an investigation into the undeclared foreign assets of the wife of
Valentin Gorbunov, the head of the Moscow City Electoral
Commission. Potupchik's recommendation was to change
the topic:

> Navalny's investigation about Gorbunov's foreign
> assets should be seen as an act of petty revenge for the
> fact that none of the members of [Navalny's] Progress
> Party was registered for the election to the Moscow
> City Duma.

Potupchik returned to the "everyone's given up on Navalny" argument on October 6, when the news broke that Vladimir Ashurkov, head of Navalny's anti-corruption foundation, had sought political asylum in the UK:

> . . . It should be noted that almost no one in Navalny's inner circle believes in his political success. That should be the explanation given for the emigration of his closest supporters: Volkov, Guriev, Ashurkov. The *okhraniteli* should declare a split in the Navalny group.

Though often outpaced by Navalny and his allies, Potupchik faced an even bigger problem—not a person or group, but reality itself, in the shape of events in the world that even the Kremlin couldn't fully control, or of hard-to-spin policies coming from other parts of the state.

For example, on August 6, 2014, the Russian government announced it would impose retaliatory sanctions on the import of European and American goods—primarily foodstuffs and other agricultural products. Potupchik's advice: ignore it!

The next day, however, as the news sank in, the *okhraniteli* had to launch a rear-guard defense against biting criticism from the opposition. Potupchik wrote:

> Statements that the West imposed sanctions on Russian officials, and Putin hit back against his own consumers should be countered, to the effect that in addition to the personal sanctions the West is trying to land a blow against whole segments of industry, major enterprises, primarily in the defense sector,

and its goal is *de facto* indirectly to hurt the incomes of the families of workers and engineers in industrial cities.

A greater challenge came four months later. The Russian ruble, which had traded at about 35 to the US dollar at the beginning of 2014, had been on a slow but accelerating decline since August 2014. On Friday, December 12, 2014, the ruble closed at 56.9 to the dollar. By Monday night, it was at 64.4.[50] Potupchik wrote that day:

> The most important and, in fact, the only topic of discussion in social networks was the sharp devaluation of the ruble—even the comments of the *okhraniteli* have a note of panic. Against this backdrop, the silence of the Ministry of Economy and the Central Bank truly looks strange. The position of these agencies must be presented in the informational space and must contain a clear description of the reasons for what has happened. Otherwise, the mood of panic will not disappear—it will continue to get stronger.

As Potupchik's occasional outbursts of frustration suggest, her allies could be at least as much of a challenge as her opponents. In the months and years after Putin's reelection in 2012, the State Duma came to be known as the "crazy printer," passing conservative and repressive legislation in rapid-fire succession, including ideological fodder of the kind described earlier, as well as a raft of measures aimed at tightening state control over NGOs and the internet. Eventually, the "crazy printer" began to drive Potupchik crazy, too. At the end of July, the Duma passed a law regulating bloggers, including the requirement that bloggers with a large readership register as media outlets, as well as punishment for what Russians call "non-normative vocabulary"—in other words, foul language. In a note that would have been both a plea to the Kremlin and a tacit message of solidarity to her online comrades, she all but begged the Duma to back off, not least because it was alienating the *okhraniteli* themselves.

Two days later, Potupchik was fighting the same battle on a different front. Regional authorities in Siberia had got a court there to order the blocking of online accounts associated with a regional protest movement. The censorship, she noted in her report of August 3, drew even more attention to the cause than had the protests.

A similar "cry of the soul" went up on December 3, after news broke of a proposal gathering steam in the Duma to ban people from working in disciplines other than those in which they had received their university degrees. Potupchik wrote:

> The appearance on the internet of information like this . . . discredits all *okhraniteli*. What's more, the reaction to such news in the information space, where people are riled up by information about the falling ruble exchange rate, about oil prices and data on a recession in Russia, is even more angry and harsh. These things aren't seen as innocent jokes anymore.

On other occasions Potupchik's demands on the state were more proactive, such as when, on September 3, she called for concrete action to defuse mounting criticism of food-price inflation in the aftermath of Russia's retaliatory ban on European and other food imports. On the whole, however, the reports suggest that, while Potupchik was very much aware of her role on behalf of the Russian state, she and Prokopenko had concluded that the only way the Kremlin would be able to win the battle online would be if it could learn to take on board not just the concerns expressed by Russians online, but also some of the values that pertain in the online world—values that privilege responsiveness over *diktat*, and give-and-take over outright coercion. Potupchik's goal, then, was not only to remake the internet in the Kremlin's image; she sought also, as much as possible, to remake the Kremlin in the internet's image.

Despite all the challenges and failures, Potupchik's efforts at framing were at least partially successful. One goal of a good frame is to get those who use it to internalize the frame as part of their own identity. If bad news stories online made this difficult to do on particular issues, the broader notion of the existence of a group of *okhraniteli*, or "guardians," dedicated to defending Russia and Putin online proved more successful. The very term *okhraniteli* came to be adopted by pro-Putin bloggers and social-media commentators as a badge of honor. Exasperated opposition bloggers and commenters, by contrast, called them *portianki*, the term for the long strips of cloth that Russian soldiers were issued to wrap around their feet and calves in place of socks, or *vatniki*, referring to the shoddy, cotton-stuffed overcoats worn by Soviet soldiers, prisoners and manual laborers. In the process, sides were drawn and the information in the online world became more structured—just as there were people and places to develop the opposition worldview, so now there were people and places devoted to creating a Kremlin-approved version of online reality.

THREE

THE RUSSIAN SPRING

On March 7, 2014, Igor Grebtsov became a little green man.

From the town of Slavyansk-na-Kubani, near the Kerch Strait that separates Russia from Ukrainian Crimea— some 1,600 miles from his home in the Ural Mountains— Grebtsov called his wife to tell her that he would not be back in time to celebrate Women's Day on March 8. At first, she thought it was a prank and called him back three times to make sure. As the reality sank in, she threatened him with divorce, but eventually relented. He would return home, nursing wounds from a tank battle in eastern Ukraine, nine months later.

After breaking the news to his wife, Grebtsov crossed into Crimea with a group of other men, mostly army veterans and reservists, and more than a few Cossacks, and settled into a hotel. The next morning, according to an interview he gave to his hometown newspaper, he and others went to witness what he called a "Banderite march"—a rally of supporters of the "Euromaidan" movement that had overthrown Ukrainian President Viktor Yanukovych.[1] Grebtsov and his comrades saw the revolutionaries as followers of Stepan Bandera, the Ukrainian partisan leader who fought against both Soviet and German domination of western Ukraine during and after World War II, but who also aligned himself with the SS at times and terrorized the Jewish population of the region. Later that day, Grebtsov enlisted in the "militia" of "little green men," the covert operation that led to Russia's annexation of Crimea. By the end of the month, he was in Donetsk, the key city in Ukraine's eastern Donbas region and the focal point of what would soon become a separatist war.

Oddly enough, it was the disconnect between what he was seeing on Russian state-controlled TV and what he was reading on independent Ukrainian websites that finally made him pick up and go to war, Grebtsov remembered in an April 2014 interview with the local newspaper *Kachkanarsky Chetverg*. "When you see that they're saying one thing here, and something totally different there, and you don't understand what's really happening, the only way to figure it out is to go there yourself," he said.

The story of how Russia went to war with Ukraine is, above all, the story of men like Igor Grebtsov. We don't know how many of the Russian fighters in various parts of Ukraine were following orders, and how many—like Grebtsov—were volunteers. But we do know that the Kremlin's decision to occupy first Crimea and then parts of the Donbas, and to plunge the region into an armed conflict that continues to this day, produced a groundswell of genuine support: in some cases, support strong enough to move men to leave behind families and put themselves in the line of fire.

"At first, I wasn't intending to enlist in the militia," Grebtsov told *Kachkanarsky Chetverg*. "The idea arose while I was there, when I saw those Banderite rallies, talked to people, learned more about the conflict." When a rumor began to spread among the anti-Maidan crowd about NATO exercises planned for March 9, his mind was made up.

"I decided to join and defend Russians," he said.

There were no NATO exercises in March 2014, but that hardly matters.

TO WAR

By the middle of February 2014, it was becoming increasingly clear that Viktor Yanukovych's grip on Ukraine was failing. Protesters had occupied Kyiv's Maidan Nezalezhnosti—Independence Square—since November 21, 2013, when President Yanukovych suspended plans to sign an association agreement with the European Union. In the ensuing days, protesters drafted demands calling for constitutional reform reducing the power of the presidency and refused to leave the square. Clashes with police ensued on November 30, leading to riots and running skirmishes that lasted well into the new year. On February 20, the Russian prime minister (and former president) Dmitry Medvedev—who had kept his own riot police largely at bay during the 2011–12 Russian mass protests—publicly called on Yanukovych to take a harder line: "Don't let people wipe their feet on you," Medvedev said.[2] That day, amid shooting from both sides, between sixty and eighty protesters were shot dead on and around the Maidan.[3]

The next day, Vladimir Lukin—a former Russian ambassador to Washington and Putin's long-time human-rights ombudsman—arrived in Kyiv, ostensibly to help mediate in negotiations between the government and the opposition; instead, he spirited Yanukovych out of the country, installing him in the southern Russian city of Rostov-on-Don. During the flight, the Ukrainian parliament voted to impeach the president. Two weeks later, Igor Grebtsov was in Crimea, and he wasn't alone.

On February 22, 2014—the day after Yanukovych fled Ukraine—someone in Russia registered the internet domain address dobrovolec.org, the name drawn from the Russian word for "volunteer." After sitting dormant for several weeks, the address eventually began to be used for recruiting mercenaries like Grebtsov. We don't know who bought the domain or why, but the facts that are available suggest a startling degree either of foresight or of planning on the part of whoever was behind it. Before those plans (or that foresight) could be put to use, however, there was work to be done.

On February 26, 2014, unrest broke out on the grounds of the Crimean Rada, the parliament of the Republic of Crimea, which, together with the port city of Sevastopol, where Russia had its Black Sea Fleet base, enjoyed semi-autonomous status under the Ukrainian constitution. On the one side were Crimean Tatars, members of an ethnic group indigenous to the region but who were deported *en masse* to Central Asia under Stalin and who had struggled to regain their lands and rights even under independent Ukraine; the Tatars were interspersed with pro-Maidan activists, waving blue and yellow Ukrainian flags. Opposing both groups was a contingent waving Russian flags. The exact composition of this latter group remains a mystery: they were mostly young and mostly Russian-speaking, but whether they were from the large Russian-speaking majority that inhabits Crimea or from Russia itself is unclear. What is clear is that fisticuffs resulted, and the opposing sides barricaded themselves into corners of the Rada compound.[4]

This, apparently, provided the opening that someone in Moscow had been waiting for. Under cover of night, masked armed men in military uniforms bearing no insignia stormed the building. The next morning, with Ukrainian police watching from a safe distance, the masked men marshaled a self-declared quorum of Rada members, who in turn voted to hold a referendum on independence for the peninsula, scheduled for May 2; the "little green men" guarded the doors and windows of the building as the voting occurred.[5] That night, another group of armed masked men in military uniforms with no insignia—delivered in army-green trucks with no markings or number plates—seized control of the Simferopol airport, the peninsula's key airfield.[6] The sun rose on February 28 to find checkpoints armed by unidentifiable "little green men" on the road between Simferopol and Sevastopol—the peninsula's main artery—and on other major roads.[7] In a hint of things to come, a number of these checkpoints were also manned by members of the Night Wolves, a Moscow-based biker gang known for its nationalism and, indeed, the only openly nationalist organization with which Vladimir Putin has ever posed for a photo opportunity.[8]

"It was truly bizarre," recalls Roland Oliphant, who arrived in Simferopol on February 26 to cover the events for London's *Daily Telegraph* and was the first Western reporter to write about the rapid emergence of the "little green men." "They were like the guards at Buckingham Palace who aren't allowed to interact with the tourists. We would go up to them, run after them, taking pictures and asking questions about where they were from and what they were doing, and they would just stare blankly at you through those balaclavas."[9]

Russia's mainstream media—led by the three government-controlled television stations—were covering events in Crimea through the same prisms that had shaped their coverage of the Euromaidan in Kyiv, but with a twist. The overarching narrative of a fascist *junta* brought to power by radical nationalists and with the backing of Washington and Brussels was diluted somewhat by Russian reporters' own bewilderment at the "little green men"—although most Russian media used the term "polite people," in reference to the masked men's evidently placid demeanor. On this front, at least, the Russian mainstream reporters knew no more than their Western or Ukrainian competitors. It was, then, perhaps unsurprising that Grebtsov and others might have been motivated by a desire to learn the truth.

Another Russian citizen who traveled to Crimea in search of the truth was the prominent opposition blogger Ilya Varlamov. In a post on his LiveJournal blog from March 4, 2014, Varlamov wrote:

The most important thing is, everything's calm. There is tension, but it's being stoked from outside. People are watching the television, reading newspapers, and then make horrified phone calls to their relatives in Crimea, saying "Is there a war there? Get out! Save yourselves!" In Crimea, Russian soldiers are sharing their cigarettes with their Ukrainian colleagues and no one has heard anything about a war or could even think about it. But there is tension.

There were, however, Russian soldiers in places they weren't supposed to be, Varlamov reported.

> Since officially these aren't Russian soldiers, the Moscow PR people, who have also come to Crimea, invented a very cool thing: "Polite people." They're creating the image of the liberating Russian soldier, who came in a nice new uniform with beautiful weapons to protect peaceful villages and cities. He's courteous, smiles, you can take a picture with him as a souvenir. He's polite.[10]

The official line—delivered emphatically by Defense Minister Sergei Shoigu and President Putin himself—was that these "polite people" were most certainly not Russian soldiers; rather, they were local self-defense forces, made up of volunteers, and the Russian government knew nothing whatsoever about how these local volunteer forces managed to acquire late-model Russian uniforms, equipment and vehicles.[11] Few if anyone bought that story, however. On March 6, the Obama administration laid the groundwork for sanctions against Russia should it move to annex Crimea under any pretense, citing what Washington saw as a covert invasion of the peninsula. As the referendum approached—brought forward to March 16—international media were filled with stories about Crimea's now ubiquitous "little green men."[12] The rest, of course, is history. On March 16, more than 95 percent of participants in the Crimean referendum voted to declare independence and join Russia; the only other option on the ballot was to seek functional autonomy through a constitutional reform in Ukraine.[13] The following day, the US, the EU and Canada imposed the first round of sanctions, focusing on Russian officials and state-linked companies directly involved in the annexation, including, incidentally, the Night Wolves. A day after that, Putin solemnly announced that Crimea had "rejoined" the Russian Federation.

PUTIN V. THE NATIONALISTS

It has become common among Western analysts and policymakers to think of Vladimir Putin as a nationalist. Such accusations usually point to his statement in 2005 that the breakup of the USSR was "the greatest geopolitical catastrophe of the twentieth century," as well as to his 2007 speech to the Munich Security Conference, in which the Russian president pointedly challenged American power in the world.[14] Russia's intervention in Ukraine would seem to prove the point. But until men like Igor Grebtsov started packing their bags for Crimea, the Kremlin went out of its way to avoid nationalism at home.

Nationalism—including xenophobia and chauvinism—has always been a part of Russian politics (distinguishing Russia, of course, from no other country on the planet).

Russian and various other ethnic nationalists were among the dissident groups that opposed the Soviet government after Khrushchev's post-Stalin thaw, meeting in apartments to hone their ideologies, building underground networks of sympathizers at home and abroad, distributing clandestine texts through *samizdat*. The ultra-nationalist and notoriously anti-Semitic movement Pamyat was among the most powerful movements to emerge in Russia after the collapse of the Soviet Union, but it was far from alone. Among the longest-lasting groups was Alexander Dugin's Eurasianist movement, drawing on the thought of earlier generations of nationalists including Lev Gumilev (1912–92) and Ivan Il'in (1883–1954), as well as more esoteric sources.

In 1993, Vladimir Zhirinovsky shocked the world when his nationalist and anti-Semitic (and ironically named) Liberal Democratic Party won the largest share of votes in the parliamentary elections. Zhirinovsky and the populist former mayor of Moscow Yury Luzhkov, among others, would periodically call for President Boris Yeltsin to intervene on behalf of ethnic Russians living in the Baltics or Central Asia—as well as for the return of Crimea—but Yeltsin demurred. More recently, groups like the Movement Against Illegal Immigration (DPNI, by its Russian acronym) emerged to oppose the migration of dark-skinned "guest workers" from the Caucasus and Central Asia. Even Alexei Navalny—nominal leader of Russia's liberal opposition—has frequented the nationalist "Russian Marches" held annually on November 4. However, Putin's Kremlin had steadfastly ignored calls from both the DPNI and Navalny to impose a visa regime on migrant workers from Central Asia.

By the time Putin rose to power in 1999, Zhirinovsky had become a mostly tame mainstream Russian politician, and the more extreme nationalist organizations were effectively suppressed by the Federal Security Service (FSB), which Putin himself had headed. Putin's administration, however, was always aware of the nationalists on its flank and from time to time launched experiments to try to keep at least the more mainstream nationalists on board.

In 2003, Vladislav Surkov, Putin's chief political adviser, brought together a group of moderately nationalist politicians to create a new political party, Rodina (Motherland), in an effort to give nationalist-minded voters a Kremlin-friendly option for that year's Duma elections; the party duly won 9 percent of the vote but was disbanded in 2006 amidst the growing ambitions of its leaders.[15] In 2007, the nationalist flag was picked up by Nashi, the youth group created by the Kremlin to channel the political energy of young people in pro-regime directions (and which had once employed Kristina Potupchik, the Kremlin internet operative we met in the previous chapter). Nashi went on the offensive against the government of Estonia, when it attempted to remove a prominent Soviet-era war memorial. Nashi activists took part in riots in the Estonian capital and hounded the country's ambassador in Moscow. They similarly harassed the British and American ambassadors. The Kremlin itself, however, maintained a polite distance and eventually brought the activists to heel.

In deciding not to allow radical nationalists to contest the 2007 parliamentary elections, the Kremlin reinforced its policy of suppressing that part of the political spectrum. Nationalism and xenophobia did not, however, go away. Even though they were subject to prosecution under laws against extremism and inciting ethnic hatred, nationalist groups proliferated, making use of online social media to grow beyond kitchen tables and clandestine clubs. Often, football fan groups served as hotbeds of nationalist senti- ment, as they do in many countries. Predominantly, the nationalists' anger was directed against migrants, including immigrants from Central Asia and internal migrants from the ethnic republics of the North Caucasus, who in turn organized themselves into communities of solidarity and self-defense (as well as organized crime).

That violence would ensue was almost inevitable. In September 2006, riots erupted in the small northern- Russian town of Kondopoga, near the border with Finland, after a bar-room fight led to the murder of two ethnic Russians by a group of Chechen and Dagestani migrants. In December 2010, some 50,000 nationalists rioted on Manezh Square, under the walls of the Kremlin, demanding revenge for the death of an ethnically Russian football fan in a mass brawl with a group of North Caucasians living in Moscow. The Kremlin responded to the rising unrest with a wave of arrests of nationalist leaders, including Alexander Belov (leader of the DPNI).[16] The result, unsur- prisingly, was to further deepen the mistrust between nationalists and the Kremlin, according to Alexander Verkhovsky, a human-rights activist and long-time Russian observer of the nationalist movement. "Because the bulk of radical nationalists are members of violence-oriented groups, the entire movement saw this policy as a 'declaration of war,' which raised the temperature of their anti-government sentiment," Verkhovsky wrote.[17]

Sensing that rising temperature, the Kremlin again decided to dabble. In an effort to show that he was tough on migrants, Moscow Mayor Sergei Sobyanin—who was running for election in September 2013—decided to organize a series of raids on goods markets, transport hubs, dormitories and other sites where immigrants could be found *en masse*; detainees were herded into makeshift detention centers and then onto airplanes out of the country, all under the watchful eye of television cameras.[18] The anti-migrant campaign that led up to the election was, in part, a response both to the memory of the Manezh and Kondopoga riots, and to the participation of nationalists in the anti-Kremlin "Bolotnaya" movement of 2011–12, Verkhovsky argues. Not only did the campaign respond to the nationalists' immediate demands, but it gave nationalist groups an opportunity to participate directly in the implementation of their desired policies, by helping the police and other authorities to identify and round up illegal immigrants.

All but one of Sobyanin's opponents in the election, meanwhile, lined up on the same side of the issue, each vying to outdo the others in anti-immigrant fervor.[19] Navalny, for one, promised (with tongue only partly in cheek) to ban public performance of the *lezginka*, an iconic folk dance from the Caucasus.[20] Sobyanin duly won the election, which in turn brought an end to the crackdown on migrants—but, of course, not to the nationalism. One month later, the working-class Moscow neighborhood of Western Biriulevo was rocked by a wave of pogroms, in the wake of the death of an ethnic Russian resident, allegedly at the hands of an immigrant from Azerbaijan. As before, the Kremlin was silent.

CRIMEA IS OURS!

When Vladimir Putin addresses the Russian parliament—whether for his inauguration, to deliver his annual "state of the nation" address, or for any other purpose—the parliament comes to him. Once all are seated in a gilded Kremlin hall, massive doors swing open and Putin, alone, enters, striding wordlessly to the podium amid the applause of his audience. The address on March 18, 2014, was no exception.

The circumstances were, however, exceptional. For the first time since the end of World War II, Russia had annexed territory by force from one of its neighbors. For all its ambivalence about nationalism, the Putin administration had just delivered on one of the nationalists' fondest dreams—taking Crimea. And it had all happened without the Russian government acknowledging what it had done. Now finally, Putin was to speak, to frame the annexation and state official Russian policy.

"To understand why this decision was made," Putin said, "it is enough to know the history of Crimea, to know what Russia meant and means for Crimea, and Crimea for Russia." He continued:

> In Crimea, literally everything is saturated with our common history and pride. It is the land of ancient Chersonesus, where the Holy Prince Vladimir was

baptized. His spiritual feat—his conversion to Orthodox Christianity—predetermined the common cultural, moral and civilizational foundation that binds the people of Russia, Ukraine and Belarus. In Crimea are found the graves of Russian soldiers, through whose bravery in 1783 Crimea was brought under Russian rule. Crimea is Sevastopol, that legendary city, that city of great fate, the fortress city and Motherland of the Russian Black Sea Fleet. Crimea is Balaklava and Kerch, Malakhov Kurgan and Sapun-Gora. Each one of these places is sacred to us, as symbols of Russian military glory and unheard-of valor.[21]

Some of this history would have been familiar to Russians, but much of it was obscure and being heard by most people for the first time.[22] As we will see in Chapter 4, to say that many Russians responded positively to the annexation of Crimea would be an understatement, but Putin and his advisers could not have known just how powerfully his words and actions would resonate. According to Gleb Pavlovsky, Putin's first chief political adviser, the approach taken in the March 18 speech was to throw things at the wall and see what stuck. Much like Potupchik's work with the online *okhraniteli* on behalf of the Kremlin, Putin's speechwriters tried a bit of everything: in the president's words, the annexation of Crimea was an act of humanitarian intervention to liberate an oppressed Russian-speaking population; an act of historical justice; even an act of Christian piety. It was justified by geopolitics, by ethnic solidarity, and by the long arc of history. Whatever the rhetoric, though, the nationalists came running.

Most Russians are not ardent nationalists. Very few would pick up and go to war. Comparatively few, in fact, would spend much time thinking and talking about war, or the potential for war. And yet, some people obviously did, and it was from that cohort that people like Grebtsov were recruited. Finding these people, of course, is a challenge. One place to do it was on the battlefields of Donbas; these, alas, were off limits to us. Another place was online. Indeed, it was in social media communities and a handful of dedicated websites that many of the recruits—and their financial and ideological supporters back home in Russia—found one another and joined the cause.

At the core of this digital nationalist movement was a group of "community" pages on the popular Russian online social network VKontakte (VK, for short). We concentrated on the largest of these, sixteen communities bringing together more than 1 million people. At their peak, these communities were generating as many as 6 million "likes" per month. To learn more about this group, we examined more than half a million posts—and several million comments—made between December 2011 and May 2016.

Nationalists being nationalists, prior to the eruption of the Euromaidan in Ukraine most of these groups spent their time talking about Russia. In fact, most of the pre-Euromaidan content wasn't overtly political: participants would share patriotic movie clips and images, indulge in nostalgia, get whipped up in the fervor around Victory Day every May 9, and so on. Notably absent from these communities was Putin: the Russian president—who had so assiduously avoided outright nationalism himself—made it into fewer than 5 percent of the posts we found prior to Crimea. Every once in a while, America or Europe—the nationalists' primary bogeymen—would come into the picture, but only in about one in ten posts. When things did get political, messages were most often imbued with a sense of historical grievance and the need for revenge, mostly for the loss of the Soviet empire. In fact, the language of revenge was present in about one in five posts prior to December 2013.

But the Euromaidan changed all of that. A popular meme making the rounds in December 2013 on the nationalist VK communities showed two photographs—one of Soviet soldiers in World War II, and the other of protesters waving the EU flag on the Maidan—with the caption, "Back then, they didn't know that seventy years later the Ukrainians would hand their Motherland over to the enemy." In fact, these online communities had begun talking more and more about Ukraine in the summer of 2013, as Russian nationalists on both sides of the border reacted to the growing likelihood that the EU and Ukraine would, in fact, conclude and sign an association agreement.[23] Attention only grew as events in Kyiv unfolded, for a while drowning out even discussion of Russia itself.[24] Much as mass anti-Georgian sentiment had been whipped up prior to Russia's short 2008 war with that country, so too did Ukraine come to capture a segment of the Russian public imagination. For Russian national-ists, the Moscow-based political scientist Sergei Medvedev wrote, talking about Ukraine became an important way of talking about themselves. In short, it was the fight in Ukraine that came to define Russian nationalism itself.

It was around this time, too, that the nationalists' rhetoric began to merge with the Kremlin's. Many of the "wedge issues" that were so powerful in countering Russia's own oppositional uprising in 2012—homophobia, antipathy to "liberal values," and the imperative of counteracting allegedly Western-backed "fascism"—worked their way into nationalists' discussions of Ukraine.[25] All of these were argued by both the nationalists and the Kremlin to be part of the West's nefarious bargain with the Maidan. In describing his comrades in Crimea and Donbas to an interviewer from his local newspaper, Igor Grebtsov put it this way:

> *Grebtsov*: These people, they came to defend Russians and the interests of their country. They came because they don't like the European life. A [Russian] guy from Germany told us how he works as a computer programmer, he's 40-something years old, raising two kids. One day his daughter brings an assignment home from school—write an essay on tolerance. The conditions: your parents are being visited for the weekend by a gay friend, and you and your brother have to occupy the guest while your parents are out doing the shopping.

> *Interviewer*: And you think that's unacceptable?

> *Grebtsov*: Naturally. In Crimea, the front line now lies not between Ukraine and Russia, the European Union or anyone else, but between normal people and abnormal people. People consciously don't want to join Europe.[26]

On the morning of February 27, 2014, the trending post in the VK community known as "Anti-maydan" (sic) was a report that special-ops troops from Chechnya had arrived in Crimea "to defend the population and restore order," linking this rumor (for which there is still no clear corroboration) to earlier reports on the occupation of the Crimean Rada in Simferopol. Later that day, however, it was overtaken by a post headlined "VICTORY!!!" and reporting the news that the Rada had announced the referendum. On March 1, by far the most popular post was a report that the Russian Federation Council had authorized Putin to move Russian troops across the Ukrainian border. The post read: "The decision has been taken. Russian troops are going to Ukraine. The decision has been taken!!! A minute ago!!!"

The nationalists' excitement at the reports from Crimea was understandable, as was their newfound admiration for Putin. The Kremlin was finally putting the force of the Russian state—indeed, the force of Russian arms—behind an agenda for which the nationalists had been agitating for years, if not decades. By contrast, Putin's set-piece annexation speech was almost a non-event. On the day of Putin's speech, one of the most popular posts in the nationalist segment of VK read simply: "Russian warriors don't start wars, they end them!" Another popular post was a joke:

Obama, Merkel, Hollande and the rest—Putin's sick of them already. They keep calling and calling, so he switched his phone to voicemail. His message says, "Hello. You have called Russian President Putin. Unfortunately, I cannot take your call at the moment.

If you want to surrender, please press 1. If you want to
threaten sanctions, please press 2. If you want to discuss
the situation in Ukraine, please press 3. All buttons
other than 1 activate our Topol-M intercontinental
missiles. Have a nice day!"

ON THE FRONT LINES

When and if a future Russian government decides to open
up its archives and declassify military and intelligence
dossiers from 2014, historians will be able to tell us how
much of what happened next in eastern Ukraine was
planned in advance.

It began on April 7, 2014, in Kharkiv, where anti-
Maidan protesters stormed the regional administration
building. Three days later, protesters overran the local
headquarters of the Ukrainian security services—the
SBU—in Luhansk. Oleksander Turchynov, Ukraine's
acting president, promised the protesters immunity from
prosecution if they would leave the government compounds
peacefully, but the gesture was in vain.[27] On April 11, anti-
Maidan protests emerged in Odessa; on April 12, protesters
tried to seize the Donetsk office of the Ukrainian prosecu-
torial service, but were turned away.

In the town of Slavyansk, however, things took a more
ominous turn: a group of heavily armed men—wearing
masks and military uniforms bearing no insignia—led by
someone calling himself Igor Strelkov, took over the local
police headquarters; the town wouldn't return firmly to
Ukrainian government control until July 5.[28] On April 14,
"Polite People"—identical to those who had been seen in

Crimea—began turning up in Luhansk.[29] On April 16, a group led by Kharkiv-based nationalist leader Alexander Zakharchenko overran the Donetsk city hall and called on the authorities in Kyiv to allow a referendum "on the territorial status of the Donetsk region."[30] The next day, "Polite People" were spotted at the Donetsk airport.[31]

An "anti-terrorist operation" launched by Turchynov on April 15 resulted in a series of embarrassing defeats for the Ukrainian military, which found itself outgunned and out-maneuvered. By the end of April 2014, much of the Donetsk and Luhansk regions were effectively outside of Kyiv's control, and skirmishes began to break out further afield, including in Mariupol (on the road from Donetsk to Crimea) and in Odessa, where running street battles ultimately led to approximately sixty anti-Kyiv protesters being burned to death on May 2.[32] Sensing Russia's hand—and corroborated by Putin's own admission on April 17 that regular Russian troops had "backed up" the local self-defense forces in Crimea—the US and EU expanded sanctions on April 28.[33] (In December 2015, Putin would publicly acknowledge that the Russian government ran the Crimean operation from start to finish.)[34]

As with Crimea, the nationalist groups on VK obsessed over reports from the emerging "front" in eastern Ukraine. From March through July 2014, "war reports" account for between half and two thirds of each month's online activity. Over the course of the spring and summer of 2014, the number of large, public community pages on VK dedicated to the emerging conflict mushroomed from three that were active prior to February 2014, to six by the end of

April, twelve by the end of May and fifteen by the end of August 2014. Whereas the pre-conflict groups bore names like "Anti-Maidan" or "Against the EU," the new groups took titles more specific to the war: "Novorossia" or the "Republic of New Russia," "Russian Spring," "Revolution East," "News Front," "South Ukraine," "Government DNR," and so on. The largest group to emerge bore the name of the war's most prominent commander: "Strelkov-Info."

But these communities were about more than banal voyeurism. On May 13, the following message begins appearing across several of the nationalist communities on VK:

ATTENTION!

Announcing the formation of a special brigade, inviting ONLY (!) people with combat experience.

Creation of the 1st SOUTH-EAST INTERBRIGADE

To save your time and ours, and for more effective cooperation, keep strictly to the form.

Form:

1. Your city (Formation takes place in Moscow).

2. Your age.

3. Military specialization category number.

4. Combat experience and skills.

5. Additional information.

6. Contact information.

Send your information to: Oborona_ua@dobrovolec.org with the subject line "Special Battalion" or write here: coordinator on VKontakte

#junta #ukraine #Novorossia #DNR #Russia #Odessa #Mariupol

Note the domain name on the email address: dobrovolec. org—the same address that was registered on February 22, the day after Yanukovych fled the country. On June 19, two more messages went out across the network, with the same contact details. One of them read:

RUSSIAN VOLUNTEERS
We need military paramedics, communications officers, artillerymen, staff officers (platoon, troop, division, battalion), mortar squads (brigade regiment), self-propelled howitzer specialists, operational department, reconnaissance, transport, missile artillery specialists, rear officers, rifle platoon and squad commanders, battalion commanders, service technicians for armored transports, armored infantry vehicles, armored landing vehicles and tanks, launch operators.

The second message that day requested help in requisitioning twenty-four pieces of heavy equipment, including generators, pumps, compressors and other machines. The text begins with the line "Reports from Strelkov, Igor Ivanovich" and notes that the supplies are needed "URGENTLY" for the troops in Slavyansk.

By mid-May 2014, Strelkov had emerged as the most prominent of the Donbas separatist leaders, although he wasn't from the region. A Russian FSB agent whose real name is Igor Girkin, he had served in Transnistria and Serbia, as well as Chechnya and Dagestan. In a breathless profile of Girkin–Strelkov published in June 2014, the newspaper *Moskovsky komsomolets*—one of Russia's most widely read dailies—wrote:

> Today, the defenders of Donbas, wielding only light arms, are taking losses in battle with regular forces of the Kyiv army and fighters from the Nazi "Right Sector," who are armed to the teeth. The rich military experience of Igor Strelkov helps to even the scales and gives south-eastern Ukraine hope for a quiet and peaceful future. The bravery of the defenders of Donbas and Strelkov's talents have melded into an armor against which the new Banderites' anger is powerless.[35]

Indeed, as support for the Donbas uprising grew online and spilled into Russia's mainstream media, neither the fighters themselves nor even the Russian government went too far out of their way to hide the connections between the two. Denis Pushilin, co-chair of the government of the Donetsk People's Republic (DNR) at the time, was most prominently known as the head of the regional branch of the Moscow-based "multi-level marketing" pyramid scheme MMM. Pavel Gubarev, who took the title of people's governor of Donetsk region, was best known as a member of the Russian neo-Nazi group Russian National Unity.[36] Another DNR commander, Alexander Borodai, told journalists on May 15 that plans for Donbas and Crimea were developed "more or less by the same cohort of people." He went on to say, "I won't hide that I worked in Crimea."[37] A day later, RIA Novosti—Russia's official state-run news agency—ran a story touting "Polite People" as the new symbol of the Russian military.[38] In another interview more than a year later, Borodai claimed that between 30,000 and 50,000 Russians fought in the Donbas and launched a Union of Donbas Volunteers to "defend volunteers, assist the families of those who died, and the people of Donbas."[39]

TURNING TIDES

On May 25, 2014, Ukrainian troops attacked separatist positions in and around the Donetsk airport.[40] Now fighting with a clearer sense of their opponent and intelligence and advice from the US, the UK and Germany, Kyiv's operation was not the abject failure that many of its earlier missions had been, but neither did it end in success; in fact, the struggle for the Donetsk airport—or, rather, what was left of it—would go on for the better part of a year. Nonetheless, the terms of the war were beginning to shift. In voting on May 15, Petro Poroshenko was elected as president of Ukraine, to be inaugurated the following month. His promise was to seek peace if possible, but to win the war if necessary.

As Poroshenko took office, Kyiv launched an offensive that would, for the first time since the war began, push the front line toward Russia. On June 21, Putin announced a general mobilization of active duty servicemen and reserves in Russia's Central Military District and used a series of exercises to reposition troops and equipment near the Ukrainian border. Battles were fierce and casualties mounted, including among civilians.

Among the most symbolic victories for the Ukrainian army was the retaking on July 5, 2014, of Slavyansk—the town where the fighting had first begun a few months earlier. The online nationalist communities were livid. One popular post on the South Ukraine page July 5 read simply: "It was not for nothing that Moscow was delivered to the Frenchman, burned to the ground. . . ."

But the most popular post written in reaction to the fall of Slavyansk was a startling combination of anger, accusation and confession. Too lengthy to reproduce here in full, it is written as though from an anonymous Russian soldier to an anonymous Ukrainian soldier:

> Ukrainian soldier, you won! Congratulations!
>
> What did you see when you entered the liberated Slavyansk?
>
> Did you see happiness on the faces of the locals? Did you see celebration? Did happy women throw flowers on your armored personnel carrier or your tank? Did they hold out their children for you?
>
> Did you see the people's happiness at your arrival? Did you feel oneness with these people? Were you happy that you—a Ukrainian soldier—were a defender, a liberator, a preserver of life?
>
> Did you feel what our soldiers felt in Prishtina or South Ossetia?
>
> Or not?
>
> Did you see demolished homes?
>
> Hospitals?
>
> Schools?
>
> Kindergartens?

Did you see fear in people's eyes? Did you see hate in those eyes?

Did you see the fresh graves? Did you count them?

What did you bring with you to Slavyansk, the city you liberated?

From whom did you liberate it, and for whom?

You were followed into the city by nationalists. You were followed by mercenaries. You were followed by Ukrainian secret services, and we know whom they serve.

And what are they doing right now, before your very eyes? What are they doing?

They are looking for unreliable elements. They are dealing in arrests, in interrogations, in revenge. They are taking their revenge on the city. They are putting the residents on their knees. They are forcing them to jump and yell "Glory to Ukraine! Glory to the heroes!" right next to the fresh graves of their relatives and neighbors.

How do I know this?

Simply because it has happened before.

And you were also followed by Ukrainian politicians and journalists.

And what are they doing now?

They are lying. They are making set-piece films. They are taking false interviews.

. . .

This is all your doing.

Almost as if foreshadowed by the nationalists' own desperate rhetoric, the Russian retreat from Slavyansk also saw Moscow switch its attention to a very different front. On July 12, Russia's Channel 1 television—the country's most popular broadcaster—showed a report alleging that Ukrainian forces had sought revenge against residents of the town who were thought to have supported the separatists. Among the interviewees was a woman who claimed that her 3-year-old son had been crucified before her eyes. It was a powerful story, evoking basic human emotions, including sympathy for the mother and hatred of the boy's killers.

But it was also a lie. A few days before Channel 1 aired its report, Alexander Dugin—the leader of the Eurasianist movement and supporter of the Donbas separatists, who had become a prominent television personality in the early months of the war—posted a story about a crucified boy on his Facebook page, as did an anonymous user on the Strelkov-Info VK page. Independent Russian journalists investigating the case, however, could find no corroborating evidence and determined that the woman in the clip had no children anywhere near the right age.[41] In December 2014, Channel 1 itself backed away from the story.[42]

Although it was obviously not the first lie told during the war, the incident of the "crucified boy" instantly became Exhibit No. 1 for the use of "fake news" and "disinformation" in warfare and political conflict. Evidently, someone at Channel 1 had decided that such stories, whether they were true or not, were needed in order to evoke in the wider Russian population the passions that were already roiling the nationalists. And clearly, since Channel 1 had picked up the story from social media feeds associated with Dugin and Strelkov, they had become accustomed to taking their inspiration from the nationalists.

The relationship of the nationalists themselves to "fake news" was, in truth, ambivalent. Their online social networks were rife with rumor and falsehood, but that does not appear itself to have been the goal. After years of feeling at turns undermined or repressed by the Kremlin, the nationalists were not inclined to trust the Russian government nor its media outlets. Indeed, discussion of media manipulation was a common topic in the nationalist VK groups long before the war broke out, accounting for about 10 percent of the posts in our database between December 2011 and December 2013. And because so much of what was being posted on these VK pages was reports from the front, many of the nationalists felt that they were privy to truths that the Kremlin was unwilling to share with its own citizens. Thus, a poll by the independent Russian research group the Levada Center in September 2014 found that only 29 percent of Russians thought that there were Russian soldiers fighting in Ukraine; few if any among the nationalists on VK would have had any doubt.[43]

In his April 2014 interview with *Kachkanarsky Chetverg*, Igor Grebtsov was philosophical about the truth. The news—trumpeted on Russian television—that Crimeans were partying in the streets until dawn after the "referendum" was a bald-faced lie, he said: there was a storm that night, with lashing rains and strong winds. Equally false, he said, was the idea that there was no fighting. But despite the ubiquity of "fake news" on the Russian airwaves, Grebtsov didn't put much stock in truth-telling. The only way to win the propaganda war, he concluded, was to fight lies with bigger lies. "If Ukrainian TV channels were lying that two [Russian] soldiers raped two girls from Crimea, then Russian TV needs to lie and say that a crowd of Banderites raped a whole kindergarten," he said.

Not everyone among the nationalist contingent on VK, of course, would have shared Grebtsov's interpretation. It is notable, however, that when the news was hard to spin in the movement's favor, it was largely ignored. Stories like the retreat from Slavyansk could be used to whip up anger and reinforce the fighting spirit. But when a surface-to-air missile brought down Malaysia Airlines Flight MH17 over Donbas on July 17, 2014, it was discussed in only twenty-seven posts—out of more than 19,000 posts in our database that month. Mainstream Russian media spun stories about how the plane had been shot down by a Ukrainian air force jet that mistook it for Putin's presidential liner, or how it was actually the Malaysia Airlines plane that had gone missing somewhere in the Indian Ocean earlier in the year and was now being used to frame Russia, but the nationalists didn't go in for that.

Neither, unsurprisingly, did the nationalists go in for the Minsk Protocol signed on September 15, 2014. Based on an initial twelve-point agreement discussed by Poroshenko and Putin, the accord called for a bilateral ceasefire, established an Organization for Security and Co-operation in Europe (OSCE) monitoring mission, and promised a process of legal reform that would grant the Donbas more autonomy, but it also clearly disenfranchised the leaders of the Donetsk People's Republic (DNR) and Luhansk People's Republic (LNR). Again, the nationalists were livid. Many, evidently, saw it as treason. On the day the Minsk accords were completed, Dmitry Dzygovbrodsky, a prominent nationalist blogger involved in the Russian Spring movement, wrote on Strelkov-Info (and in his own LiveJournal blog):

> The forces in Moscow and Kyiv who thought that they could continue to play with the people, as they have for the past twenty-three years, have still not learned that historic processes are at work here, as they were in 1917 and 1789. And [no one] can keep these processes under control. Never. *Vivat* Novorossia!

In an interview published on September 16 on the Strelkov-Info VK page, separatist leader Pavel Gubarev was more measured:

> Peace talks are always a good thing. In that sense, I support the Minsk agreements. But with two caveats: the independence of the Donetsk and Luhansk People's Republics must be the starting point for these negotiations, and the ceasefire must be observed *de facto*.

Mostly, however, they ignored the topic. Minsk figured in only 6 percent of the posts in our database in September 2014. It got more attention in February 2015 when, following renewed fighting and the evident reinforcement of the separatists, the agreement was revised on terms much more favorable to the DNR and LNR; but even then, it figured in only 15 percent of posts that month. The largest pro-separatist community on VK at the time, Strelkov-Info, ignored Minsk altogether. Instead, September 15 and 16, 2014 were filled with reports from the front, such as this:

> A mysterious sniper is picking off Banderites in Slavyansk. In the Slavyansk area an unknown sniper is destroying Ukrainian occupiers in cold blood and in the light of day. . . .

Or this:

> Letter from Mariupol
> I can say this, after the liberation of Mariupol from the ukro-fascist "defenders" I can guarantee a serious surprise—the Novorossia battalion made up of Mariupol residents will be the largest and the most merciless. . . .

Mariupol never fell.

HOME TO ROOST

On May 20, 2015, Oleg Tsarev—a Ukrainian politician who joined the separatist movement and was "elected" in June 2014 speaker of the Parliament of Novorossia, which brought together separatist leaders from the DNR and LNR—announced that Novorossia was done. In messages put out on the movement's VK pages and other social networks, and in subsequent interviews, Tsarev explained that the idea of Novorossia as a unified, independent republic "doesn't fit into the peace plan."[44] The first Minsk protocol was effectively dead in the water by the end of 2014, scuppered in large measure by the separatists. In February 2015, however, France and Germany brought the warring sides back to the table, and a new agreement—Minsk II—was hammered out, in a fashion much less advantageous to Ukraine.

For many among the nationalists, however, Minsk II was still a step too far, and Tsarev's announcement was yet a further confirmation of Moscow's treason. Within the nationalists' communities on VK, the news had an explosive effect, and the size of the blast can be measured in words. Across the sixteen "communities" we followed online, the remarkable convergence of rhetoric that had seen the nationalists talk about the war and the world in virtually identical terms from the start of the war in April 2014 and until May 2015 disintegrated.[45] As the Kremlin sought to dampen down the passions of separatism and empire that had only recently united the nationalists and aligned them with Putin, discord among the nationalists once again became the norm.

That is not to say that the nationalists somehow reverted to their *status quo ante*. Ukraine had changed too much for that to be possible. Ukraine in fact continued to dominate the conversation even after Tsarev announced the Kremlin's betrayal, outpacing even Russia among the topics discussed. Fascism and the vocabulary of revenge remained popular framings for the conversation. But topics from Russian domestic politics that strayed into the debate—such as the discussion of homosexuals—fell away, as did mention of Putin himself.

If Putin was once again pushed to the margins of Russia's nationalist discourse by the dawn of 2016, the Russian president certainly responded in kind. Dugin, a darling of the nightly TV news and debate shows at the height of the war, disappeared from the airwaves. Girkin–Strelkov, too, faded into relative obscurity, and by the end of 2016 almost the entire leadership of the DNR and LNR had been purged.[46] Left in place was a leadership with the will and resources to fight. But unlike Strelkov's troops—who attacked Mariupol on the day the first Minsk protocol was signed—the local commanders were also ready to stop on command from Moscow. Closer to home, too, the Kremlin took few chances, arresting the leaders of two nationalist groups, the Russian March and the Orthodox State (so named in a purposeful parallel with the Islamic State).[47] Having brought nationalist forces out into the streets of Moscow and other major cities for a wave of Anti-Maidan marches in February 2015—marches that were headed by the Night Wolves, carrying portraits of Putin and the father of Chechen President Ramzan Kadyrov (but not of Ramzan himself)—the government evidently did not want to see disaffected nationalists return to the streets of their own accord.

After Igor Grebtsov finished his part of the war in Ukraine—with a medal for his service in Crimea, and a shrapnel wound for his service in Donbas—he returned to his hometown of Lesnoi and took a job as an editor at *Kachkanarsky Chetverg*, the newspaper that had interviewed him during the war. It was a hero's welcome, and he filled numerous pages of the paper with his recollections from the front. In March 2015, the Moscow-based

journalist Maria Eismont traveled to Kachkanar to interview him and his colleagues, resulting in a long profile
published by the online news magazine Snob and the
online television channel Dozhd.[48] In her profile, Eismont
writes:

> Grebtsov has a lot of photographs on his computer of
> pro-Ukrainian rallies in Crimea and he happily shows
> them, commenting: "This guy here, who was talking a
> lot, we detained him and shipped him to Ukraine.
> There were a lot of slogans about us being occupiers
> and all that, but there's one slogan I agree with: 'The
> referendum is a step toward war.' We wanted war, the
> people who were living in Crimea and then went to
> Donbas wanted war. Yes, the referendum was a step
> toward war, toward the war for Ukraine as a piece of
> Russia. If someone thinks otherwise, we disagree."

Further in her article, Eismont recounts a party she
witnessed at Grebtsov's apartment. Grebtsov's friends had
gathered around the table, and the host, as he was wont to
do, was telling war stories, when one of his friends, a
younger man named Mikhail, spoke up:

> "That's the problem, that we think that Ukraine is our
> Ukraine," [Mikhail] said. "But it's not ours! It's an
> independent country, Igor. It's an independent country
> that has its own rights. If it wants to join the European
> Union, let it join the European Union."
> "There is no Ukraine," Igor replies. "There is
> no war between Russia and Ukraine. There's a war

between Russia and the US, and the Ukrainians are just pieces of meat."

"Oh come on," said Mikhail, not giving up. "Ukraine has a right to be independent, has a right to join the European Union. Or it always has to be an appendage of Russia?"

"If Russia's not opposed, let it join."

"So you think that any country that was part of the Soviet Union still has to be ours?"

"No. Any country for which even a drop of Russian blood has been spilled should be part of Russia."

"But what if it doesn't want to be with us?"

"You know, Misha, it's like with women. Not all the women we've slept with wanted to sleep with us. But we were men and convinced them otherwise."

The men—and there were only men around the table—laughed loudly.

"What you're talking about," said Mikhail through the laughter, "sounds more like rape."

Eismont's profile made Grebtsov famous well beyond the provincial Ural Mountain towns of Lesnoi and Kachkanar. For Ukrainian partisans, Grebtsov was an enemy to be liquidated: he deleted his social media accounts and went into hiding after a call for his head went out on the internet.[49] But for Eismont's readers and viewers—mostly among the liberals of Moscow and St. Petersburg—Grebtsov was a mirror held up to Russia's demons.

FOUR

THE GATHERER OF LANDS

For Leonid Volkov, Crimea was a problem.

At 37, Volkov was the presidential campaign manager for opposition leader Alexei Navalny and himself an increasingly prominent politician from the Ural Mountains city of Ekaterinburg. On the face of it, as the 2018 elections drew closer, Volkov should have been riding high. The economy was a shambles: two years of economic contraction, four years of declining real incomes and a complex web of sanctions and counter-sanctions all meant that just about no one in Russia was better off than they had been before Putin returned to the Kremlin.

In short, grabbing the political sympathies of someone like Elena should have been easy. A 20-year-old film student in St. Petersburg, Elena told us she was looking forward to graduating, getting a job—something better than her part-time job in an elementary school—and moving out from her parents' apartment. From where she and her friends sat however, the immediate future did not look particularly bright.

"Whoever you ask, everything's bad—the wrong job, salary's too small, no spaces in the kindergarten," Elena said. "Ordinary people are dissatisfied, and it seems to me that our country's policies are more oriented to foreign policy. They're not that interested in the people."

Indeed, the Kremlin and its friends on television and online worked hard to drown the economic sorrows in a sea of geopolitical glory. Success in Ukraine and in Syria— even the upcoming 2018 FIFA World Cup, for which stadiums and hotels were being built or refurbished across the country—were all proof of Russia's hard-won geopolitical glory. As Kristina Potupchik would remind the *okhraniteli*, there was a price to be paid for these things, but it was worth it. The jewel in the crown, of course, was Crimea.

"There are good things and bad things about it," Elena told us. "Of course, a whole lot of money is being pumped into Crimea from the budget, and again we're forgetting about the countryside. And our country has this habit of focusing on one place. First it was Sochi, everything was pumped into that city [for the Olympics], and now it's Crimea. All the money is just gone. . . . Well, most of the money goes there. On the other hand, it's a good resort, and it will bring a decent income. And it's nice that it's ours now. . . . Crimea, for me, is close to my heart. So many movies were made there, it just seems like it's our piece of land, which just kind of went away for a while."

And that—the warm fuzzy feeling that Elena and tens of millions of other Russians got from Crimea—was Volkov's headache. "Crimea is ours"—*Krym nash*, in Russian—emerged as such a frequently repeated mantra, that it has become something of a joke. There is a Russian saying, however, that there is a bit of truth in every joke. However much *Krym nash* might seem like a cliché, the sentiment is very much genuine, even for those uncertain about their economic future. Volkov himself likened it to the "magic bean" that a player in a video game might grab, prolonging his life and powers.

"Crimea, of course, was a real gift of fate for Putin," Volkov told us, sitting in Navalny's campaign office. "Just remember, when Crimea happened. In the fall of 2013, his ratings fell below 60 percent for the first time since 2000. It was 50-something, not 60-something or 70-something. And of course that was linked to our tremendous rise after the election in Moscow, when we showed ourselves to be the leading political alternative.... And then Putin grabbed that magic bean and ate it. And we can see how it galvanized his dead political system for another two to three years and gave his political corpse a little more life. And that's bad, because for all these years—these extra years of Putin—we're going to have to pay the bill. They're not just sitting there, hands folded. They're stealing, stealing. Stealing millions. But what can you do? That's just the way it is."

In this chapter, we unpack the "gift of fate for Putin" that was Crimea. We look at how television was used to build a simple, powerful and almost completely false narrative of the Ukrainian revolution and the annexation of Crimea. With the help of leaked emails, we see the efforts the Kremlin made to recreate the same narrative online, and the problems it faced in doing so. Then we see how that narrative resonated with the Russian public, binding millions of Russians to the regime with an emotional connection that arose from their sense of participation in the war in Ukraine and annexation of Crimea. This deep emotional commitment lasted for years, making Crimea not just a gift for Putin, but a gift that kept on giving.

A LYING WORLD

Revolutions are complicated, and the revolution that took place in Kyiv and across Ukraine in February 2014 was no exception. The Revolution of Dignity, as some of its participants called it, was a peaceful protest asserting the values of civic participation against a corrupt and violent authoritarian president. Citizens gathered to express their contempt for their rulers and to develop programs for clean and honest governance. They endured the attacks of riot police and stood firm. In the end, the tyrant fled and the obscenity of his corruption and the rotten nature of the system were laid bare for all to see.[1]

While this heroic narrative is true, another version of events also contains some truth. The revolution was won in the end by an armed insurrection, some of whose participants used nationalist slogans and rallied under the image of World War II genocidaires. Mock lynchings of terrified public officials were held in Ukraine's western provinces. In one particularly awful incident in Odessa, dozens of opponents of the revolution were burned to death in a building where people had sought refuge after a street fight. In two eastern provinces (Donetsk and Luhansk), citizens were organized in military units to oppose the revolution, often with the involvement of forces supported by—and possibly directed from—Moscow.

The complexity of the process divided even the most dispassionate observers. Bitter discussions broke out even in scholarly communities that pride themselves on civility and the importance of evidence over emotion.

Russian television viewers, however, were spared all this complexity. Instead, what viewers saw was a Western-backed fascist junta taking power in what was portrayed as a coup, threatening the lives of millions of Russian speakers living in eastern Ukraine and Crimea.

In this context, the Russian response—the armed annexation of part of Ukrainian territory—would have looked entirely justified. The official narrative showed Putin's flair for connecting together different strands of Russian history. The annexation was not a hostile act of territorial expansion, but the historic correction of a Soviet-era mistake that had estranged Crimea from its "rightful" place as part of Russia. Researchers who have studied the way Russian television covered the events stress what they call a "national irreden-tist" framing of stories that defined people according to the language they spoke rather than their ethnicity—the majority of people living in eastern Ukraine speak Russian but describe themselves as ethnically Ukrainian. Underlying this approach was an implicit claim that these territories rightfully belonged to Russia, not Ukraine. The coverage also sought to make a clear distinction between Russian speakers who should somehow be united, and Ukrainians and Europeans who were somehow different and should be opposed.[2] Simultaneously, the land grab was presented as saving citizens from fascism, playing on a central narrative of Russian statehood since World War II. Moreover, the whole process was somehow miraculous. Crimea was won without a shot being fired.[3] Putin, like his late medieval predecessor Tsar Ivan III, was righteously gathering together "Russian" lands under Moscow's control.

This narrative—simple, straightforward and almost entirely false—was repeated over and over as state television breathlessly pushed the Kremlin's story. News broadcasts were extended from thirty minutes to an hour and the Sunday news shows were extended from one hour to two. And it was all Ukraine, all the time. According to Russian media researcher Arina Borodina, the two most watched evening news shows—*Vesti* and *Vremia*—had an average of ten segments of seven to ten minutes each covering Ukraine. As Russian children discovered, nothing was too sacred to be moved in favor of coverage of Ukraine: one of Russia's most loved traditions, a children's bedtime show called *Goodnight Little Ones* (*Spokoinoi nochi, malyshi*) was even moved from its usual spot on Russia 1 to a completely different channel.[4] Overall, ratings data show about a 30 percent increase in time spent watching television news compared to the year before.[5]

Moreover, television did not operate in a vacuum, but instead the narratives developed there reproduced themselves online. The "anti-fascist" and anti-Western tropes of television soon came to dominate cyberspace, too.[6] Overall, Russia became afflicted by what political observer Kirill Rogov called "Crimea Syndrome" in which even staunch critics of the regime were caught up in the intensity of the moment.[7]

WHEN IT RAINS

In her online work for the Kremlin, Kristina Potupchik found herself writing quite a bit about Ukraine. In its hottest phase at the time the reports in the Humpty Dumpty leak were written, the war in Ukraine features in virtually every document. In the recommendations she would write to the *okhraniteli* ("the guardians") at the end of each report, describing the day's agenda and providing guidance for spin, the *okhraniteli* were told to remember that events were to be placed in the context of a struggle against fascism. Fascism was important in two ways. By dismissing the post-Euromaidan government in Ukraine as a gang of fascist thugs, the *okhraniteli* would play their part in delegitimizing the revolution in Ukraine. Just as important, however, was that framing the struggle in Ukraine as a struggle against fascism linked the politics of the day with the glorious victory in World War II. Russia was not grabbing land from its neighbor for selfish reasons, but instead, Russia was once again taking on the historic struggle to save the world from fascism.

But the nationalists—even as they rallied to the Kremlin's cause in Ukraine—were not easy allies for Potupchik and the *okhraniteli*. Yes, the annexation of Crimea and the war in Donbas had created common ground between the Kremlin and a nationalist constituency with which it had long been at odds. The nationalists were brought on board by a sense that the Russian state was finally doing what the nationalists had long been asking for: behaving more assertively internationally, building a bulwark against Western expansionism, and intervening robustly on behalf of

Russian (or, at least, Russian-speaking) populations in the post-Soviet space. But the relationship was both conditional and uneasy: the Kremlin was skittish about a movement it had previously sought to suppress (and which had protested violently under the Kremlin walls as recently as 2010), while the nationalists were wary of the Kremlin's own fickle loyalties.[8]

While Potupchik aimed to integrate the nationalists into the broader community of *okhraniteli*—and often referred to them as *okhraniteli* in her reports—the problem she faced was that the nationalists, fueled by their own passions and accustomed to having their own opinions, would react to events on the ground in eastern Ukraine in ways that were not always productive. An episode in early July 2014, after the Russian-backed separatist commander Igor Strelkov ordered his militia to retreat from the strategic town of Slavyansk, is illustrative. On July 6, Potupchik wrote:

It should be noted that the maneuver by Strelkov and his militia to abandon Slavyansk and retreat in the direction of Donetsk and Luhansk was received by the *okhraniteli*, who had earlier supported south-eastern Ukraine, in different ways. The spectrum of opinion ranges from sharply negative to positive, and the same goes for the related interpretation of Putin's policies and support for his person. We need to develop a common position on the actions of the south-eastern militia, in such a way that these interpretations would be beneficial for Russia and would be in accordance with the actions of the Russian authorities. This would allow us successfully to resist the opposition in discussions.

By November, Potupchik declared victory, in a note that seemed designed more for her bosses than for the *okhraniteli*:

> We have *de facto* captured the theme of support for Novorossia from the nationalist community. Moderate nationalists are essentially performing along *okhraniteli* lines, and their activity neutralizes the oppositional wing [of the nationalists], who are supporting Ukrainian neo-Nazis.

Spreading "Crimea Syndrome" throughout Russian society would, however, take more than just a concerted message on state television and on the internet. It would require clearing the field of competing voices.

In fact, the Kremlin had begun to move hard against independent voices even before Crimea. And Dozhd—the online and cable TV channel created and edited by Mikhail Zygar, whom we met earlier—was at the top of the hit list.

Zygar was—and remains—proud of what he and his colleagues had built. From their point of view, being independent wasn't about being part of the opposition. As protesters filled the streets of Moscow, St. Petersburg and a few other large cities in 2011–12, millions tuned in to find both sides of the political divide represented on air. Alongside protest leaders like Navalny, Ksenia Sobchak and Gennady Gudkov, Zygar and his team brought in government minister Mikhail Abyzov, Russia Today editor-in-chief Margarita Simonyan and nationalist cinema director Fyodor Bondarchuk, among others.

"That was a giant achievement, I believe, because no other television channel could allow itself to pose a question—in a live broadcast—to a government official or a Church leader on the topics that really mattered to people," Zygar told us. "The opposition was something we covered, because the whole idea was that we didn't place any limitations on ourselves. But we absolutely did not consider ourselves to be an oppositional channel. I had a mantra that I kept repeating to the journalists at the time, which was that we are in no way an oppositional channel: we're a normal channel, which provides an opportunity for all sides to have their say. A typical, normal television channel, which has to follow the principles and standards of the profession. And that was what separated us from all of the state-run channels."

The approach paid off. After Bolotnaya subsided—and even as Putin returned to the Kremlin and began his crackdown on the opposition—Dozhd continued to grow, reaching 20 million monthly viewers all across Russia by late 2013. In November of that year, the government announced a competition to select ten channels that would be included in the country's first nationwide digital television service. When the jury from the national television academy voted, Dozhd came in eleventh place, losing by one vote to Muz-TV. Sympathetic (and incensed) jurors made it clear to Zygar that Vyacheslav Volodin—who was running domestic politics for Putin's Presidential Administration at the time—had called in the fix.

The Kremlin, it seemed, had decided that Dozhd's openness—regardless of its balance and objectivity—was oppositional enough. After locking the channel out of the digital TV package, the government pushed through legislation restricting the ability of cable channels to sell advertising. And then, in January 2014—a month before the Sochi Olympics and two months before Crimea—the Kremlin seized an opening. A history-focused talk show produced jointly with the monthly magazine *Diletant* posed a question to viewers: should the USSR have surrendered Leningrad to the Germans, to avoid the loss of life? It was a needlessly provocative and polarizing question, and blowback was inevitable, but Kremlin-backed media and talking heads fanned the flames. Within the span of a week, Dozhd was dropped from virtually all cable packages and became available only online.

Thus, with new allies on board and the decks cleared of opposition, the Kremlin was ready to ride the most powerful political wave it had ever faced. Neither Potupchik nor even Putin could have known, however, just how big the wave would get.

THE POLITICAL MIND

To understand the response in Russia to events in Crimea, we need to look inside the political minds of Russian citizens. We need to unpack the psychology of the experience, and consider the interactive, social, situational nature of what happened in Russian politics over the spring and summer of 2014. In other words, to understand what went on, we need to understand the politics of emotion.

Anyone who stumbled upon a recent issue of the leading academic journals on politics might be forgiven for thinking that political science has become a branch of applied mathematics. The pages are filled with impenetrable graphs, lemmas and calculations of equilibria from mathematical models. This comes as a surprise to most non-specialists. What has mathematics got to do with politics?

The answer is rationality. Political science, like economics, is fundamentally about what drives human behavior—a tricky question, but one that economists felt they had solved a long time ago. The answer was to assume that people were fundamentally rational—they prefer more money to less and less work to more. From that basic premise—and with lots of ingenuity—economists were able to construct elegant models of human interaction, from the "animal spirits" of financial markets to the careful calculations of marriage.

Political scientists—who had once cut their teeth on a combination of legal studies and moral philosophy—began to experience equation envy. While few would deny that political behavior was often irrational, perhaps it would be useful to follow the economists and also just assume that people were politically rational, with deviations from rationality averaging themselves out over time.

Assuming that politics was a rational pursuit turned out to be pretty useful. Armed with this assumption, significant progress was made in understanding issues such as how political parties position themselves with respect to one another, the conditions under which countries democratize, when people are likely to engage in political protest, and what conditions are more likely to trigger ethnic conflict. We also gained fascinating insights into particular historical episodes. One of the best analyses of the collapse of the USSR—an event that surprised almost everyone—was the product of modeling how rational people would behave if they worked in a bureaucracy where their bosses suddenly stopped monitoring their behavior.[9]

However, if the claim that rationality is the basic source of all human behavior sounds too good to be true—or too simple to be right—that's because it is.

Economists had not so much solved the problem of understanding human behavior, as assumed it away. As critics pointed out, the rationality assumption was likely to fit some circumstances better than others. And, indeed, over the last decade or so, the tide of narrow rationality seems to have turned across the social sciences, in favor of a more sophisticated approach to human psychology. Economists, for example, have begun digging into the ways in which people actually make economic decisions, giving rise to the hot field of behavioral economics. Political scientists, in turn, have started to detail how "affect"—the way we feel—impacts everything from political attitudes and voting behavior, to terrorism and international relations. There is also important research on subjects such as violence, ethnic conflict and political protest that demonstrates the importance of understanding emotions.[10]

This emotional turn in the study of politics should not surprise anyone who has been paying attention to the world in recent years. If the global financial crisis was not enough to make people rethink assumptions about rationality, the political consequences of that crisis, in particular the return of far-right political parties in Europe, the rise of Donald Trump in the United States and the advent of Brexit in the United Kingdom, certainly should be. As a result, what were already developing but certainly not mainstream research programs on the psychological and emotional elements of politics have rather suddenly moved to a very prominent position.

Incorporating emotions in our analysis, of course, does not mean throwing out rationality. In fact, social scientists have been careful to recognize that while emotions and rationality are not the same, they are related. What's important are the ways in which they combine and interact to shape our behavior.[11]

Originally, most scholars assumed that people make rational judgments about a person or a situation, and then later develop an emotional relationship—positive or negative—to that judgment. Evidence now suggests that this is not how the political mind works.[12] Emotion often comes into play before a person has the chance to think through an issue. Indeed, experimental research suggests that some information about politics is seen primarily through an emotional lens, rather than a rational one.[13] In fact, people are often able to express a view on a subject even when they cannot recall any information whatsoever about it.[14] This, of course, does not necessarily mean that they are irrational. Instead, people may use emotion to substitute for information: they learn about something, develop an emotional response to the issue and even allow those emotions to be altered by new information, but what they remember is sometimes the emotion, not the information.[15] Consequently, while people are often unsure of the details of a memory, they are rarely in doubt about how they felt about it.[16]

There is currently no consensus about how our "rational" and "emotional" thought processes interact. In fact, the very definition of thought (whether it needs to be conscious or not) is changing rapidly as neuroscience advances.[17] What seems obvious, however, is that how people feel and how they think are inextricable from one another. And so, if we want to understand politics—and if we want to understand Russian politics in particular—we need to understand the role of emotions.

LOVING THE LEADER

The emotion that people most closely associate with dictatorship is fear. Popular depictions of authoritarian rule, from George Orwell's *Nineteen Eighty-Four* to Mario Vargas Llosa's *Feast of the Goat*, show citizens caught in a terrifying world of violence and intimidation, designed to create obedience to the ruling regime and its system. And it is unquestionably true that fear is a major part of how authoritarian leaders stay in power.[18]

But fear is not the only emotion at work, and perhaps not even the most powerful. Russia's Putin—like many other authoritarian leaders in the world today—is more likely to be embraced by his citizens than to be feared by them. There are, certainly, exceptions. But if we want to understand Putin's power, we need to recognize that millions of ordinary Russians feel pride, trust and even hope when they think of the political leadership of their country. And we need to understand why.

When Joseph Stalin died in 1953, people all across the USSR fell into mourning. Indeed, hundreds, perhaps thousands, of people were crushed to death as crowds gathered in Moscow and other Soviet cities to mourn the passing of one of history's most brutal dictators.[19] For Svetlana Alexievich, the Nobel Prize-winning chronicler of the aftermath of Soviet totalitarianism, this was no surprise. As one of her interviewees told her after the demise of the USSR, "You forget about the long lines and the empty stores faster than you do about the red flag flying over the Reichstag."[20] Indeed, much of the attachment to Stalin and to his successors was built upon pride and patriotism over Soviet victory in World War II. Although Stalin's leadership in the war is widely criticized in scholarly circles, the victory over fascism became one of the founding myths of the Soviet state—and of post-Soviet Russia, too.

Another chronicler of totalitarianism, Hannah Arendt, argued powerfully that it is fundamentally wrong-headed to see totalitarian rule as imposed by a runaway, terroristic state on a resistant society. A German Jew who fled during the war and eventually found her way to New York, Arendt devoted her life to the question of how tyrants like Hitler and Stalin were able to do what they did. Without absolving the dictators themselves of blame, Arendt argued that the system of rule in Nazi Germany and the Soviet Union was produced from within those societies themselves. In difficult political times, people looked for comfort to leaders who offered them certainty and a release from their responsibilities. People did not merely put up with despotism: many revered the despots.

Moreover, Arendt argued that "mass support for totalitarianism comes neither from ignorance nor from brainwashing," nor from ideology nor people's material interests.[21] What wins the love of the masses, instead, are fictions worked up by the leadership. These fantasies do not even need to make sense. What matters is that they resonate in some vague but convincing way with the present experience of the populace. In this way, authoritarian leaders create "a lying world of consistency which is more adequate to the needs of the human mind than reality itself," enabling the regime to shut the masses off from the real world.[22]

The appeal of such fictions is greater when mainstream politicians struggle to create a realistic agenda actually capable of solving social problems. Societies are vulnerable, Arendt warns, when political parties and social groups have difficulty organizing and mobilizing people around a concrete policy agenda. In this context, the state appeals not to the material interests of particular constituencies and classes, but instead uses propaganda to create a largely fictional narrative in which individual and collective interests are submerged into a single national struggle. Creating that sense of national struggle—the myth that binds everyone together—depends tremendously on social norms and what people perceive to be the views of others. The more a citizen's friends, neighbors, colleagues and relatives buy into the lie, the more likely that citizen is to believe it, too—and the less likely he is to ever see the truth. Sound familiar? It probably should to citizens of many countries today—including Russia.[23]

There are many differences between the societies that Arendt studied and today's Russia. Putin is neither Stalin nor Hitler. Nevertheless, Arendt's insights are powerful. The idea that what people believe depends in part on what they think others believe, that fictions can be more compelling than truth and that emotions may matter more than interests, guide our argument here. In the rest of this chapter, we will show how the Kremlin's lies can have tremendous emotional power to change people's views of the present, the future and even the past.

PREJUDICE AND PRIDE

To see how this works, remember Natalya, the 44-year-old enthusiastic Putin supporter from Yaroslavl whom we first met in Chapter 1. Despite her clear views, Natalya told us that her interest in politics is a relatively new thing.

"I never used to watch the news very much," Natalya recalled. "But starting in 2014, I just got hooked on the news, I started watching it constantly. It was Crimea, of course! It started with that, in November, with that conflict in Ukraine, and I felt sorry for the Ukrainians, that they were going through what we went through back with the Bolsheviks."

Given that Natalya's political education came against the backdrop of Crimea and the Donbas, it is perhaps unsurprising that she is virtually a model Putin voter. She supports both the law on religious sentiment ("Well, if they're going to go dancing in churches, then yes," she says) and on LGBT "propaganda" ("Why are they even living in our country? They should leave, with those kinds of thoughts. Go to Europe"). She supports increasing restrictions on the internet, primarily to prevent terrorism, but also to clamp down on all kinds of foreign elements; she's particularly upset about the presence of Jehovah's Witnesses in Yaroslavl. ("What do we need them for? All these societies, saying people should be free, whatever their religion? They're a bit aggressive.") And, of course, she supports Putin.

To study the role of emotions, we did two things. First, in October 2013, we surveyed some 1200 internet users, with at least some post-secondary education, living in one of Russia's thirteen cities with a population of more than 1 million. Following the revolution in Ukraine, we asked the same people the same questions again in June 2014, to see whose answers changed and how. Some 715 people answered questions both times.[24] We complemented our survey with longer structured interviews, in which respondents are able to give lengthier, more elaborate answers to our questions.

In looking at the answers, it is striking how many of the elements of Arendt's world can be seen at work—large numbers of people buying into the world of fiction created for them by state television and becoming increasingly emotionally attached to a leadership that provided a story of national, unifying struggle against a historic and largely confected enemy. Moreover, as Arendt stressed at the time, this is a collective process in which citizens' emotions are reinforced by interacting with others and with the public sphere.

At the core of this process in Russia is television. Although there certainly were "volunteers" like Grebtsov, who experienced the annexation of Crimea and the war in Ukraine in a very direct and personal way, for the vast majority of Russians this was a war experienced on television. According to data collected by the widely respected Russian polling company, the Levada Center, a majority of Russians get their news and information from one single source—television. The next biggest source people cited was "friends and relatives," who presumably also got their news from television.[25] So what was happening on Russian television? Precisely what Arendt would have called the creation of "a lying world of consistency."

From our research, we can see how enthusiastically and widely Russians like Natalya were caught up in the moment. One indicator of this is President Putin's popularity ratings, which soared from the mid-60s to the mid-80s. This included the recruitment into the ranks of Putin supporters of many who before Crimea had been quite critical. In our online sample of educated urban Russians before Crimea, only 53 percent had expressed approval of President Putin. But when we asked the same individuals again in June 2014, Putin's approval had soared to 80 percent—almost the same as the population as a whole.

More significantly, though, this increased approval came alongside a major shift in broader feelings about the president. Before Crimea, we asked respondents to what extent they felt a feeling of pride when they thought about Russia's leadership. The response was underwhelming, to put it mildly: only 15 percent expressed any pride at all. After Crimea, however, the numbers changed dramatically. Now fully 37 percent said they were proud of their president.

The same transformation was true of other emotions. Before Crimea, only a quarter said they trusted those who led Russia; after Crimea, about a half of those same people said they trusted Russia's leaders. We asked, too, about whether the leadership inspired hope for the future. Before Crimea, only about one in five felt it did. After Crimea, that number was also nearly half. The same story can be seen in the negative emotions we asked about—anger and contempt. Before Crimea, fully 36 percent of our respondents said they were angry at Russia's leadership and 22 percent reported despising Russia's leaders. Afterwards, just 18 percent expressed anger and 11 percent contempt—half of the pre-Crimea numbers.

What was it about the Crimean experience that made Putin go from being tolerated to being an object of pride, hope and trust for nearly half of our educated urbanite population? Was it the very fact of the successful annexation of Crimea itself, or was there something else going on?

One element of the story was probably the straightforward fact that the demonstration of military prowess impressed many Russians, particularly given that Russia had been strategically on the defensive for most of the thirty years since Gorbachev came to power in 1985. Here was evidence of Russia's turnaround that was hard for Russian patriots to ignore. Ever since his first years in the presidency, when Putin still cultivated his image as a pro-Western modernizer, Russian nationalists had treated him with suspicion. Yet, with hardly a shot fired and in a matter of days, a part of Ukraine that had been coveted both by ethnic nationalists and those who wanted to recreate either the Russian empire or the USSR (both kinds of people exist and they share a lot of goals) had been "returned" to Mother Russia.

Looking at our data, there is clear evidence that nationalists were more likely to feel emotionally closer to Putin after Crimea than they had before. And it does not matter much what kind of nationalists we analyze—those who feel strongly attached to the Russian state, those who identify very strongly with Russian ethnicity or those for whom Russian Orthodoxy is a big part of their identity. All were able to find in the Crimean annexation and the subsequent war in eastern Ukraine reasons to identify more emotionally with their president.

Interestingly, the data suggest that the Crimean annexation did not actually make Russians more nationalist, or at least not much more. In 2013, fully 38 percent of our respondents said that being part of the Russian state was a very important part of their personal identity. By 2014, this proportion had risen slightly to 45 percent. There was even less change in other measures of nationalism. The proportion saying that Russian ethnicity or Orthodox Christianity were a very important part of their personal identity was the same in both rounds of the survey.[26]

EFFERVESCENCE

Annexing Crimea and invading other territories in Ukraine was bound to be popular with Russia's nationalists. But most Russians are not radical nationalists—and yet tens of millions of them became caught up in the Crimean "moment" and the ensuing war in Donbas. Even if their participation was mostly on the sofa, in front of a television screen or a computer monitor, many Russians felt an emotional pull, as if they had actually been there.

What happened to Russians as a result of Crimea—what others have called "Crimea Syndrome"—bears a striking resemblance to a phenomenon first described more than a hundred years ago by the pathbreaking French sociologist Émile Durkheim.[27] Studying the religious rituals of Aboriginal groups in Australia, Durkheim noticed something fascinating. The key to making something sacred was togetherness: engaging with other people in the same unusual moment that transgressed the rules and tedium of everyday life. The euphoric feeling that this extraordinary togetherness causes—the same powerful emotional excitement that we get from being "in sync" with others, whether in a church pew, the mosh pit at a rock concert or in the stands for a football match—is what Durkheim called "collective effervescence."

Born to a rabbi and a seamstress in the eastern French town of Épinal in 1858, Durkheim came from a line of rabbis and even attended rabbinical school himself, but he was of a profoundly secular turn of mind. For the young Durkheim, the key intellectual challenge of the era was to understand human beings and their interactions, and to do so in a way that was based not on the religious categories that had dominated thinking about society for millennia, but instead to take an empirical—what today we might call data-driven—approach.

Durkheim made many important contributions to our understanding of social (and anti-social) behavior, but the one that is critical in helping us understand the Russian experience of 2014 is a book he published in 1912, just five years before his death: *The Elementary Forms of Religious Life*.[28] *Elementary Forms* is an effort to understand the origins of religion and is primarily based on the study of religious rituals, which Durkheim understood as moments in which people step outside of the bounds of ordinary everyday life and embark together upon something extraordinary or sacred.

While his work on "collective effervescence" focused on religious rituals in Australia among small groups of partici-pants, he was keenly aware of the larger context. Talking about the Crusades of the twelfth and thirteenth centuries, the French Revolution and other such periods, Durkheim noted that there "are periods in history when, under the influence of some great collective shock, social interactions have become much more frequent and active. Men look for each other and assemble together more than ever. That general effervescence which results is characteristic of revolutionary or creative epochs."[29] For many Russians watching on their televisions and talking with their families and friends, the spring of 2014 was just such a moment.

Writing at the dawn of the twentieth century, Durkheim emphasized the importance of being there, of experiencing the moment yourself. More recent research, however, has shown that in the modern world of television and social media, people often have the sense of participation in events even when that "participation" is limited to watching television or discussing things online.[30] A recent study looking at protests in Ferguson, Missouri, in 2014 after the fatal shooting by police of the African American teenager Michael Brown found that people on Twitter using the hashtag #Ferguson experienced a sensation of participation in the events even from afar. And, in a sense, they were right: tweeting and retweeting, watching live streams of tear gassing and arrests all offered these mediatized participants the feeling of collective engagement, of community, of Durkheim's collective effervescence.[31] In the twenty-first century, you don't have to be there to be there.

The effects of mediated participation on emotional connections can be clearly seen in our data. Russians who watched more state television were substantially more likely to feel an increase in pride, trust and hope connected with their political leadership than those who watched less. Moreover, Russians who increased the amount of state television news they watched—regardless of whether they used to watch a lot or none at all—were even more likely to feel more pride, trust and hope. The same was true of Russian citizens who discussed politics frequently with their family, friends, neighbors and colleagues or who began to discuss politics more with those around them. Finally, another good predictor of increasing emotional engagement was interest in politics—people who either were more interested in politics or who became more interested in politics over this period were more likely to become increasingly proud, trusting and hopeful.

And this emotional engagement was extremely significant. With some further digging in the data, we found patterns that suggest that increasing emotional engagement with the regime has important effects on how people evaluate the political world they live in, the future of that world and, fascinatingly, even their estimation of their own past.

When we asked our survey respondents about their approval of Putin and their likelihood of voting for him in the future, we found that those who were more engaged in politics, watched more political news on television and discussed it more with friends were not only more emotionally attached, but were also more approving of Putin and more likely to vote for him. This effect was there, however, even for people who did not become more emotionally engaged but simply participated more than before.

However, we then asked some broader questions about how citizens understood the world in which they lived. Here we found change only among those who had become more emotionally engaged with the regime. And the effects of this emotional attachment were impressive. Those who felt more emotionally connected also reported that they thought high-level corruption to be less of a problem than they had done back in October. Given that it is unlikely that any of our respondents have personal experience of high-level corruption and that the Crimea annexation in itself vastly increased opportunities for high-level corruption, this is surprising.

Once we probed a little deeper, the power of emotional connection became even clearer. People who had become more emotionally engaged also thought that low-level corruption—the kind of petty corruption that many citizens of Russia experience and observe directly—had become less of a problem. This was true even though there are no objective data that show a fall in corruption in Russia between October 2013 and June 2014.

Higher levels of emotional engagement also made people more positive about the future and even, strikingly, the past. Survey respondents who reported more emotional engagement became more optimistic about the prospects for the Russian economy, even though experts, including those featured on Russian state television, felt that the Crimean annexation and conflict in Ukraine, not to mention international sanctions, were likely to be a significant drag on Russia's economic prospects. Finally, those who were more emotionally engaged improved their recollection of how their families had fared during the economic crises of the 1990s: those reporting increased emotional engagement were less likely to report that the 1990s had been tough on their families and more likely to report that their families had done well out of the changes. The manufactured story that Russians consumed about Crimea and Ukraine made so many things better—the present, the future and, even, the past.

A VERY PLEASANT SURPRISE

Given how radically Crimea reshaped Russia's political landscape—flipping Putin's political fortunes virtually overnight—it is tempting to wonder whether it was all planned in advance. "Little victorious wars," after all, are a tried and true part of the political arsenal in many countries. But as they made their preparations to seize Crimea, it seems unlikely that the Kremlin knew exactly how powerful the effect on public opinion would be. The Kremlin has always taken public opinion seriously, commissioning endless surveys and focus groups, trying to gain insight into risks and opportunities. The head of FOM—Russia's largest polling agency—is among Vladimir Putin's longest-serving advisers. But one doesn't usually run territorial acquisition through a focus group.

"They didn't know," Gleb Pavlovsky told us. "They couldn't have known. It was a surprise for them. But a surprise that they liked."

A one-time anti-Soviet dissident, Pavlovsky rose through the ranks of Boris Yeltsin's political advisers in the late 1990s and helped organize the rise of Vladimir Putin as Yeltsin's successor. He went on to be instrumental in the creation of the United Russia party and in Russia's initial reaction to the 2004 Orange Revolution in Ukraine. At Putin's behest, Pavlovsky went down to Kyiv to support Viktor Yanukovych, the chosen successor of outgoing Ukrainian president Leonid Kuchma. Kremlin backing, stuffed ballot boxes and Pavlovsky's advice were not enough to help Yanukovych withstand the popular uprising that swept Viktor Yushchenko and the so-called "Orange Coalition" to power. Pavlovsky was replaced shortly thereafter by Vladislav Surkov, after which he gradually reverted to outright opposition to the regime he helped create.

It is thus perhaps ironic that Alexander Dugin—the firebrand radical whose "Eurasianist" ideology found its greatest application in the annexation of Crimea and the war in Donbas—blames Pavlovsky for Russia's dismemberment of Ukraine. "Putin used to send oligarchs and liberals to solve the problem of Ukraine," Dugin said. "There was Marat Guelman [a flamboyant and liberal modern art promoter and gallery owner], there was Gleb Pavlovsky, that pure globalist liberal, the other oligarchs, the corruptioneers, and so on, dealing with Ukraine and trying to bring back Ukraine to Russia. When Yushchenko came to power, before the Maidan, that was the major situation. At the same time, we worked with the patriotic wing, patriotic forces of Donetsk, of Crimea, of Kyiv, as well as nationalists in Ukraine, trying to find a way to understand. The majority of what was done was on behalf of the liberals. They didn't make anything positive. They lost everything. And so in the end our plan was accepted."

Whatever their ideological differences, though, Dugin agrees with Pavlovsky that the decision-making process that led first to the annexation of Crimea and then to war in Donbas was haphazard, driven more by *ad hoc* analysis than by grand strategy.

"Crimea wasn't decided beforehand," Dugin recalled. "It was one of many plans, and because all the liberal suggestions, liberal globalist suggestions around him, had failed, he took this plan. And then only part of it, because the plan was to liberate eastern Ukraine. Or the other version was to acknowledge Yanukovych as the legitimate leader, he would ask for our military intervention, as in Syria. In Syria, that was repeated, because Assad controlled only a small part of Syria and invited us, and little by little we have changed the situation. The same could have happened in Kharkiv, for example, or in Donetsk, with Yanukovych. To legitimize the Russian military presence, or the creation of a Ukrainian federation, to save Ukraine. There were many, many solutions, and there was no iron will to take Crimea and leave Donbas in an indefinite state, and to leave the other parts to Ukraine. It was a kind of result of a combination of these situational solutions."

Putin is not the first world leader to benefit from a war. British Prime Minister Margaret Thatcher's popularity soared after military victory versus Argentina in the Falklands War of 1982. So, too, did George W. Bush enjoy a huge bounce following the September 11, 2001 attacks on the United States. Indeed, these sorts of "rallies around the flag" are reasonably common.

But Putin's rally is different, the clearest evidence of which is the fact that it has lasted so long. After soaring from the mid-30s before the war to 59 percent in June 1982, Thatcher's approval rating had returned to the 40s by November of that year and continued to decline until 1985.[32] In September 2001, Bush's approval ratings rocketed from the low 50s to 90 percent, but by 2003—as support for the so-called "War on Terror" began to wane— he was back in the 50s again.[33]

Putin, by contrast, saw his approval rating go from 65 percent in January 2014—before the peak of the crisis in Ukraine—to 86 percent in June, three months after the annexation of Crimea. In April 2018, however, Putin's approval was still running at 82 percent, according to reliable independent polling.[34] Moreover, despite almost a decade of economic stagnation and increasingly severe Western sanctions, some 60 percent of Russians still felt the country was moving in the right direction. Before Crimea this number was only 40 percent. In other words, more than four years after the annexation of Crimea, Putin's popularity continued to defy the usual laws of political gravity.

Undoubtedly, one important element is the role of the media. Russia is an authoritarian regime with a press and a parliament that consistently and almost universally support the president and his policies. The UK and the US are democracies (warts and all), with competing political factions that seek to undermine one another in the eyes of the public and, indeed, to gain control of the state. Studies of the Bush and Thatcher "rallies" generally find that this airing of public criticism by members of competing elites is one of the key factors that begins to bring approval ratings back down to earth. All politicians tend to rally to the side of the government in moments of national crisis like 9/11, but they return to their critical role as soon as they possibly can.

In an authoritarian regime like Russia's, elite criticism of government policies is muted at best. There are few voices—if any—that criticize policy over Crimea or even explore the nuances of the policy, and those that do exist are not widely reported on. This lack of public political competition has to make a difference.

Nevertheless, the puzzle of the durability of the surge in support for President Putin and the overall direction of the country remains. Four years is a long time, and many things have changed in Russia over that period—but few things have happened that one would think would lead to increasing faith in the leadership. In this context, thinking about Crimea and Durkheim can help to solve the riddle.

One of the key arguments that Durkheim made about participation in collective rituals is that they create new identities and senses of belonging that outlast the act itself. Rituals—those acts of moving together—break down barriers between participants and create a new sense of solidarity. People are changed, transformed by the experience. Soccer fans know this well—the profound emotional arousal of watching a game live together, singing together, crying together and sharing symbols of a collective history creates lasting bonds that go well beyond any particular moment of any given match. Sociologists know about it too (in part from studying soccer fans).

The importance of the collective emotional experience we describe tends to be underappreciated by political scientists and has been largely missing from most analysis of the Crimean annexation and Ukrainian war and their effect on Russian society and politics. Yet, both our survey data and our interviews indicate that the experience of spring 2014 was for many Russians an identity-shaping moment, in which citizens began to think differently about their state, about Putin as a leader—and about their own role in the story.

In part this was because, from a foreign policy perspective, the annexation of Crimea represented the first time since the collapse of the USSR that Russia was not surrendering territory, but expanding. For the first time in thirty years, Russia appeared to be moving from playing defense to playing offense.

Moreover, this was not just any piece of territory, but a piece that could be reimagined as a crucial part of Russian heritage. In his presidential address on March 18, 2014, marking the "reunification" of Crimea with Russia, Putin argued that "everything in Crimea speaks of our shared history and pride," noting that it was in "ancient Kherson" (on the Crimean peninsula) that Grand Prince Vladimir was baptized in 988 and so brought Christianity to ancient Rus, the historical precursor of both Russia and Ukraine.[35] This theme was developed later in his state of the nation address in December 2014, when Putin went so far as to describe Crimea as having "invaluable civilizational and even sacral importance for Russia, like the Temple Mount in Jerusalem for the followers of Islam and Judaism."[36] The fact that polls suggest most Russians knew little about Prince Vladimir's baptism (and even less about "ancient Kherson") did little to dampen the fervor.

After all, there was a much more recent connection with Crimea in many Russians' minds. The port city of Sevastopol has been the site of tremendous suffering and tremendous courage at least twice in recent history, first in the Crimean War and then, even more horrifically, in World War II. The resistance to the Nazis of this "Hero City," as Putin reminded his citizens in his May 9, 2014 Victory Day speech, was a critical part of how World War II is remembered and commemorated in Russia.

The nightly ritual of hours of television news coverage of war and "liberation" helped to link the contemporary events in Ukraine to the great crises of the past, etching in turn the events of spring 2014 more deeply in the hearts and minds of many citizens. The more involved people became, either by watching television or by discussing politics with friends and family, the greater the effect. This was a collective moment of enthusiasm and patriotic energy—in other words, collective effervescence.

The consequences of this period have been profound. One consequence, as Durkheim would have expected, is that creation of a new sense of group identity. We see clear evidence of this in the much higher degree of emotional attachment between Russian citizens and their leaders. Another consequence, research suggests, is that once the initial moment has passed, it takes only mundane, ritual- ized reminders—Putin's speeches perhaps, or the mantra of *Krym nash*—to reaffirm individuals' sense of connection and well-being.[37]

There are other implications, too, for the relationship between Putin and Russian citizens. The Ukrainian crisis was the most serious faced by Russia since the end of the Chechen Wars of the 1990s. It was also a crisis with an extremely clear geopolitical context—Cold War-style (superficially at least) competition with the United States over the political orientation of lands historically and geographically close to Russia. Political science research has shown the importance of such crises in turning otherwise unremarkable political figures into charismatic leaders, beloved by their people. After all, for a leader to be charismatic there must be an audience willing to see them as such. Charisma is a relationship between a leader and a set of followers.[38] As a result, charismatic leaders often emerge in times of crisis because successful management of a crisis turns formerly ordinary politicians into charismatic leaders. As our evidence suggests, this was certainly part of what happened in Russia during the spring of 2014. The Ukrainian crisis helped complete Vladimir Putin's journey from gray KGB operative to the charismatic "gatherer of lands." That mantle—once reserved for the fifteenth-century Grand Prince Ivan III, who defeated the Golden Horde and tripled the territory of Muscovy—was placed squarely on Putin's shoulders by the likes of Dugin.

However, when we met Dugin—some four years after the annexation of Crimea—he was angry, but not at the West. Putin, he said, had betrayed the cause.

"To tell the truth, in Novorossia [Dugin's term for eastern Ukraine] the revolt was much more popular,"

Dugin told us. The Kremlin, he said, should have pressed the fight. Yes, he argued, there were achievements in Crimea, but "Crimea could easily be an integrated part of Ukraine, because of the passivity of the population. The real revolt, the real popular, anti-Kyiv, pro-Russian revolt was precisely in Donetsk. . . . Their referendum was much more legitimate than in Crimea, to say the truth. But the truth—this truth—was prohibited."

Prohibited, Dugin said, by Putin.

Russia emerged from the crucible of annexation and war and global geopolitical confrontation a different country: one in which support for Putin would be based not on the fortunes of the economy or the successes of his policies, but on emotion, on pride and on a rekindled sense of Russian identity. But Putin, too, emerged from this conflict a new man. It was, to be certain, an empowering moment for the Russian president. But in bringing Russians together in a new sense of community, it would place upon him certain obligations: he could not, after all, risk alienating his newly galvanized nation. Being the gatherer of lands, it turned out, has its downsides.

FIVE

PUTIN'S GREENGROCERS

When we met her in St. Petersburg in February 2018, just a few weeks before Vladimir Putin's reelection to the presidency, Marina was having mixed feelings about the upcoming vote.

"I can't say that we don't have free elections," the 54-year-old office worker told us. "I mean, no one forces you to go vote. Go if you want, don't go if you don't want. So, that makes them free, right? Nobody holds a gun to your head and says, 'go vote for X,' right? ... But at the same time, somehow, I don't know why, but we really don't have any choice. We already know perfectly well who the next president is going to be. It's not a secret for anybody. You could put twenty candidates up against him. And people who maybe don't even want to vote for that candidate will vote for him anyway, I think, because we just don't have another option."

Marina paused.

"At least," she continued, "not yet."

Putin, of course, surprised nobody, winning 77 percent of the vote on March 18, 2018, with 68 percent of registered voters turning out to the polls—according to official figures. His closest opponent, the Communist Party candidate Pavel Grudinin, got 12 percent. Alexei Navalny, Putin's most ardent opponent and the almost undisputed leader of the opposition, was not allowed to run. The only openly oppositional candidates on the ballot—the television personality Ksenia Sobchak and the 90s-era economic reformer Grigory Yavlinsky—got less than 3 percent of the vote between them. Independent observers and number crunchers estimate that as much as ten percentage points of both Putin's result and the turnout may have been the result of electoral manipulation. Even if that's the case, though, Putin's victory was resounding.

One of those who voted happily for Putin was Vasily, a 41-year-old factory worker in St. Petersburg. Political scientists and pollsters often ask people whether they think the country is headed in the right direction: their answers can be a useful barometer of the level of optimism in a society, and the level of support enjoyed by rulers, elected or otherwise. But it can also be useful to ask people *why* they think the country is—or isn't—headed in the right direction. That's what we asked Vasily.

"It all starts with the president," he explained. "I respect our president and his work. We have a great example of a president, I think, someone we should look up to. And regardless of the difficulties, we overcome them one way or another. Of course, not everything is smooth, there are rocks under the water, sure. But on the whole, everything is headed in the right direction."

We pressed on, however, asking Vasily how he would describe that "right direction."

"It's a direction," he said, pausing to think, "in which, let's say, other countries start to respect us, to respect Russia. Not like it was before, when people could just kick Russia around."

What about at home, though?

"Well, the economic situation, if I judge by my own situation, it's all the same problems," he said. "My economic situation, for example, is that I get a utility bill every month of 7,000 rubles, which I think is a lot. The prices in the stores are going up uncontrolledly. All the same problems. For us, for simple people, nothing is getting better. Things are getting worse, I'd say."

Indeed, just to pay his bills Vasily has had to take on extra shifts at work and to seek out odd jobs here and there. He's hoping to get some additional training, in order to go after higher-paying jobs. If in three years' time he's earning considerably more than he is now—as he hopes he will be—he doesn't think it will be because of anything that Putin will have done.

"That has its upsides, though," he said. "Nobody gives you a handout. It keeps you in good form, doesn't let you relax."

Even for an enthusiastic Putin voter like Vasily, though, the silver lining came with a cloud. Looking ahead to the 2018 elections, he told us he was reminded of *The Truman Show*, the 1998 movie in which Jim Carrey's character plays a man unwittingly living in a reality TV show.

"I believe, of course, that it's all honest, but all the same, I don't know, just my intuition," he mused. "My intuition tells me that everything's already decided, really. . . . Right now, our country reminds me—everything that's happening, the elections—it's like we're all really in a big TV show. When Ksenia Sobchak announced her candidacy, that just made me think, it's all really just some kind of TV show. I understand that Vladimir Vladimirovich [Putin] will be president again, that's just ... inevitable. But for the first time it just made me think that this is all just some big TV show. Everything that happens, it's all just for show."

Why do ordinary Russians—people like Vasily and Marina and tens of millions of others—willingly take part in this show? On the other side of the barricades, why did hundreds of thousands of others take to the streets in 2011–12, when Putin made his return to the presidency? And why have thousands more protested Putin's rule over the last two years? Finding reasons to support Putin or oppose him is not hard. Indeed, in their conversations with us, Marina and Vasily and many other ordinary Russians identified arguments on both sides of the debate. But that doesn't explain why each of them accepts a particular role in what we—and, indeed, they—understand to be a show.

IN HARMONY

Walking through the streets of Communist-era Prague, the dissident Václav Havel once asked a similar question: Why did greengrocers and other shopkeepers almost uniformly display Communist propaganda in their windows? Does the fact that a store manager places a sign declaring "Workers of the world, unite!" in his window, or a portrait of the leader behind the counter, mean that the manager's a true believer?

"I think it can be safely assumed that the overwhelming majority of shopkeepers never think about the slogans they put in their windows, nor do they use them to express their real opinions," Havel wrote in 1978, ten years after the Soviet Union crushed the Prague Spring and plunged Czechoslovakia into a renewed neo-Stalinist dictatorship. Arrests for "political crimes" were common; Havel himself spent more than four years behind bars for speaking his mind.

> That poster was delivered to our greengrocer from the enterprise headquarters along with the onions and carrots. He put them all into the window simply because it has been done that way for years, because everyone does it, and because that is the way it has to be. If he were to refuse, there could be trouble. He could be reproached for not having the proper decoration in his window; someone might even accuse him of disloyalty. He does it because these things must be done if one is to get along in life. It is one of the thousands of details that guarantee him a relatively tranquil life "in harmony with society," as they say.[1]

Moreover, Havel pointed out that, in the context of authoritarianism, the decision of an individual citizen "to live in social harmony" has an effect that stretches well beyond his or her private life.

"The greengrocer declares his loyalty (and he can do no other if his declaration is to be accepted) in the only way the regime is capable of hearing; that is, by accepting the prescribed ritual, by accepting appearances as reality, by accepting the given rules of the game," he wrote. "In so doing, however, he has himself become a player in the game, thus making it possible for the game to go on, for it to exist in the first place."

Havel was not alone in thinking that dictatorship requires the participation of its citizens to survive. Hannah Arendt—the influential theorist of twentieth-century totalitarianism, whom we met in the previous chapter—similarly teaches us that building a dictatorship requires not just passive acceptance of the regime by the population, but the integration and normalization of that regime in the psyche of its citizens.

Nevertheless, in Czechoslovakia—indeed, throughout the Eastern Bloc—there were individuals for whom "living in truth" was more important than "living in harmony with society." Many of these dissidents, like the playwright Havel, or like the novelist Alexander Solzhenitsyn and the physicist Andrei Sakharov in the Soviet Union, hailed from what there is known as the intelligentsia, or what we might today call the creative class. When Russians rose up in 2011–12 in what came to be called the Bolotnaya movement, many inside and outside the movement insisted it was, once again, the creative class on the march; Vladislav Surkov, Putin's master political operator, called them "angry urbanites" but meant largely the same thing. In truth, it was neither only the creative class who had participated, nor even all of Russia's educated urbanites. If the opposition needed confirmation of that fact, all they had to do was look at the Moscow mayoral elections of September 2013. While the favored candidate of the opposition—Alexei Navalny—won a respectable 27 percent of the vote, Putin's man, a Siberian by the name of Sergei Sobyanin, still won handily. If some urbanites were angry, others clearly were not. To understand why, we need to delve into the minds of ordinary Russians.

DO RUSSIANS LOVE THEIR CHILDREN, TOO?

Attempts by Western researchers to understand the psychology of ordinary Russians have not always—or even often—ended well. Too many of these attempts have focused on trying to figure out what makes Russians different from everyone else, looking for elements in the Russian psyche (or soul) that would explain everything from Ivan the Terrible to Stalin to Putin. It is not hard to see the problem that arises when you pose the question that way: all of a sudden, you reduce tens of millions of people to one single psyche.

Perhaps the most infamous of these efforts was a project that came to be ridiculed as "diaperology." After the end of World War II, the US defense establishment began to worry about the threat posed by its wartime ally, the Soviet Union. Not without good reason, Washington feared that Moscow would pursue an expansionist policy in Europe and globally, enforcing its will through force of arms if need be. (The fact that Washington intended to do the same only served to heighten the fear of confrontation.) As the world slipped into the Cold War, then, America decided it was time to get to know the Russians.

To do this, the US military called on the services of Margaret Mead. One of the most famous scientists of her era, Mead's fieldwork among the indigenous peoples of Samoa and Papua New Guinea in the 1920s made her a household name in the United States—a rare accomplishment not only for a woman in that day and age, but for an anthropologist to boot. In 1943, *The Washington Post* declared Mead one the "outstanding women of the modern world," alongside Eleanor Roosevelt. With only eight women on the list, that was quite an honor.[2]

When the United States entered World War II in 1941, Mead was quickly drawn into the war effort, trying to put her anthropological knowledge and skills to use to understand, and so defeat, Germany and Japan. This presented at least two problems. First, Mead had dedicated her career to promoting an egalitarian understanding of other cultures. Now, her goal was to help defeat them in battle. Second, Mead made her name by immersing herself in the cultures she was studying, but with a war in progress immersion in Germany and Japan was out of the question. If the first problem was overcome by a sense of patriotic duty, the second required inventing what she called "the study of culture at a distance"—a technique that involved interviewing émigré nationals in the style of an anthropologist, while also reading extensively like a historian or literary scholar.[3]

Mead and her collaborators believed that each country had a "national character" that was the result of the particularities of a country's history and culture. This "national character" consisted of typical behaviors and styles of thought that were both shared by citizens of the country and were also unique to that country. Understanding "national character," Mead thought, would help hone wartime propaganda efforts and, hopefully, post-war reconstruction and reconciliation.[4] The US military quickly recognized the potential value of this research in conducting psychological warfare and provided extensive funding.[5]

As attention turned to the Soviet Union—a country she had never before studied—the challenge before Mead was formidable: how to decipher the "national character" of a people whose language she did not speak and who lived in a country she hadn't visited and never could. This was indeed anthropology at quite some distance.

Mead and her main collaborator on the project, Geoffrey Gorer, decided to focus on understanding the relationship between Russians and authority. What were the characteristics of the Russian "national character" in relation to authority, and where did these attitudes come from? And what did they tell us about how best to handle relations with the USSR in what would soon come to be called the Cold War?

It was taken for granted that what mattered in dealing with the USSR—a federation made up of different republics and hundreds of nationalities and ethnic groups—was the so-called "Great Russian" national character. This was despite the fact that Stalin, who was running the country at the time, was himself not Russian, but Georgian. (Gorer was said to have been completely blindsided when this fact was brought up at the inaugural seminar of Harvard University's Russian Research Center in January 1948.)[6]

The key to the Russian national character that Gorer and Mead stumbled upon was stunningly novel: the relatively common practice in Russia of swaddling infants.

Gorer claims to have made his breakthrough during a team discussion of "typical gestures" made by Russians, which seemed to him to have a peculiarly symmetrical shape. This symmetry, added to "squarely set shoulders" and a resting position that had the shoulders supposedly further back than amongst non-swaddled peoples, was apparently immediately identifiable to Gorer, who, despite having been completely unaware of swaddling before, "could, after three months' interviewing, tell at a glance, and with practically no errors, if a Russian had been swaddled as a child."[7]

As Gorer himself understood, the swaddling theory was unusual to say the least. It had no precedent in anthropology, psychology or, for that matter, any other field. In no other country or culture that practiced swaddling—and there are many—had researchers ever concluded that it mattered for determining "national character" or anything else of significance. Nevertheless, Gorer was convinced of its importance. Rather than seeing a parent or nanny or some other human as the embodiment of authority, Gorer and Mead argued, Russians grew up understanding authority as an unflinching, unmovable, emotionless constraint—much like the cloths in which infants were so often tightly bound. Moreover, the effort of pushing unsuccessfully against the constraints of swaddling was believed to result in feelings of rage, futility, exhaustion and, ultimately, infantile depression. This experience of pointless struggle, according to Gorer, accounted for "three sets of facts [about Russians] for which we have plenty of data: the pleasure in painful emotions, the fact that Great Russians viewed weakness as absolute and not relative, and 'avalanche fantasies' [a fear that the slightest deviation from a position of equality will lead to total subordination]."⁸

The sweeping nature of these claims, the flimsy nature of the evidence on which they were based and, no doubt, the professional jealousy of Russia experts dealing with a set of well-funded neophytes, meant that Gorer and Mead's theories quickly became the subject of ridicule from more established scholars in the field. Hence the "diaperology" moniker. But whatever their motives, the skepticism of most researchers toward Mead's project was well-founded. The whole project was misconceived from the very beginning and was based more on fantasy than research.

The fact that the research was nonsense, however, did it no harm in policy circles. Quite the contrary. Policymakers favoring a hard line against the Soviet Union seized on the work as supporting the conclusions they wanted to reach—that without firm and constant pressure against them, "the Russians" were inevitably an expansionist people, who would interpret any sign of weakness as an invitation to total subordination. As a result, as far as scholars of Russia are concerned, the very idea of studying personality in Russia—even if done in a way that has nothing to do with Mead and Gorer's work—is tainted.

Nevertheless, this skepticism is wrong. With modern techniques and real science, political psychology can take you a long way in today's Russia.

LEARNING TO LISTEN

People are different. Some people love to take risks. Others are inherently cautious and play it safe. Some naturally seek out compromise, while others enjoy a good fight. And it all starts very young. Some children are rambunctious and strong-willed, others are quiet and attentive. Moreover, it often seems that these characteristics are intrinsic to each child. As parents, we are often surprised to see how different our own children can be from one another, despite having the same ancestry and upbringing. We all, in short, have our own personalities, unique combinations of attitudes and affinities—likes and dislikes—that make us who we are.

For more than a hundred years, scientists have wondered about the effects of personality on human behavior and have argued about how to understand personality and how to study it. It turns out that the best way is to listen to how people talk. It's an old idea—called "the lexical hypothesis" by its inventor, the nineteenth-century British polymath Sir Francis Galton—and it begins from the thought that if humans behave in a certain kind of way on a more or less regular basis, then words should exist that describe that kind of behavior. Consequently, if we could collect all of the words from the dictionary that describe what people are like, then we would have a complete description of human personality.

Following Galton's idea, British and German scholars began to produce lists of words that described different aspects of personality. The problem, of course, is that there are a lot of words in the dictionary that do this— thousands in fact. What to do with all those words? Galton had argued that the words should be grouped together into sets that referred to the same underlying personality trait. But what did that underlying structure of traits look like?

How many traits should there be? At the end of the nineteenth century, neither the theory nor the technology was available that could answer these questions, so the pursuit of personality through words languished.

Math provided the answer. In the 1930s, a University of North Carolina psychologist and mathematician, Leon Louis Thurstone, developed a new statistical technique called "factor analysis" to test Galston's "lexical hypothesis." Based on a limited set of terms, Thurstone argued that the words clustered reliably into five groups that reflected five underlying personality "traits." Determining exactly which traits these were, though, would take more data and more money. The money eventually came (once again) from the US military.

In the 1950s, the US Air Force had a problem. Training officers was very expensive, and identifying people who would do well in training and in service was hard. As a result, a lot of investment was wasted on people who burned out. Consequently, in order to improve its success rate, the Air Force decided that it needed to begin measuring not only applicants' intelligence (which was relatively easy), but also their motivation and character (which was harder). To develop a test, they turned to psychologists Ernest Tupes and Raymond Christal. Tupes and Christal conducted a number of different studies on Air Force officer candidates and serving officers, both male and female and with a broad range of educational levels.[9] What emerged from these studies was a system of five basic personality traits that was both stable and, more importantly, useful in predicting officer performance on the job. These traits were Openness, Conscientiousness,

Extraversion, Agreeableness and Neuroticism—often known by their acronym, OCEAN.[10] Over time, these traits have come to be known as "The Big Five," both because the five traits cover most of the variation in human personality, and because each label itself is quite expansive.[11] Thus was born the modern science of personality psychology.

Psychologists who study the Big Five think of these personality traits as basic ways in which individuals see the world, interpret their surroundings and guide their behavior. Within each individual, research suggests that these traits are quite consistent over time—thus confirming the conventional wisdom that our personalities don't change much as we age. Moreover, humans, it turns out, are pretty good at assessing each other's personality—our assessments of our own traits tend to match pretty closely the assessments that others make of us.

When we think of our family, friends and colleagues, we often make implicit assessments of their personality traits in thinking about how to deal with them. We usually have a good idea of who would be up for a new adventure to some exotic locale. These people, who like to try new things, probably score highly on the trait of "openness." By contrast, those less adventurous friends who would prefer to return to the same place they have been going to for twenty years are probably low on openness. At work, we know who is likely to care about the details of a project and who will work hard to follow the rules, even if those rules are complex. These people are typically high on the "conscientiousness" scale; those who would be more inclined to focus on the big picture and to try to find a short cut around annoying rules are probably nearer the other end of the scale on "conscientiousness." We all have friends who are talkative and outgoing and enjoy the company of others. These people score high on "extraversion" and are quite different from those low on extraversion, who typically would prefer to keep their thoughts and their time to themselves. Some people worry a lot about fitting in socially and getting along with others. Other people do not. This is the trait of "agreeableness," which will figure prominently in our story. Finally, there is "neuroticism." People who score highly on this trait seem anxious and are easily upset, while their opposites are calm and relaxed.

Where do traits come from? Here the research is less clear. There is some evidence that personality traits are partly genetic and partly the result of early childhood experiences.[12] There is also some evidence presented by neuroscientists that differences in traits across different people are associated with differences in brain activity when cognitive and emotional processing is taking place.[13]

Wherever they come from, though, we know that personalities matter. Studies that follow the same individuals over time, for example, show that children who are more conscientious tend to live longer.[14] Amongst the elderly too, conscientiousness is a good predictor of longevity—even when we take into account things like smoking and cardiovascular disease.[15] This is particularly striking, because other research shows that highly conscientious people also smoke less, eat better and exercise more, increasing their longevity advantage.[16] (The research also suggests that, once you're old enough to read this book, there's very little you can do to increase your conscientiousness score.)[17]

And it's not just conscientiousness. Catholic nuns who are more extraverted live longer than nuns who are less, again taking into account age, education and cognitive ability.[18] Meanwhile, in a finding that will surprise no one, many studies suggest highly neurotic people live shorter lives than their more emotionally stable peers.[19] (Although personality scientists believe that it is possible for adults to reduce their level of neuroticism.)[20] In reviewing hundreds of studies of this kind, Brent Roberts from the University of Illinois and his colleagues concluded that the effects of personality on mortality were at least as large as those of socio-economic status and intelligence.[21]

Personality traits affect not only the length of your life, but how you live it. People who are more neurotic are more likely to experience divorce, while more conscientious people and those who are highly agreeable are less likely. Moreover, people who are more neurotic are more likely to have similar problems repeat across multiple relationships in their lifetime.[22] Studies show the effects of personality on self-esteem, feelings of well-being, religiosity and values, health, mental illness, relationships, romance, job choice, professional success, and the propensity to volunteer or commit crimes.[23] It should come as no surprise, then, that personality also affects politics in powerful—and sometimes surprising—ways.

AN ABSOLUTELY NORMAL PERSON

Andrei had just returned from a trip when we interviewed him in January 2018. He didn't like what he had seen and was eager to tell us about it.

"I just came back from Russia," said the 29-year-old Muscovite. We interviewed him in Moscow. Like most Russians—but perhaps unlike most foreigners—he understands the difference: Moscow is not Russia. "Where are we headed? It depends what you mean. If you mean are we headed toward an economic state where everything works, like in Europe, then we're headed in the opposite direction, aren't we? There is no order anywhere, not so far as I can tell, not in any sphere. We're not headed in any direction. And I'm a patriotic person. I'm for Russia, for spending my vacations in Russia, for . . . damn. I'm satisfied with everything, nothing is changing, that's just the way things are for us. Stability, I don't know, anti-stability. What's our road? Deep . . . anarchy. I don't know. I just don't think we have a road. We're just standing in place, and that's all. In ten years, nothing has changed."

That professed—if frustrated—satisfaction masks anxiety, however.

Of late, Andrei says he's been perturbed by the state's efforts to increase internet surveillance, particularly of mobile messenger apps such as Whatsapp or Telegram.

"When I heard about that kind of thing in America, when the FBI and the CIA could just follow whoever they wanted, I was like, 'Sure, fine,'" he said. "But when it affected me, I mean my personal correspondence, when I write to my girlfriend, for example, and we have our, you know, conversations … No, please, you can keep tabs on the people who need to be kept tabs on. People working in the government, high-ranking officials, because, you never know, maybe they're working for another country, or stealing money with their friends. Please, investigate them. But when it comes to ordinary citizens, who don't come into contact with state secrets or anything like that, that's no good."

By contrast, Anna—a 37-year-old retail worker, who also lives in Moscow—is generally positive. When she looks at people a bit younger than she is, she sees them placing more value on education. "And what does a good education tell us? About brains, about our future as a country, which might finally be what it should be," she said.

And then, of course, there's Putin's foreign policy.

"Russia's such an enormous, great power, and the fact that Putin's trying to stand up," she said, trailing off. "With all of these accusations about our Olympics, it's really just offensive. … I'm a patriot of my country. And likewise with these American wars of ours, I think we're moving in the right direction, because we need to respect ourselves, and make others respect us, too. We're a power. So, I think that we're right to be maybe even a little bit aggressive, maybe we're not always understood, maybe it's even risky, but if we stand up for our interests abroad, then … Oh, well I haven't ever even been to the States, although I really wanted to, because of the climate. We have these harsh winters, after all. But now, with all of this oppression of Russians, it's just offensive, and I think that, with our strategy, we're invincible, and there are a ton of arguments why we can't be broken."

That said, there is one policy area in particular that concerns Anna, who moved from a provincial city to the capital in 2001: the number of people following in her footsteps, particularly from other countries of the former Soviet Union.

"I'm not a racist, I'm not a homophobe, I'm an absolutely normal person, but I think that while Russia should let migrants in, there need to be limits," she told us. "We should let in people who have something to add. People with education. Or maybe some small percentage of street-sweepers. But from what I can see, it's just a flow of unemployed people. And there's competition for every good job."

Andrei and Anna live in the same city, were born in the same generation, see and experience the same things, more or less, and yet, their attitudes—while overlapping—sound and feel very different. Andrei, with his sharp edges and critiques, sounds like he might one day be persuaded to vote for opposition leader Alexei Navalny; Anna, on the other hand, sounds like a Putin-voter through and through. What can personality tell us about the differences in political outlook between Andrei and Anna?

Hundreds of studies, in fact, have linked two personality traits in particular to politics. Openness is generally argued to be associated with what Americans call liberal political positions (better known in Europe as left-of-center positions). By contrast, conscientiousness is usually thought to go along with conservative (or right-of-center) positions.

Exactly why this should be the case is a matter of debate. One reason might be that there is a natural affinity between certain personality traits and policies. People who prefer order and stability—those who are high on conscientiousness—may prefer conservative, traditional values and be worried about processes, like immigration for example, that might challenge their values. Those who are relatively open to new experiences, by contrast, will instinctively be more welcoming of change and innovation. This contrast between openness and conscientiousness maps well onto the basic divide that has structured the traditional politics of left and right in Western democracies.

However, it is probably exceptional that personality directly shapes politics in this way. For one thing, the connection between a given policy and its outcome would need to be (or at least appear to be) pretty simple and straightforward, so that even citizens who are not that interested in politics (i.e., most people) can easily understand what is at stake. Second, direct effects are more likely when citizens see a clear connection between their own personal interests and the policy in question. This is more likely to be the case when people have real and easily identifiable gains and losses that are at stake and so have some incentive to think about the policy.

There are certainly times in politics when these conditions appear to hold. Immigration policy—Anna's concern—is probably the most obvious example. It is fairly rare, though, for non-experts to be able to identify the direct effects of government policies on their lives, and even experts usually disagree. The truth is that political combat is most often about how issues and their effects are framed. Politicians, interest groups, the media and activists wage vigorous "framing competitions" all the time, in an effort to present issues to the public in one light or another, and these competitions shape how people see the gains and losses involved in different issues.[24] In this sense, the effects of personality on politics are likely to be skewed by the context and the rhetoric in which issues are presented and discussed.

In other words, the relationship between personality and politics flows through information. Not everyone gets the same political information. In fact, the kind of information people get is quite strongly patterned, and it is by now well understood that people tend to choose the sources of information they pay attention to as a function of their political preferences. People who watch Fox News in the United States, for example, tend to be conservative before they tune in.[25] Once they are watching of course, Fox then provides them with a highly selective set of political issues and a strongly conservative slant on those issues. This helps people relate their general political orientation to specific policies and issues. The same process works with personality. As we will see, highly conscientious and highly agreeable people in Russia tend to get more of their news from state television, exposing them to pro-government positions on a whole host of issues and shaping their attitudes on those issues much more than people who are less conscientious and less agreeable. Thus, personality, too, becomes subject to power—specifically the power of the state to set the agenda and control the messages people receive.

PICKING SIDES

To help understand what makes people like Anna and Andrei different, we conducted a series of online opinion polls over a number of years, focusing particularly on that sector of the population that had been most prominent in the protests against President Putin and against election fraud in the period from December 2011 to May 2012—in other words, the creative class we discussed earlier.

The reasoning was simple. From Cairo to Kyiv, the biggest threat to authoritarian rulers has come from urban protests in the capital cities. And for a brief moment in early 2012, even Putin's robust dictatorship seemed under threat from such protests. Consequently, if we want to understand the sources of support and opposition that would be critical to the survival of the regime, it seemed that the people we should care most about were internet-using urbanites.

As mentioned earlier, in October 2013 we polled some 1,200 educated urbanites from around Russia about their values, politics and media use—and we also asked them about personality traits.[26]

Back in 2013, educated urbanites were, as we had expected, much less likely to support President Putin than the rest of the country. At that time, some 48 percent of our respondents approved of the president, compared to 64 percent in reputable national polls asking the same question.[27] Similarly, only 27 percent of educated urbanites thought the country was headed in the right direction, compared to 40 percent of the population as a whole. The remaining respondents were divided—47 percent thought the country was going in the wrong direction, and 26 percent said they did not know.

Unlike the image of a country united against a foreign, gay threat that the Kremlin was trying to promote at the time, educated urban Russians were pretty evenly divided between supporters, opponents and people who appeared either not to know where they stood, or not to care. Those divisions were also evident on some of the key wedge issues that the Kremlin had aggressively put on the political agenda. While the Kremlin railed against the threat posed by minorities, urbanites were more or less evenly divided on the question of minority rights.[28] Kremlin-sponsored legislation to criminalize causing offense to Orthodox believers was similarly divisive, but while a majority of Russians at large supported it, half of our urbanites opposed it.[29] The issue of gay rights was more sharply tilted in favor of the Kremlin, though even there fully a quarter expressed outright opposition to Kremlin-supported anti-LGBT legislation.

Nevertheless, despite the divisions among urbanites on key political issues of the day, there was enormous unity on questions related to nationalism and identity. A plurality of our respondents said that Russian national identity and Russian citizenship were very important to their sense of self (though for many one was more important than the other).[30] With respect to migrants, fully three quarters said that the Russian government should take measures to deport most immigrants from the country, but almost two-thirds agreed with the idea that people of any nationality should have the right to become Russian citizens. On foreign policy too, although war in Ukraine was still unimaginable at the time, the effects of the image of Russia under attack from a hostile United States being projected on state television were plain to see. Only 1 percent of our respondents said the US was an ally of Russia, and only 8 percent thought it a partner. Fully 41 percent considered the US an enemy.[31]

What explains these differences among the pro-regime, anti-regime and indifferent urbanites? We found two consistent answers—economics and personality. Even in authoritarian Russia, economics still matters. People who said their financial situation was getting better were about twice as likely to report having voted for President Putin as those whose personal finances were getting worse, even once we take into account a host of other possible factors that might shape preferences, like age, gender, wealth, Moscow or non-Moscow residence, and whether or not they work in the public sector. But the economy is only part of the story. The rest is personality.

For each of the "Big Five" traits, we asked survey respondents to place themselves on a simple seven-point scale, according to how much they felt the descriptions we offered described them personally. Using a standard method from personality psychology, we asked two questions for each trait.[32] The characteristics we asked about were:

Openness: "open to new experiences, complex"; "conventional, uncreative"

Conscientiousness: "dependable, self-disciplined"; "disorganized, careless"

Extraversion: "extraverted and enthusiastic"; "reserved and quiet"

Agreeableness: "sympathetic, warm"; "critical and quarrelsome"

Neuroticism: "calm, emotionally stable"; "anxious, easily upset"

Given what we know about personality and politics in the West, we expected that we would find conscientiousness to be a good predictor of support for Putin's avowedly conservative regime and policies, while openness should predict opposition. Our expectations were only partly borne out. How conscientious a person was—the extent to which they thought of themselves as "dependable, self-disciplined" and not as "disorganized, careless"—did predict well whether a person was likely to approve of Putin or to vote for him. In fact, people who scored high on conscientiousness were almost twice as likely to vote for Putin as those low on conscientiousness.[33] Conscientiousness also predicted support quite accurately for the anti-LGBT legislation: more dependable and self-disciplined people were about three and a half times more likely to support anti-gay legislation than the self-described disorganized and careless. The effects of conscientiousness were greatest when predicting support for legislation outlawing offending the sensibilities of religious believers. People higher on the conscientiousness scale were about five times more likely to support the controversial legislation introduced after the Pussy Riot affair. Similar effects were observed for other traditionally conservative attitudes, such as the importance of a strong military.

But that's where Russia's similarity to the West ends, when it comes to personality and politics. Openness seems to have no effect. People who think of themselves as more creative and unconventional—the very definition of the "creative class" perhaps—were not systematically more likely to oppose President Putin and the conservative wedge issues the Kremlin used to shore up his base. In fact, systematic predictors of opposition were rather hard to find. The one trait that did seem at least sometimes associated with lower approval of President Putin was neuroticism—people who thought of themselves as more "anxious" and "easily upset," and less "calm" and "emotionally stable"—but this effect was not consistent across the range of political views and values. Moreover, among the "Big Five," neuroticism is the one trait that evidence suggests is most likely to change over a person's lifetime. It is easy to imagine why oppositionists in Russia might feel "anxious" and "easily upset."[34]

AGREEABLE AUTHORITARIANS

The most surprising and important finding, however, relates not to openness, but to a trait that rarely seems to matter much for politics in other countries: agreeableness.[35] Respondents who were high on the agreeableness scale—who think of themselves as sympathetic and warm, rather than critical and quarrelsome (and yes, there are plenty of people who self-identify as quarrelsome)—were seven times more likely to vote for Putin than those who were low on agreeableness, and they were four times more likely to give Putin a high approval rating. They were also three times more likely to support both the legislation against giving offense to Orthodox believers and the anti-gay legislation. All told, agreeableness turns out to be the personality factor that best predicts a person's politics in Russia.

Why does Putin draw such support from the most "sympathetic and warmhearted" of his citizens? Most of us, after all, would think of Putin as being rather cold and quite unafraid of a fight. And why do these same people support legislation that allows the state to lock up gay and lesbian people? On the face of it, that sounds unsympathetic and highly judgmental.

The reason is that Russia—fairly obviously—is not the West. Unfortunately, most of the research on personality and politics so far has taken place either in the United States or in Western European countries like the Netherlands: in other words, in liberal democracies. Russia, of course, is not a liberal democracy and in fact has never in its history been either liberal or a democracy. Certainly, Russia experienced—enjoyed seems too strong a word—a political opening in the 1990s, in which there was considerable political competition. President Boris Yeltsin was, after all, elected in presidential contests that were genuinely competitive, even if that competition was sometimes skewed. Opposition parties not only participated in, but actually dominated the three national parliamentary elections that were held in that decade. At the time, too, both print and broadcast media promoted vigorous debate, even if ownership was dominated by a small handful of billionaires and political content in the media rarely strayed too far from their interests.

Nevertheless, Russia never was more than a warped facsimile of democracy. The rule of law was weak, and violence, fraud and money were more important than democratic procedures in crafting the 1993 constitution and reelecting Yeltsin in 1996. Russia's brief dalliance with more competitive politics was gradually snuffed out over the years after Vladimir Putin first became president in 2000. By the time Putin ran for a fourth term in March 2018, there was absolutely no suspense about the outcome. Long before this time, however, the very notion of legitimate political competition and a loyal opposition had largely disappeared from Russian politics. Candidates and parties can run against the ruling United Russia party and even against President Putin, but these candidates are hand-selected and very careful to play softball politics. Even the most critical candidate on the 2018 presidential ballot, Ksenia Sobchak, admitted that she was running not to win, but to improve her chances of being chosen as Putin's successor when (or if) he finally decides to stand down.

The result is a politics that is intensely focused around the person of the president, and one in which criticism and disloyalty are closely associated with each other. To take a stand and criticize the president is to risk social censure, and, for more prominent people, death threats and physical attack. Boris Nemtsov, the most prominent and charismatic of Russian oppositionists, was murdered on his walk home outside the Kremlin on February 27, 2015, an assassination that most saw as a direct result of his opposition to the war in Ukraine. Navalny and his supporters, too, have been harassed, arrested, beaten and sprayed with toxic chemicals.

Aside from politics itself, the media environment in Russia also differs from democracies in important ways.

One of the characteristics of media in non-democratic political systems is that news tends to be heavily weighted to one side—the government's side. This is not to say that there are no alternative media sources available. Dozhd, the independent online broadcaster that hosted engaging talk shows focused mostly on Russian politics, was, until the crisis in Ukraine, available on satellite television in Russia's big cities. Supporters of Dozhd raised over $1 million in a crowdfunding effort to save the channel after it was forced off cable television, and it is still available to subscribers online. Meduza, a lively, independent online magazine and news aggregator, is widely available to Russians, despite being based in Riga, Latvia. Run by Russian journalists who left the major Russian news website Lenta.ru after the firing of its editor-in-chief, Galina Timchenko, Meduza's very existence—a website run from a foreign capital by exiled journalists—is proof of the problem.

The result is that while both official media run by the Putin regime and independent media are available, the playing field is far from level. There is simply vastly more pro-regime information available, and it is much cheaper and easier to access. This means that only people who are especially motivated to access oppositional voices are likely to come across them. That this is the case is illustrated by an online poll conducted by Meduza on March 13–15, 2018, on the eve of the presidential election. While not scientific, the views of the nearly 85,000 Meduza readers who responded are fascinating—and wildly at odds with those of the population as a whole. Nearly 60 percent of respondents favored revisiting the status of Crimea as part of Russia, while 64 percent were in favor of allowing gay marriage. Three-quarters opposed the military draft in place in Russia and nearly three-fifths supported the legalization of soft drugs.[36] These views could hardly be more different than those of the Russian mainstream (though interestingly, more than 70 percent of Meduza's respondents favored stricter immigration legislation, a view shared by a substantial majority of Russians at large).

A final crucial fact about the Russian context that shapes how personality and politics interact is the absence of real ideological divides and the importance of nationalism. Unlike in the United States and western Europe, there is little evidence that ideology has much to do with support for political parties or voting behavior in Russia.[37] Ideological debate over the nature of power, the role of the state or the meaning of citizenship is mistrusted, and in its place politicians compete in their enthusiasm for Russian patriotism. This patriotism, in turn, often stresses the uniqueness of Russians versus the West.[38]

This process of distinguishing Russians from the West has two related effects. One is to downplay political and cultural differences among Russians, stressing their supposedly shared perceptions and collective uniqueness. The other effect, perhaps even more insidious, is to stigmatize those people who do have non-mainstream views as somehow non-Russian, foreign, even anti-Russian. This can have profound consequences for how Russians relate to one another. According to recent focus groups among young Russians conducted by one of the leading scholars of Russian media, Ellen Mickiewicz of Duke University, participants felt that people who have an "opinion corresponding to the majority" were more trustworthy, and that it was less risky to work with people with conformist views than with others.[39]

Taken together, these elements—autocracy, state-dominated media and non-ideological, patriotic politics—mean that the basic political dividing lines in Russia are very different than those we have traditionally seen in the Western democracies. Loyalty to the president and loyalty to the state become fused. To disagree and to challenge is to take a strong and potentially dangerous stand. Politics is not about policy and who gets what, when and how, as it has been classically conceptualized in democracies. Instead, as with generations of dictators throughout history, politics under Putin's authoritarian regime is about identifying friends and enemies, "healthy" supporters and "deviant" oppositions. As a result, the political effects of personality in Russia are different than they would be in the West. Instead of politics being a contest between conservatism and change, which draw upon the traits of conscientiousness and openness, politics becomes about conforming to socially accepted standards of opinion and attitudes—or rejecting those standards. This is very different psychological terrain.

This is where agreeableness comes in. Highly agreeable people care more about the opinion of those around them than less agreeable people, and they are strongly motivated to maintain positive relations with others. In a context in which citizens are asked to show their loyalty to their country and to their people through their views on political issues, highly agreeable people are likely to experience strong internal pressures to accept what they are told is the patriotic, communitarian, "normal" position. Moreover, highly agreeable people are likely to be, on average, quite mainstream in their selection of information and news sources, which in turn enables them to be well tuned to what the prevailing positions are expected to be on different issues—even issues to which they personally have probably not given much thought.

Take, for example, Anna. On our agreeableness scale, Anna scores a six out of seven. And, indeed, her daily life seems saturated with conversation and opinion. As a retail worker, Anna works two days on, two days off, and on her off days, she watches a lot of television, especially the talk shows on NTV. She's active online, with friends on Facebook and VKontakte, and while she says she doesn't seek out politics, it often comes up in conversation at home, at work, with relatives and with friends. She doesn't feel that she always has to agree—she and her mother, for example, disagree about whether Lenin should remain in his mausoleum on Red Square, and her husband takes a harder line on most issues than she does—but she is often on the lookout for what others are thinking.

"Of course, I listen to other people's opinions," she told us. "At work, for example. I pay attention to the opinions of the people I look up to. People who, you know, are deeper, who read more. Honestly, the things they're talking about, they're interesting to me, but I'm not going to go that deeply into them. I find it interesting, important, I'm not apathetic, and an opinion just begins to form. Mostly I just listen to people who know something."

By contrast, Andrei scores only a two out of seven on our agreeableness scale. Of course, correlation is not causation, and that's especially true when you're trying to understand the views and behaviors of a single individual. The reasons why Andrei sees the world the way he does are complex and ultimately inscrutable. But over the course of his hour-long interview with us, one gets the sense of a man who is not entirely comfortable in his own society. He refuses to watch Russian television, which he regards as entirely untrustworthy. But neither is he an acolyte of the opposition media; the newspapers he most frequently reads—*Izvestia* and *Komsomolskaya Pravda*—are very firmly in the pro-Kremlin camp. Mostly, though, he gets his news online, not from formal media sources, but through search engines: he'll hear about something in a conversation or on the radio, and then he'll search for it on Google or its Russian equivalent Yandex (and has noted that they often give him different results), reading until he figures out what's what to his own satisfaction.

Thus, whereas Anna takes the Kremlin's position fervently on the wedge issues of the day—the anti-LGBT and anti-blasphemy legislation in particular—on the issues where the Kremlin wants him to have an opinion Andrei is almost blissfully ignorant. Before we asked him, he had heard only of the LGBT law (which he said he would strongly support), although he didn't know it had already been passed. He had heard nothing of the anti-blasphemy law (which, when described to him in the law's own terms, he said he would oppose).

This raises an interesting paradox. Normally, most psychological studies describe agreeable people with terms like warm, kind and sympathetic.[40] Supporting laws that criminalize open conversation about homosexual relationships or allow someone to be prosecuted for blasphemy would, by contrast, seem unkind. The answer is that being agreeable isn't about being nice so much as it is about appearing to be nice. In a study by the psychologists William Graziano, Jessica Kieras, Renee Tobin and Mary Rothbart, children were asked to pick a favorite and a least favorite toy from a box and then say what they liked or disliked about them. Psychologists, being disagreeable people, then randomly gave the kids one of the selected toys as a gift—either the most favored or the least favored one—and watched very carefully to see the reaction. As you can imagine, the kids who received the least favored toy were disappointed and visibly so. And for most of these kids, their disappointment lingered on their faces. But a minority—the most highly agreeable children—were almost immediately able to mask their initial disappointment and ended up expressing reactions that were just as positive about their least favorite gift as they had been about the toy they really wanted. Graziano and his team call this the "effortful control of frustration."[41]

How does working hard to control your frustration relate to support for Putin's policies? Getting along—and seeing the positive in any situation—takes work, and agreeable people are more likely than others to make that extra effort. As they make that effort, though, they're reading their social surroundings to determine what's expected—and what's expected is not necessarily nice. In another series of experiments, Graziano and his colleagues showed that agreeable people—when placed in an environment in which various kinds of discrimination are exhibited by most people around them—are at least as willing to discriminate as everyone else.[42] In other words, it is not that highly agreeable people are less prejudiced, but that they are more willing to hide their true feelings and behave like everyone else in order to fit in.

In the Russian context, this means that being high on the agreeableness scale—wanting to get along and avoid social conflict—was the leading predictor of voting for Putin and of approving of the Kremlin's ideological positions. This is because highly agreeable people, like Anna (and unlike Andrei), were more likely to get most of their news from official sources and less likely to use opposition-oriented media. Russian Orthodoxy was also more important in the lives of highly agreeable people than less agreeable people. Exposure to state-sanctioned media campaigns and the Church clearly led them to stronger support for Putin but also to more homophobic attitudes. In those contexts, it was not only permissible to express fear and prejudice against gay people, it was encouraged.

A NORMAL DAY

When it comes to politics, Andrei is both vociferous and vociferously uninterested. Looking ahead to the 2018 presidential elections, he told us he planned to go to work.

"It's just a normal day," he said.

The only time he did vote, he told us, was when he was in the army. "It was against my will," he said.

If forced to vote, however, he would support Putin, mostly because he despises the opposition.

"The leaders we have, they're bad, but at least they're already in power, and life is kind of okay," he said. "At least on the surface. But these guys [in the opposition], they're clowns. ... I don't even consider them to be an opposition. It's just a band of crooks, who are really being fed from somewhere overseas. It's not even really a secret anymore, it's that, what's his name, the one they sent to prison, who's now in Latvia or somewhere. I forgot his name." (A few minutes later, Andrei remembered: Khodorkovsky.)

Clearly, one does not need to be agreeable to support Putin (even if only for the lack of a better alternative), and neither is disagreeableness a direct route to the opposition. But to the extent that agreeableness has helped support Putin's political fortunes, it holds a trap.

If Russia's most agreeable people are among Putin's biggest supporters—and if the reason they support him is not because of anything he's done for them materially or even ideologically, but because that's what the social context demands—what happens when the social context begins to shift? Ironically, despite the importance of loyalty in structuring Russian politics, an "agreeable" electorate is not, in fact, an inherently loyal electorate. Or, rather, its loyalty is to fitting in—to what Havel called "living in harmony with society"—rather than to Putin himself.

"I just don't see any real opponent to our president," the highly "agreeable" Anna told us ahead of the 2018 presidential election. Strikingly, her support for Putin was devoid of any of the aggression and anger that characterized Andrei. "Because there's no worthy competitor. If there was a worthy competitor, maybe our political situation would change, we might have a different leader. But these [people on the ballot] aren't competitors. They're too little. . . . That's just my point of view. I don't see a worthy opposition to Putin. When I do, then I'll say, 'That's my president.' Of course we need young blood. We need to change."

SIX

RUSSIA AT WAR

"He's dead."

It was Evgenia Albats, the usually irrepressible editor of the opposition-minded Russian newsweekly *The New Times*, who said it first. Along the length of a lunch table in Boston, phones had begun to buzz.

"Boris is dead," she repeated. "They killed him."

RUSSIA RISES

The story of Vladimir Putin's power—the story of how Putin's strength is created by the emotions and support of millions of Russians and the acquiescence of millions more—is not the only story in Russian politics. It is not even the only story that matters. Putin's power was built in the face of opposition and, despite everything, that opposition has persisted. Millions of ordinary Russians continue to see a different future for their country, and the challenge they pose to the Kremlin remains formidable. Their story needs to be told, too, not least because they will play no less of a role than Putin's supporters in writing the next chapter in Russian history.

Boris Nemtsov, however, will not feature in that future. A Yeltsin-era governor and deputy prime minister with an infectious smile, he—like many of Boris Yeltsin's young reformers—was associated by most Russians with the chaos and deprivation of the 1990s. But standing shoulder to shoulder with Alexei Navalny and Sergei Udaltsov throughout the Bolotnaya protests, and risking life and limb as the police charged into the May 6, 2012 rally, Nemtsov gradually began to restore his standing. While Udaltsov languished in prison and Navalny was tied up in seemingly endless prosecutions, Nemtsov led the charge against the war in Ukraine. In July 2013, he was elected to the Yaroslavl regional Duma, making him one of very few opposition leaders to actually hold office. In addition, he headed the People's Freedom Party (Parnas, by its Russian acronym), the only true opposition party officially recognized by the Central Electoral Commission and thus "licensed" to put names on the ballot. Plans were being laid to field a broad slate of opposition candidates in the 2015 parliamentary elections.

It was the anti-war movement, though, that really put Nemtsov back at the forefront of Russian politics, as the most prominent politician of any stripe to speak out force-fully and consistently against both the annexation of Crimea and the intervention in the Donbas. The first major anti-war rally in Russia was held on March 15, 2014, just three days before the annexation of Crimea. Smaller-scale, unsanc-tioned anti-war and pro-Ukraine rallies had been held before in Moscow, attracting no more than a few hundred people at a time. March 15 was a bitterly cold day, and the rally itself was beset by technical difficulties, which particularly affected the sound system. As a result, many participants left early.

Nevertheless, by 1.45pm there were already 5,000 people on the streets. Nemtsov and Ilya Yashin held a banner reading "Russia and Ukraine without Putin!" By 3.45pm there were as many as 50,000 people. Groups represented included a particular slice of the Russian political spectrum—liberal groups like Solidarnost, the Progress Party and Demvybor, and some anarchists. Opposition politicians and activists, war reporters and even members of Pussy Riot took the stage.[1] Sergei Kurginian—a Kremlin-friendly nationalist voice who had headlined many of the anti-opposition, fake pro-Kremlin demonstrations ("Putingi") in 2012—reprised his earlier role, leading a pro-Kremlin rally at the same time as the Peace March, but it attracted only a fraction of the participants, despite the obviously greater popularity of its message.

A second Peace March was scheduled for September 2014. By then, peace rallies—which had been something of an untested idea in the spring—were clearly becoming an opportunity for the opposition as a whole to regroup, and perhaps regain some of the momentum that had been so sorely lacking since Putin's inauguration in May 2012. Almost all of the major liberal opposition political groupings announced their intention to take part, including Yabloko, RPR-Parnas, the Progress Party, the Green Alliance, the December 5 Party, and Solidarity. The agenda, too, began to grow beyond simply opposition to Russia's intervention in Ukraine; the application for permission to protest railed against "growing fascism in our country, [and] the heavy economic consequences."[2]

Nemtsov was rapidly emerging as the most prominent voice in the anti-war movement, and he in turn helped to attract a small handful of celebrity supporters, including the rock singer Andrei Makarevich and the actor Oleg Basilashvili.[3] Still, in an interview with Dozhd the day before the march, Nemtsov kept the focus very much on the war: "If a lot of people come out to the march now, it will be a very powerful signal that the decision in Minsk, the Minsk ceasefire, must be maintained. That's a very serious thing. It is very fragile, and there are a lot of people who want to break it and start [fighting] all over again. Nonetheless, the opinion of citizens—and first and foremost of Muscovites—can play a very important role. We can, in fact, save people's lives. You understand, coming out to this march, we are saving the lives of those boys, saving families, children, women, men, fathers, mothers, saving everybody. That is a very important reason to come out."[4]

The turnout for the September Peace March was on a par with the spring event, bringing out somewhere in the range of 50,000; a smaller rally was held in St. Petersburg.[5] In other cities, however, local authorities refused to allow anti-war marches to go ahead, including in Ekaterinburg, Novosibirsk and Barnaul.[6]

The day he died, Nemtsov gave what would be his last interview to Ekho Moskvy, a state-owned radio station with a reputation as one of the few broadcast media where opposition leaders could still get a hearing in Russia. After the relative success—in terms of mobilization, if not results—of the March and September 2014 Peace Marches, the opposition settled on a deliberate (if leisurely) pace of one major march every six months or so; the next was scheduled for March 1, 2015. This time, though, the government threw a spanner into the works, denying permission for another rally in central Moscow, and instead offering a location in the bedroom suburb of Marino, about as far as it is possible to go from the Kremlin and still technically be in Moscow. In his Ekho Moskvy interview, Nemtsov explained that, while some groups (including Yabloko) pulled out in protest at the government's move, the rest of the movement decided to go ahead with the march in Marino, while simultaneously expanding the agenda yet further. Instead of calling it a Peace March, the rally was dubbed the Spring March, trying to steal back the moniker of "Russian Spring" that had been adopted by the nationalists and Donbas separatists, and railing against the government not just for the war, but for the economic hardship the conflict was wreaking on ordinary Russians, and for the cover it provided for corruption and abuse of power.[7]

SHOTS FIRED

As Nemtsov was preparing to give the interview that no one could know would be his last, a two-day conference at Tufts University was about to get under way. Given that the conference was organized by students, it was a remarkable affair, attracting some of the biggest names in Russian academia, politics and journalism. In one of the morning panels on the first day, Evgenia Albats shared the stage with Oksana Boyko, a talk-show host on Russia Today, the Russian state-backed international broadcaster often accused of propaganda. The fireworks were spectacular, and it did not end well for Boyko, who was forced to admit that Russian state television had fabricated much of its coverage of the early months of the Donbas conflict.

Albats had lunch that afternoon with exiled opposition politician Ilya Ponomarev, Ukrainian revolutionary leader Mustafa Nayyem, and a number of political analysts, including your co-author. (Boyko lunched in a different room.) The news was broken in a text from Yashin, Nemtsov's comrade from the anti-war movement, who had taken a call from Nemtsov's companion as she stood help-lessly watching him bleed out on the asphalt. It happened at 11.15pm: shots fired from a passing car. Had it been a different time of day, the shadow of a Kremlin tower would have fallen squarely on the spot. Albats boarded the next plane to Moscow. Boyko, perhaps wisely, skipped the rest of the conference.

Nemtsov was not the first opposition figure to be killed in Russia: opposition politicians, including Galina Starovoitova and Sergei Yushenkov, had been murdered, as had journalists including Anna Politkovskaya and Anastasia Baburova, and human-rights activists Stanislav Markelov and Natalia Estemirova, to name just a few. But Nemtsov's murder was immediately seen as different: he was among the top two or three names in Russia's current opposition, a former deputy prime minister who could not be regarded as a minor figure of little importance, as Putin had earlier dismissed Politkovskaya. Russia had become the sort of country where opposition leaders were gunned down.

In the next issue of *The New Times*, Albats recalled a conversation she had had with Nemtsov only the week before. "How come," she had asked, "Navalny keeps getting thrown in jail, and they never touch you, even though you write harsher and harsher things about Putin, the Kremlin and Donbas?"

"Because I was deputy prime minister," Nemtsov answered briskly. "You have to understand, they do understand that power will change hands eventually, and they don't want to create a precedent for whoever comes to power later and might start shooting at those who served Putin."[8]

The Spring March planned for March 1 became a memorial procession for Nemtsov. With hastily granted permission from the city authorities, the event was moved to the very center of the city, and participants walked in silence to lay flowers on the spot where Nemtsov was killed. They carried signs and banners adding the Cyrillic soft sign to his given name, transforming Борис into Борись—the imperative form of the verb "to fight."[9]

UNDER THE GUN

Looking back from the vantage point of Putin's fourth term in the Kremlin, it's easy to conclude that Russia's opposition was doomed from the day he came back to the presidency and crushed the Bolotnaya protest movement. But for many, that was not the feeling at the time. Putin was back in office; people were in jail; restrictions on the media and on civil society had been tightened—but all the same, many liberals believed things were still looking up.

"In the fall of 2013 there was still a sense of ongoing liberalization, just of everything continuing to open up," Mikhail Zygar recalled, looking back on a time when he was still editor-in-chief of Dozhd. "There had been [Moscow mayoral] elections in the summer, where Navalny came in second and almost forced a runoff. In the fall, they let both Khodorkovsky and Pussy Riot out of jail. Everyone was looking forward to the Olympics. Everyone was looking forward to more openness and more liberalism. We were certain that our wave was cresting. We didn't feel the sword of Damocles hanging over us."

In fact, the opposition had already been dealt a number of blows. Putin returned to the Kremlin in May 2012 with a heavy hand, persecuting opposition leaders and activists, tightening control over the media and the internet, and harassing NGOs and civic groups. That's not to say that the Kremlin had made no concessions to the Bolotnaya opposition movement: regional gubernatorial elections were reinstated (having been ended after the Beslan terror attack in 2004), and barriers for political parties to gain access to the ballot were reduced somewhat. In April 2012, Yevgeny Urlashov ran on an opposition ticket for mayor of the city of Yaroslavl and won; fifteen months later, he was bundled into a police van and jailed on corruption charges.

The first criminal investigation against Alexei Navalny—the lawyer and anti-corruption blogger who emerged as the charismatic leader of the opposition, overshadowing even Nemtsov—was launched in July 2012, on charges that he had defrauded the Kirov regional government when he had served as an adviser in the privatization of a forestry company, Kirovles. In December of that year, he and his brother, Oleg, were charged with embezzlement in a different case, relating to a contract with the French cosmetics company Yves Rocher (despite the fact that the company reported taking no losses in the matter). In July 2013, Navalny was convicted and given a five-year jail term in the Kirovles case, only to have the prosecution request and receive a suspended sentence the next day, after which he returned to Moscow to contest the mayoral election there. In December 2014, Navalny was given a second suspended sentence in the Yves Rocher case, while his brother, Oleg, was sent to prison for three and a half years. Other movement figures also faced prosecution. In August 2012, two members of Pussy Riot were sent to jail. And Sergei Udaltsov, leader of the radical National Bolshevik Party and among the most vociferous figures in the Bolotnaya movement, was arrested as one of the May 6 protesters and sentenced to four and a half years in prison.

In addition to those and other activists—particularly in Russia's far-flung regions—pressure was brought to bear on public figures who sympathized with the opposition. Thus, in the spring of 2013, the government opened an investigation into a group of Russian and international experts who had been asked by former Russian Constitutional Court judge Tamara Morshchakova—at the behest of then-President Medvedev—to write confidential opinions regarding the convictions of the oligarch Mikhail Khodorkovsky. Among them was the economist Sergei Guriev, rector of the New Economic School, who had written economic policy for Medvedev but had, more recently, publicly supported Navalny. Fearing prosecution, he fled the country in April 2013, shortly before the investigators announced pending charges for attempting to subvert the course of justice. Suspicion fell on others, as well; thus, Igor Fediukin, deputy minister of education, came under fire for his perceived collaboration with the Dissernet project, an initiative led by opposition figure Sergei Parkhomenko aimed at uncovering academic fraud and plagiarism among the ruling elite.

Fediukin was forced out of office the same week Guriev fled the country. The result was that the fear of prosecution began to hang over even those liberals who had stayed away from political opposition *per se*.

Meanwhile, the government tightened its control over the information space, both legislatively and managerially. In July 2012, two months after Putin's inauguration, the government adopted a new law and set of regulations creating a state-run blacklist of internet content that the government found undesirable. Formally, this was targeted at content deemed to promote extremism, narcotics or suicide, or to contain child pornography; however, the system could be—and soon was—used to target protest-related content as well. In March 2014, Roskomnadzor, the agency charged with maintaining and enforcing the blacklist, blocked access to the opposition-minded news sites Grani.ru and EJ.ru, as well as to the blogs of Navalny and opposition leader Garri Kasparov.

In addition to laying the groundwork for control and censorship online, the government moved to tighten control over a wide range of media outlets. The effort began close to home, in December 2013, when Putin issued a decree dismissing the leadership of RIA Novosti—a state media holding known for high professional standards and a modicum of balanced reporting. The agency's new head, Dmitry Kiselev, was instructed to promote the interests, views and messages of the Russian government. In March 2014, Roskomnadzor threatened to block the major news website Lenta.ru, provoking its owner, Alexander Mamut, to fire the editor. The rest of the editorial staff resigned in protest, and a new staff follows a Kremlin-friendly line.

Gazprom Media altered its own management structures to enforce tighter control over the Ekho Moskvy radio station, known as a voice for opposition-minded journalists, activists and politicians. The next month, Pavel Durov—the founder and CEO of VKontakte, Russia's largest social networking site, who had refused to provide user data to the security services—was pushed out and fled the country. And in September 2014, the Duma passed a law restricting foreigners from holding more than a 20 percent stake in any Russian media outlet, calling into question the future of some of the country's leading independent publications, including the newspaper *Vedomosti* and the Russian editions of *Forbes*, *GQ* and other magazines. The result was a gradual but significant erosion of diversity across the Russian media space.

Finally, in the year or so after Putin returned to the Kremlin, the Duma came to be known in opposition circles as the "crazy printer," for the speed with which it seemed to be producing legislation cracking down on civil society organizations, and indeed anyone at all who worked with foreign governments and pro-democracy groups, or who simply had the temerity to publicly espouse unpopular opinions.[10]

THE WAR COMES HOME

And yet, the opposition persisted—just not in the form it had taken before.

The 2011–12 Bolotnaya protest wave had galvanized what had already been emerging as a wide-ranging anti-regime movement. This involved the amalgamation of longstanding issue-oriented NGOs and civic groups, newer groupings that arose as a response to the 2011 Duma election, and the networks of prominent anti-government activists and journalists into a civic network—a network of networks that was, at the peak of mobilization, much more than the sum of its parts.[11] But, like many protest movements, it was a product both of and for the moment. When that moment passed, the movement faded—as movements do—but it did not go away. Instead, as our research shows, it reconstituted itself in new forms, forms better suited to a longer-term fight and with clearer leadership.

The Bolotnaya mobilization that began in December 2011 had brought together a range of NGOs and social movement organizations, including those that had been active in Russia across various issue areas for quite some time, and organizations created immediately before and during the election period. Thereafter, some of these newer organizations fell by the wayside, while others persisted and new ones were created, with an eye toward longer-term contestation of a rapidly retrenching Putin government.[12]

As the momentum from Bolotnaya began to fade, though, new organizations emerged, less "of the moment" and more focused on longer-term agendas and—almost inevitably—on leaders. Three of these groups emerged around Navalny himself: the Foundation for the Fight Against Corruption (FBK), Navalny's investigation and advocacy organization, known for its dramatic exposés; the aptly named Team Navalny, a central structure for on- and off-line organizing activities, created with a clear view toward eventually contesting a presidential election; and the Progress Party, Navalny's formal political platform, which attempted to field candidates in the 2015 regional and 2016 parliamentary elections, but which was never formally registered by the Central Electoral Commission. Separately, an online movement with the unwieldy name "We are against interference in the internal affairs of Ukraine" emerged in March 2014 to organize the first Peace March and continued to serve as the major anti-war platform in Russia; many of the leaders were activists in Nemtsov's Solidarity movement.

Between 2012 and 2015, we tracked these and other groups on Facebook, where they were most active. Although we could only see what people were doing publicly (and made no attempt to access their private communication), we were able to look systematically at some 200,000 messages communicated between some 45,000 people over that period, across all of the communities and movements described above.

As we would expect, discussions in the network grew quieter over time, declining to barely more than a murmur by the end of 2013.[13] But just as Russia's adventures in Ukraine sparked mass mobilization among nationalists, so too did it bring out the opposition—both into the streets, and onto the internet.[14] Crimea and the Donbas clearly breathed new life into the opposition, more than doubling the size of the network we were monitoring from the beginning of 2014 to the summer of 2015.[15]

In the summer of 2014, more than two years after Putin's inauguration, when coercion and ideological counter-mobilization had taken hold, many people even inside the opposition began to fret that the movement was dead. Thus, it was somewhat surprising that we found almost three times as much activity in the network as we had right before the 2012 presidential election. Less than 1 percent of this activity, however, was in the communities that had been created during Bolotnaya or before it. Virtually all of the participants were engaged in the new anti-war community.[16] And while Bolotnaya-movement and other groups were more active in the fall than in the summer, the anti-war community itself still accounted for 98 percent of activity.

Thus, through at least September 2014 the anti-war movement was the single most important recruiter of new supporters to the opposition. While most of the Bolotnaya and pre-Bolotnaya groups were being kept alive by skeleton crews of activists, the anti-war movement was bringing in thousands of people who had not been active before.[17] That does not mean, however, that the anti-war movement was an altogether separate phenomenon. It was, as Bolotnaya had been before, the form that Russia's opposition took at the moment. Among its most prominent activists were Boris Nemtsov and Ilya Yashin, veterans of opposition party politics, alongside journalists and activists who had been prominent in the Bolotnaya movement. They brought with them to the anti-war community ideas, frames and tropes that were familiar from the 2011–12 protest wave, and which meant that the anti-war movement took on many of the same ideas and aesthetics. Tellingly, Nemtsov himself began researching a high-profile report on the war, to be titled "Putin: War"—an obvious sequel to his "Putin: Results" report that had provided a compendium of evidence for high-level corruption during the 2011–12 wave. This meant, among other things, that Bolotnaya-era participants could fit harmoniously into the movement, while, as the anti-war community dwindled into 2015, its supporters could flow just as easily into other oppositional communities.

FRIENDSHIP PARK

For Nikolai Epple and his neighbors, the war was local.

A thirty-something journalist and literary translator—among his proudest achievements is a translation of G. K. Chesterton's *Basil Howe* into Russian—Epple moved in 2011 to Rechnoi Vokzal, a relatively quiet district in far northwest Moscow. It was sentimentality, in part, that had motivated the move from central Moscow out to the far end of the metro's green line; Epple had grown up there. But it was also the park. Epple and his wife had recently had a baby, and Park Druzhby—"Friendship Park," one of Moscow's many green spaces—would be right on their doorstep.

In August 2015, though, the park began to become less friendly. Epple and other residents found a corner of the park—a field popular with dog owners and model aircraft enthusiasts, and a hill popular with sled-borne kids in the winter—cordoned off and piled with construction supplies. That was when Epple remembered his neighbor.

"My wife works at a children's club," Epple recalled in an interview. "And this neighbor, his kids go to that club. And he's an activist, kind of a professional activist. He's always doing battle against something—against parking, against some procurement contract, just always against something. I always thought he was kind of a crazy person, but for a while there had been this conversation in his circles about the park. No one really paid attention to it. I mean, we always live with this sense that the state's going to come and take something. But he had been talking about the park for a while."

And then the bulldozers came.

"There were ten of us at the start, who went out to the bulldozers," Epple said. "Maybe not even ten. And then people just started coming. Facebook played a very important role, because it was really the pictures on Facebook that pushed it.... The core were mothers with baby carriages. That made for good pictures. And they were very dedicated. People would come, and they would call their friends. And then on the second day, on the third day, when it began to resonate, other people started coming: bloggers, journalists. Though at first it was locals, who read about it on social media."

At stake was a private football field and sports complex, to be built on dubious permits by a contractor with alleged ties to the authorities.[18] After being stonewalled by the authorities and United Russia officials, Epple and his neighbors—who manned a permanent tent camp outside the construction site even as the nights grew colder into fall—welcomed help from the liberal party Yabloko, from the Communists, and from Progressive Law, a legal aid fund set up by Navalny's Progress Party. In short order, however, flyers started appearing in the neighborhood and articles were printed in the local newspaper and on the Russian social networking site VKontakte accusing Epple and the Friendship Park protesters of being a "fifth column" in the service of the State Department.[19] By late August, the city sent in the police to break up the protests. When that failed—in part because the police themselves were loath to intervene (and one officer was fired as a result)—private security services descended on the camp in a series of raids, sending some protesters to the hospital.[20] The protesters themselves responded by branching out, seeking support from others who found themselves in a similar relationship with the state. Some of these came together in a new city-wide movement "Za Park" ("For the Park"), including a movement organized to prevent the construction of a new church in the Losiny Ostrov (Moose Island) park in northeast Moscow.[21]

"It was about a week into it, when we sat down, and there was a core team, some kind of structure, we sat and started thinking that we need to make connections, to exchange experience," Epple recalled. "It took about another week before we really started to get in touch. And then, maybe in a month or two, there was already this association [Za Park]."

Perhaps more worryingly for the Kremlin, however, Epple and his comrades decided to send a delegation to the so-called "Green Column" in the "March for the Turnover of Power" in September 2015, organized by Navalny.[22]

"That was interesting," Epple recalls. "Because we took a long time to decide whether we would just go as individuals, or whether we would go to represent the park. Some people said, we don't need this Navalny or even politics in general. They'll break us up. Others said no, we have common ground. It was a real debate. In the end, we decided to represent the park."

It was, Epple said, the outcome of a natural progression of thought.

"A lot of people started off neutral," he told us. "But after two weeks of sitting in the park, of talking through the night? People who hadn't thought through for themselves 'what's going on with politics?', 'what are my convictions?', 'who is closest to my opinions?', after two weeks of talking people moved toward this kind of liberal democratic position. At the beginning, everyone more or less didn't like [Moscow Mayor Sergei] Sobyanin, but that was disconnected, I mean, not politically motivated. It was just, 'he's the boss, who we can identify, and who is a jerk.' And then over the course of two weeks, those who didn't have a view, they got one—about democracy, about elections, about how things are the way they are because Putin has been in power for twenty years. And it just built up. It became clear what we needed to do."

DAY OF THE SNAIL

"We are not a fifth column," Sergei Voloshchuk told the Russian newspaper *RBK* in November 2015. By "we," Voloshchuk was referring to the thousands of long-distance truckers who had converged on Moscow, St. Petersburg and other major cities to protest a new tax being levied by the government on their trade. "I love my country and I hate America. . . . But right now, we're fighting for our rights and the rights of all Russians."[23]

Just months earlier, Voloshchuk and many of his comrades had taken part in the so-called Anti-Maidan, a series of rallies in Moscow and elsewhere in Russia designed to show loyalty to the Kremlin and put a stop to any talk of Ukraine-style regime change in Russia. (Never mind that such talk was mostly in the imaginations of Anti-Maidan organizers.) Participants—who included the Night Wolves biker gang favored by Putin and a group of heartland industrial workers who had threatened to come to Moscow and beat up anti-regime protesters in 2011—carried portraits of Putin and former Chechen leader Akhmat Kadyrov as strong-armed talismans against what they saw as Western encroachment and interference.[24] But in November 2015, Voloshchuk and other truckers were huddled in the cabs of their big rigs in makeshift camps outside the Moscow beltway, their PR efforts supported by friends of opposition leader Alexei Navalny, their food and clean water carried in by sympathizers from environmental and LGBT groups—and opposed by their erstwhile allies from the Anti-Maidan.

On December 4, after their warnings went unheeded, Voloshchuk and his comrades struck. They declared the "Day of the Snail," making good on their threat to drive their trucks slowly around Moscow's MKAD beltway—a massive ten-to-twelve-lane highway vital to the capital's transportation—and effectively paralyze it. The reason for their anger was something called "Platon," an automated road-tax system for heavyweight trucks. Part of the problem was the cost. Most of the striking truckers were privateers, owner-operators of small businesses, who thus could not easily pass on the cost of the tax to their clients. But the other part of the problem was that Platon reeked of corruption: it was to be operated by a private company called RTITS, majority-owned by Igor Rotenberg, the son of Arkady Rotenberg, a close friend and associate of Putin; RTITS would, of course, get a large commission for the taxes collected. One popular protest banner seen on striking trucks read, "The Rotenbergs are worse than ISIS" (and this not long after Russia had gone to war against ISIS in Syria).

The government, of course, should have known better than to pick a fight with the truckers. Organized, networked and with a culture of solidarity and mutual assistance, they were exactly the kind of social group you would expect to react robustly to policies they don't like. But the government had also been here before. In 2005, when they tried to ban right-side-drive cars—of which Russia at the time had approximately 2 million, mostly imported used from Japan—a driver named Vyacheslav Lysakov created a campaign called "Freedom of Choice," organized drivers to shut down traffic in central Moscow, and won a repeal of the ban. (Lysakov was later recruited into Putin's Russian National Front, a campaign organization parallel to United Russia, and abandoned the movement.)[25] And the government compromised on Platon, too, keeping the system in place (and thus making good on its commitments to the Rotenbergs), but reducing the tariff by nearly 60 percent and putting a moratorium on fines for noncompliance.

For all its vaunted strength and autocracy, in fact the Russian government frequently backs down in the face of concerted protest—frequently, but not always. In February 2017, Moscow Mayor Sergei Sobyanin drew up plans to demolish as many as 8,000 apartment buildings in the city. Some of these plans had been around for a long time; much of the city's housing stock, particularly so-called *Khrushchyovka*, or Khrushchev buildings, designed in the 1950s, were nearing the end of their useful lives and had long been slated for removal. But the demolition plans had never been on such a scale.

Here, too, the response could have been predicted. As it became clearer exactly which buildings were on the demolition list, a group of apartment owners came together—on Facebook, of course—to try to stop it. By April, according to our data, there were as many as 3,000 active members in the online movement; by July, the number reached 8,000. On the streets, by the government's own data, there were some 500 protests in the first half of May alone, encompassing as many as 35,000 people.[26] In a partial compromise, the city government cut the list of proposed demolitions to 4,543 and agreed to allow homeowners to vote, requiring at least 60 percent of homeowners in each building to vote "yes" for demolition to go ahead. In the end, 4,079 buildings voted "yes," and as many as 900,000 Muscovites stand to be relocated—forcibly or otherwise—at some point in the next several years.[27] The holdouts will hope that they fare better than Epple and his neighbors at the park.

"In the winter, at the district council somewhere they decided they needed to pick up the pace, because we were blocking the trucks every other night, everyone was tired, and even the construction drivers were quitting," Epple recalled. "And that's when the police really got tough. Right before New Year's they wanted to arrest us and lock us up for fifteen days. Everyone. Not just the core, but just accidental people, who were scared. At the beginning, in the summer, there was just this feeling of surprise, that there were so many of us, we were staying through the night and not leaving. There was inspiration, not fear. And then they brought in the police, and a private security group, and it got serious. People here remember that the state is powerful, and it's best not to get involved."

THE PEOPLE V. DIMON

Even as he continued to do battle with prosecutors, Navalny and his team doubled down on their anti-corruption campaigns. Drawing on legal documents and public records sourced from around the world, Navalny traced the allegedly ill-gotten gains of people at the commanding heights of Russian political and economic power. Presented in increasingly slick multi-media packages—and often with well-produced videos for those unwilling to read through the small print—the investigations aimed to uncover not just corruption, but hypocrisy. Thus, as Russia spiraled deeper into conflict with the West, Navalny reveled in uncovering the Russian elite's real estate holdings in Miami.[28] In December 2015, Navalny's target was Justice Minister Yury Chaika and his son Artyom, whom Navalny accused of using his father's position as cover for a massive corporate raiding and extortion operation.[29] In the summer of 2016, Navalny turned his attention to First Deputy Prime Minister Igor Shuvalov, whom Navalny accused not only of amassing unreasonable amounts of luxury real estate, but also of flying his wife's prized show-dogs around the world on private jets.[30]

The biggest broadside, however, came in on March 2, 2017, when Navalny released his "Dimon" investigation, using the street-slang diminutive of Dmitry—as in Medvedev.[31] Backed up by reams of paper, and illustrated in a fifty-minute video complete with aerial drone footage, the investigation pointed to an international empire of real estate and business interests, tying in some of Russia's most prominent oligarchs in the process. It was the highest in Russia's "vertical of power" Navalny's exposés had yet climbed.

Investigative work was only one of Navalny's fronts, however. Having been convicted of fraud in the Kirovles case in 2013 and given a suspended sentence—on charges the defense insisted were trumped up—Navalny appealed up through the Russian court system and eventually to the European Court of Human Rights in Strasbourg, which in October 2016 found the Russian verdict to have been "arbitrary and manifestly unreasonable."[32] In November, Russia's supreme court accepted the decision from Strasbourg, quashed the verdict and ordered a retrial. Having been freed of this conviction, Navalny could now run for the presidency—something he announced he would do in December 2016.

Running for the Russian presidency, needless to say, is not a simple task, particularly if you're not nominated by one of the "licensed" political parties. Just to get on the ballot, Navalny would have to collect 7,500 verified signatures supporting his candidacy in each of at least sixty-five regions (out of eighty-five recognized by the Russian government, including Crimea and Sevastopol)—for a total of almost half a million signatures nationwide. Achieving that required infrastructure. On February 4, 2017, Navalny's campaign opened its first regional hub, in St. Petersburg; two weeks later, a second hub opened in Novosibirsk, followed a week later by a third in Ekaterinburg, and a fourth ten days after that in Nizhny Novgorod. In March, the campaign began opening three or four new regional hubs each week, and Navalny himself traveled to many of them, greeting volunteers, giving public speeches (when allowed by local authorities) and generally rallying the troops.[33]

It was the "Dimon" investigation that brought the two fronts together. In the face of official silence about the investigation's charges, Navalny effectively invited his supporters—and the Russian public at large—to be incensed, and proposed that they be incensed together, on March 26. And they were. Rallies were held in as many as eighty cities around the country, bringing together more than 60,000 people, according to independent estimates.[34] In Moscow, where the rally had not been sanctioned by city hall, more than 900 people were detained, and some—including Nikolai Lyaskin, Navalny's Moscow campaign director—were severely injured.[35] At least three protesters were sentenced to prison terms of 2–3 years, in an apparent effort to repeat the deterrent effect of the Bolotnaya trials of 2012–13.[36]

The March 26 rallies marked something of a turning point in Russian politics. Two things happened that had not happened before, at least under Putin. First, not since the miners' strikes and other industrial disturbances of the 1990s had the number of protesters outside Moscow outnumbered those protesting in the capital itself. And unlike in the 1990s, the regional protesters this time around didn't have the backing of competing parts of the political establishment.[37] Second, these were the first major protests that weren't directly provoked by the state. Unlike the benefits protests of 2005, the political protests of 2011–12 or even the truckers' protest of 2015, the anger on

March 26, 2017 was proactive, rather than reactive. For the first time, large numbers of people had come out into the streets to demand something they wanted, rather than to prevent something they didn't want.

From Navalny's point of view, then, the anti-demolition movement provided an opportunity to capitalize politically on yet more public dissatisfaction with the government. At the largest anti-demolition rally, held on May 14, 2017 on Prospekt Sakharova, the same place where the largest anti-Putin protest had been held in December 2011, Navalny was in the crowd and expected to take the stage. Before that could happen, however, he was corralled by police; by some accounts, it was the organizers themselves who had asked the guards to shepherd him away. Navalny's over-tures to the truckers, too, were generally rebuffed. (That didn't, however, stop the anti-demolition protesters, the truckers or Epple and his neighbors from being tarred as part of a nefarious, American-backed "fifth column.")

But Navalny didn't need to get in through the front door. By declaring an us-versus-them politics, Putin's Kremlin had provided not just a basis for his own re-legitimation, but also an identity around which opposi-tional forces could coalesce. Doubtless, Putin and his advisers knew this would happen, and it may even have been the point: in 2012 and 2013, the Kremlin maneu-vered opposition leaders into taking positions in support of LGBT rights, blasphemers, Americans and others who were guaranteed not to win them votes. But the knock-on effect appears to have been broader. Raising the stakes of contestation across the board pushes the likes of Epple and his fellow park defenders—or Voloshchuk and his fellow truckers—into positions they would never before have taken. The opposition was taking shape, and Navalny—by design or by accident—was at the heart of it.

TIES THAT BIND

The spring and summer of 2017 were rich with protests. After the success of Navalny's "Dimon" rallies in March, Mikhail Khodorkovsky's Open Russia—run from the ex-oligarch's exile in London—organized nationwide protests under the hashtag-banner #Nadoel (from the Russian for "fed up") on April 29. The anti-demolition protests grew in scale until their major rally on May 14. And Navalny brought people back out into the streets for Russia Day on June 12, before the summer holidays sent everyone packing off to the dacha.

Having tracked the post-Bolotnaya opposition on Facebook from 2012 through 2015, we picked up the trail again in 2017, as Navalny's bid for the 2018 presidential elections began to take shape, and as the debates over the Moscow demolition project came to the fore. Taken together, we were able to capture almost 300,000 interactions among around 30,000 people, from February through July 2017. In other words, just judging by online activity alone—which, obviously, is an imperfect reflection of what happens offline—the opposition space in 2017 was much larger and livelier than it had been at any time since Bolotnaya.[38]

The activity was not, however, evenly distributed across the network. In the period we studied, there were three times as many individuals in the Navalny network as in the anti-demolition network, but more than twice as many interactions in the anti-demolition network as in the Navalny network. In other words, fewer people were interacting more in the heat of the anti-demolition movement—driven as it was by fast-moving events and the "now-or-never" prospect of losing your home—than in the relatively slower burn of the Navalny network. But even communication in the Navalny network itself was four times as intensive as the entire opposition network (including the anti-war network) had been in 2012–15.

Given privacy concerns and the often anonymous nature of social media, it is difficult to know much about the individuals in these networks, but, because we tracked the opposition over time, we do know a bit about their history with the movement. Roughly 20 percent of the individuals who showed up in the 2017 data had been present in the 2012–15 data, with the highest proportions coming from the Bolotnaya-specific groups and the anti-war movement. Oddly enough, however, it was the anti-demolition movement—which had conspired to keep Navalny off the stage and position itself as apolitical—that drew most heavily from earlier phases of opposition mobilization.[39] By contrast, Navalny's network did a (very) slightly better job of drawing in new entrants.[40] There was, as well, considerable overlap between the two movements in 2017.[41]

In addition to the Facebook data we collected—which mostly showed us organizational activity but didn't focus specifically on protests—we tracked the spring–summer 2017 protests and their run-ups on Twitter (which is generally more responsive to specific protests and rallies than Facebook), gathering some 110,000 tweets from

March through June 2017. As with the movements as a whole, there was considerable overlap of participants from one set of rallies to another.[42] Thus, Navalny's rallies—and even Khodorkovsky's—contributed large numbers of sympathizers to the season's mobilization as a whole. The same was not true, however, of the anti-demolition movement, which—as far as our data show—contributed only 3 percent of the participants of the June Russia Day rallies.

One reason for that discrepancy is suggested by investigating the structure of the protest networks themselves. Sociologists have since the 1970s understood what Mark Granovetter called "the strength of weak ties." As Granovetter showed, while strong ties within a community can support cohesion and solidarity, the tendency to interact primarily with people whom you know well and who know your other interlocutors well often leads people to interact less with people from outside their immediate community. Thus, communities with relatively weaker ties—in which not everyone knows everyone else, but in which more people are likely to interact with a broader range of interlocutors—tend to be better at mobilization, because they find it easier to reach out to potential supporters and spread their message far and wide.

An analysis of the Navalny and anti-demolition networks suggests that Navalny's movement has considerably weaker ties, and thus, from a mobilizational point of view, is considerably stronger than the anti-demolition movement. By one measure, the anti-demolition network on Facebook was three times as dense as the Navalny network.[43] In other words, much more of the communication in the anti-demolition network was going on between people who already communicated with each other a great deal, while Navalny's activists were reaching out more broadly, and thus drawing in a greater diversity of supporters. By another measure, the anti-demolition network on Twitter—which is arguably the better social medium for disseminating the mobilizational messages in the heat of protest—was almost four times as dense as Navalny's network.[44] Again, this means that the online networks around Navalny were considerably better at spreading messages to new audiences, while the anti-demolition messages were more likely to reverberate among those already recruited to the cause. Several other measures support the same conclusion.[45] Thus, by virtually any measure known to the (admittedly imperfect) science of network analysis, the anti-demolition movement—which strived to be apolitical and thus keep the door open to those who might not share Navalny's worldview—was actually less structurally open and diverse than the communities that came out for the "Dimon" and Russia Day rallies, or even Khodorkovsky's #Nadoel protests.

But when it comes to content—what the networks were saying, rather than whom they were saying it to—the networks had striking similarities. A systematic analysis of the vocabulary used across the Facebook and Twitter networks we collected shows that—while the two social networking sites tend to favor different kinds of language (Twitter, obviously, demanding shorter words and sentences)—within each site the different communities used remarkably similar language.[46]

The conclusion, then, is that in terms of participants and content, issue-oriented protest groups like the anti-demolition protesters or the truckers are very closely linked to Navalny's larger—and heavily politicized—opposition movement. Structurally, however, the issue-oriented groups are more insular, suffering (to turn Granovetter on his head) from the weakness of strong ties. If some protest leaders were fretting that Navalny's political ambitions might have been detrimental to their cause, then, they need not have worried—at least so far as the public response was concerned. If anything, in the spring and summer of 2017 Navalny's political appeal appears to have been a powerful unifying factor—something clearly of concern to the Kremlin.

HATE/LOVE

The state, of course, fought back. A court in Kirov made minor procedural adjustments to the prosecution that had been rejected by Strasbourg and reinstated the verdict, again handing Navalny a suspended sentence and thus raising formal questions about whether he could run for office. As Navalny continued to tour the country, opening hubs and giving speeches, he and his allies were increasingly harassed by pro-Kremlin activists, who frequently resorted to violence. In one particular attack on April 27, chemicals poured onto Navalny's face—which had happened repeatedly in the past—caused such damage to his right eye that he had to fly to Spain for surgery.[47]

Throughout the spring and summer of 2017, the tactics of the Kremlin and its supporters played perfectly into Navalny's own plans. Rather than take direct aim at Putin, Navalny's favored approach had been to lay bare the malfeasance of just about everyone around him—and thus to push the Kremlin into the untenable position of defending the indefensible. In fact, the heavy-handed policing on March 26—when Navalny called people into the streets not to support his candidacy, but to demand answers from Medvedev about corruption—seemed to be exactly what Navalny was hoping for. After all, beating people in the streets to prevent the opposition from coming to power was one thing; beating people to protect the ill-gotten gains of your cronies was another thing entirely.

Another assist for Navalny's efforts came from an equally unlikely quarter: Russia's school principals. Under pressure from regional and local administrations, school principals—mostly outside Moscow—felt obliged to find and deter potential activists among their pupils. In one case, after the FSB had come into a school to detain a young man involved in organizing the local March 26 protest in Bryansk, in far western Russia near the border with Belarus and Ukraine, the principal was forced to call a meeting in a (vain) attempt to soothe the nerves of the activist's classmates. The meeting, of course, was captured on someone's smartphone and immediately uploaded to social media, where tens of thousands of teenagers heard their elders tell them they were too young to have political opinions.[48] Similar videos emerged from schools around the country. Needless to say, teens turned out to the March protests—and those that followed—in record numbers.

But just as Navalny had ramped up his challenge, so too had the Kremlin's supporters become more "robust" in their approach. It wasn't until nearly a year after the first major Peace March that the Kremlin's supporters decided to rally their own troops on the streets of Moscow. The so-called

Anti-Maidan rally brought some 35,000–50,000 people out into the streets of the capital, led by a diverse bunch of speakers, including Senator Dmitry Sablin, biker Alexander "Surgeon" Zaldostanov, conspiracy-theorist and author Nikolai Starikov, and others.[49] According to the blogger Ilya Varlamov—the same who had documented the appearance of the so-called "little green men" in Crimea—the rally was well attended, with representatives from across the spectrum and the country: student groups, "patriotic clubs," the Republic of Chechnya, Zhirinovsky's Liberal Democratic Party, workers from the Uralvagonzavod machine building company who came to prominence for their calls to use force against the Bolotnaya protesters, and even the Red Cross volunteer corps. Participants carried portraits of Putin and Akhmat Kadyrov—the assassinated former Chechen leader and father of current Chechen President Ramzan Kadyrov—and declaimed that Putin and Kadyrov (the younger) would never allow a "Maidan" in Russia.[50]

There were some reports that the Kremlin's internal politics division was mobilizing so-called "administrative resources" to boost turnout to the Anti-Maidan and other pro-government rallies. While it seems likely that this is the case at least to some extent, the amount of genuine vs "astro-turf" mobilization is difficult, if not impossible, to assess. But unlike in 2012, when the pro-Kremlin "Putingi" had very little ripple effect, the Anti-Maidan fit into a growing eco-system of ideologically driven mobilization that, while broadly in line with the Kremlin's objectives, was more concertedly anti-opposition than it was pro-regime. A case in point is the Russian Orthodox activist Dmitry Tsorionov, better known by his *nom de guerre*

Enteo, who created and led a group he called "God's Will," known primarily for its theatrical attacks on art and culture deemed to be degenerate or blasphemous. The pinnacle of Enteo's campaign came on August 14, 2015, when he and his comrades raided an exhibition of the work of the sculptor Vadim Sidur and others, held in the Moscow Manege gallery, immediately opposite the Kremlin.[51] By 2017, the Anti-Maidan movement and sister organizations the National Liberation Movement (NOD) and the so-called South East Radical Bloc (SERB), had emerged as bugbears for Navalny and his campaign, harassing and often assaulting him as he toured the country to drum up support, claiming all the while that his agenda was to push the boundaries of Ukraine's erstwhile Orange Revolution into Russia itself.[52]

To be sure, much of what they do is violent, destroying property and causing physical bodily harm. But with all of it, including the famous green dye attacks on Navalny himself, there is an element of theatricality, and perhaps not by accident: Anti-Maidan leader Sergei Kurginian is a theater director, and SERB leader Igor Beketov (who has taken the stage name Gosha Tarasevich) is a former actor.

The theatricality seems to borrow heavily from the performance art of another group—Pussy Riot and its progenitor, the Art Group Voina of Petr Verzilov and Petr Pavlensky (who notably nailed his scrotum to Red Square, sewed his lips shut and set fire to the door of the FSB headquarters in Moscow, albeit not all at the same time). Indeed, Tsorionov-Enteo was kicked out of God's Will— the group he created—when he fell into a romance with Pussy Riot member Maria Alekhina.[53]

TEAM NAVALNY

Leonid Volkov—the 37-year-old former computer programmer from Ekaterinburg who manages Navalny's national campaign—sat at the end of a long table in southern Moscow, his back to the window, juggling a laptop, two smartphones and a tube from which he squeezed a yellowish substance onto a cracker.

"Hematogen," he said, barely cracking a smile. "The secret of Team Navalny."

Volkov's performance-enhancing drug of choice is more often given to children than to adults, a sticky sweet paste often mixed with chocolate that is meant to raise blood oxygen levels. (The only thing it's scientifically proven to do, alas, is cause diarrhea.) Whether or not it's the hematogen at play, though, Volkov's energy level is impressive.

We met Volkov on June 6, 2017—six days before the planned Russia Day rallies—in what he carefully described as "the federal headquarters of the campaign for Alexei Navalny to be allowed to run in 2018." The room occupied a corner of a large, modern office building near the Avtozavodskaya metro station. Sparsely furnished with long white plastic tables, plastic folding chairs and white boards, the room held maybe eighteen people that afternoon, but it could clearly accommodate many times that. Three doors down the hallway was the much livelier office for Navalny's anti-corruption group, FBK; in another corner was the studio from which the NavalnyLive Youtube channel was broadcast.

Throughout our conversation, Volkov would disappear into other discussions—on his computer and on one of his smartphones—and return after a pause, only to duck out again a few minutes later, all while never shifting more than a couple of inches in his chair. Just as we were getting started, he fired off instructions to a Whatsapp group of campaign coordinators. A few minutes later, his phone began buzzing with messages.

"They don't believe it's me," he said. After a few seconds of consternation, he shot back to the group: "Fuck off." That did the trick.

"This," he said, lifting his head and waving an arm across the room, "is simply one of two independent political agenda-setting centers in Russia. I mean, look at the political system in any developed country, and parliamentary parties, non-parliamentary parties, regions, governors, labor unions, civic organizations and so on—they all set their own agenda. In Russia, that has all been eviscerated. Are governors independent political actors? No. Are political parties independent political actors? No. Labor unions? You're joking. Non-profit organizations? You're joking. One way or another, in Russia now and for a fairly long time there have been only two significant centers of political agenda-setting. One of those is the Kremlin. It doesn't matter what you call it: the Presidential Administration, United Russia, the government, it's all the same. And the other one is here."

By that point in the summer, the campaign already had forty-four offices around the country, laying the groundwork for the petition drive that would begin in January 2018; in all, the campaign aimed to open seventy-seven such offices. In each case, the organization sought out local activists who could manage things in each city and region, in close coordination with HQ in Moscow.

"The federal HQ—or even regional HQs—should be seen first and foremost as a service center," Volkov explained. "Our goal in the end is to make it so that any volunteer—whether he's got fifteen minutes a day or one week out of the month and he wants to do one thing or another, he wants to hand out flyers or agitate online—he can come into the office and find a way to take part in the campaign. Every volunteer should be able to find a place in this campaign. And so, when it comes to decisions, a lot of decisions are made by the volunteers themselves, and a lot are made by the regional offices themselves. But the political decisions, the really meaningful decisions one way or another are made by Alexei."

One of those decisions—or, really, several—concerned the planned June 12 Russia Day rally. As in March, activists in more than 100 cities around the country planned protests, many of which were sanctioned by the local authorities.[54] Unlike in March, however, the Moscow authorities decided this time to play along—kind of. Moscow city hall approved a march along Prospekt Sakharova, but put pressure on vendors of stage and audio equipment, effectively making it impossible for Navalny or other speakers to communicate with the crowd. As late as June 11, Navalny was playing coy—demanding that the pressure be lifted and so that audio equipment could be procured and threatening to shift the protest "to another format" if his demands weren't met.[55] They weren't.

Early on the morning of June 12, Navalny sent word through social media that instead of converging on Prospekt Sakharova, protesters should converge on Moscow's main drag, Tverskaya Street, leading from the Kremlin to Pushkin

Square. Tverskaya, however, was already occupied by official Russia Day celebrations, which included arts and crafts booths, historical reenactments, and so on. It was thus in the midst of this general merriment that the protesters unfurled their banners, causing police to charge into the holiday crowds, corralling protesters and bystanders alike into detention vans. Navalny himself was arrested as soon as he left his apartment building, and both he and Volkov were charged with calling for unlawful public protest.

When we met Volkov on June 6, though, none of that history had yet been written. If he had an inkling of what was to come, he didn't let on.

"I don't know how to predict turnout for protests," Volkov said. "No one knows how. . . . My expectations were wrong before March 26, I didn't know there would be [so many]."

Volkov stopped and surveyed the room before continuing. Campaign workers huddled over screens large and small; conversations were barely audible.

"It's quiet now," he said, looking into the middle distance. "I think there's going to be a whole lot of people on June 12. I'm afraid to be wrong. We'll see. But however many there are, they're all ours."

SEVEN

RUSSIA'S PUTIN

After leaving Dozhd and publishing a best-selling book, *All the Kremlin's Men*, Mikhail Zygar was bored. We spoke with him the day after one of Vladimir Putin's marathon "Direct Lines" with the nation, when the president speaks—usually for three to four hours—on live television, taking carefully curated questions from generally fawning elites and ordinary citizens alike.

"All of the Russian media spent the day covering Putin's direct line," he said, smiling broadly. "I felt like the happiest man alive, because I didn't have to watch that bullshit. It bears no relation whatsoever to reality. Not one word that was said yesterday shed one bit of light on anything at all."

It was a symptom of a larger problem: after the excitement of 2011–12, when ordinary Russians rose up and forced the Kremlin to react—in effect, dictating the political agenda from the streets, if not necessarily in the way many protesters would have hoped—the Russian mainstream media had gone from talking about everything to talking about nothing.

"At some point around 2015, everything just stopped," he recalled. "After Crimea, after Ukraine, Russia just totally froze."

If arguing about the present wasn't working anymore, Zygar thought, maybe debating history would do the trick. Throughout 2017—to mark the centenary of the Bolshevik revolution—he and a team of programmers and writers produced a blow-by-blow social media feed of the run-up to and aftermath of the February and October Revolutions, replete with Tweets and Facebook posts from poets, revolutionaries and royals alike. It was a smash hit, engaging more than 100,000 readers by the beginning of the year.[1] In 2018, he and the team turned their attention to doing the same for the fiftieth anniversary of 1968, including the uprisings in France, Mexico, Czechoslovakia, the United States and elsewhere, which so radically changed the face of post-war politics.

His focus on yesteryear, though, doesn't mean Zygar has given up on tomorrow.

"That the majority of Russian society doesn't believe in politics, that's one fact," he told us. "But on the other hand, in my view, society is becoming more responsible, somehow. It is beginning to believe in its own strength more than before. There are a tremendous number of charitable organizations, volunteer groups. The way people are solving important social problems, for example the problem of orphanages, which the state is never going to solve, is pretty powerful. More than ever before. And that's exclusively down to the efforts of society."

It can be difficult to be optimistic about Russia. In part, this is because putting a good spin on all the bad news— the repression and human-rights abuses, the economic malaise, the geopolitical isolation—is the stuff of propaganda, not of analysis. And the forces arrayed against the people in whom Zygar has placed his own hopes are so tremendous that one despairs at their prospects.

Indeed, in all of the interviews we conducted for this book—and, in fact, in most of our daily interactions with our friends and colleagues in Russia—it is hard to find much optimism. Desperation is more the order of the day. Take, for example, Galina, a 30-year-old market researcher in Yaroslavl. It's her parents who are mostly on her mind. Her father is retired and collects a modest state pension. Her mother still works—albeit as a junior nurse by rank—in a local hospital. She's had a raise, but her weekly paycheck is still only in the range of 1200 rubles (around $20). Galina herself has been lucky enough to get a raise in the past year, which allows her to help her parents make their meager ends meet.

"It's just crazy," she said. "Given the resources in the country, we could live better."

Or take Marina, the 54-year-old office worker from St. Petersburg, whom we first met in Chapter 5.

"Prices have gone up for everything," she complained. "I mean, what I paid for my apartment [utilities] five years ago was a fraction of what I'm paying now. And naturally my salary hasn't grown by anything like that much. And it's not just me—everyone I know is in more or less the same situation."

Marina paused.

"I really hope things don't get worse," she continued, with a resigned laugh. "Honestly, I don't want them to. But I don't think they'll get better. At least, I find it hard to believe that they would."

And yet almost all of the people we interviewed in early 2018—including both Galina and Marina—told us they would vote for Putin that March. Looking ahead to those elections, Marina had told us that she would vote for Putin in large measure because she saw no other option—at least, she said, "not yet." Galina told us she was swayed by her boyfriend, whom she described as an entrepreneur and an assistant to a regional parliamentarian.

"He's always watching the news," she said. "Well, he's a patriot. Very strict about it. Not me."

That, in many ways, is the central conundrum of this book. Galina, Marina and tens of millions of other Russian citizens know that the system is broken. That it is rigged. That it delivers them neither prosperity nor security. And yet, like the greengrocers in Václav Havel's Communist-era Czechoslovakia, they toe the party line. Why?

FIGHTING FOR AUTOCRACY

The wrong answer to this question is the conventional one. Most journalists and many academics approach Russian politics by asking how a powerful and often brutal state apparatus controlled by a relatively small group of KGB officers and billionaires has succeeded in imposing and maintaining power over a hapless and oppressed Russian citizenry. Emblematic of this thinking is a commonly referenced joke Putin made in a speech to his Federal Security Service (FSB) colleagues just before becoming president. "A group of FSB operatives, dispatched under cover to work in the government of the Russian Federation, is successfully fulfilling its task," Putin deadpanned. As is so often the case with Putin, it was hard to tell where the joke ended and the reality began. But for many commentators, journalists and scholars these remarks captured the essential reality of politics in the country: the Putin regime represents the revanche of the KGB, once again dominating and policing a subdued population.[2]

To think this way is to misunderstand how power is produced in Russia and how it is exercised. It is critical, as we have argued in this book, to understand that power is not only imposed from above, but is shaped by the demands of Russian citizens and by a competition between the state and its challengers for the support and allegiance of those citizens. The Kremlin works to mold what Russians want through many means, particularly through its monopoly on television. But Russians in turn affect what the Kremlin does. In fact, for many Russians, Putin is a useful part of the political landscape, someone who reflects their values and rules through the kind of policies that they would like to see. Moreover, to a very significant extent, Putin's authority within the elite is a function of his popularity in the country. Putin needs support from the Russian people, and he works intensively to identify how to win and retain that support. In other words, while it is true that Russia is shaped by Putin, it is no less true that Putin is shaped by Russia.

Let's take one of the central claims of the Putin administration, and one that you hear frequently from people in Russia: President Putin "raised Russia from its knees." He forced the world to reckon with Moscow once more. He stuck it to the West. We could debate whether this claim is in fact true. What is not in doubt, however, is that it is a politically powerful claim, earnestly believed by many millions of Russians. And in prioritizing an aggressive foreign policy, Putin is responding to—and seeking the support of—a large constituency within Russia itself. According to surveys conducted by the American sociologist Theodore Gerber, opposition to foreigners "sticking their noses" into Russian domestic politics is very strong.[3] This is probably true in all sorts of countries around the world—it is certainly true in both the United States and the United Kingdom, as allegations of Russian support for Trump and Brexit will witness—but in Russia a personal sense of attachment to the state and to the nation seem especially important.

In our own surveys, even before the annexation of Crimea some 43 percent of our respondents reported that being ethnically Russian was very important to their own personal sense of who they are, and 49 percent felt that way about Russian culture. A similar 38 percent reported that belonging to the Russian state was very important, while slightly lower numbers said the same about Russian Orthodox Christianity (25 percent). While we do not have comparable identity data from other countries, these figures indicate between a quarter and a half of Russians look directly to the state and nation when forming their own sense of personal identity.

What is striking, though, is how little these proportions changed in our sample after the annexation of Crimea. As we argued in Chapter 4, this suggests that the key point about the Crimean annexation and war in eastern Ukraine was not that they led to a huge upswing in Russian nationalism, but that these actions played into themes that were already strong in Russian society before the annexation. This was not Putin controlling Russia and moving it reluctantly in an unwanted direction. However deplorable it may appear to foreigners, the annexation was highly popular.

Moreover, as we showed in Chapter 3, there were many nationalist groups within Russia that had previously been skeptical of what they saw as a Western-oriented President Putin. For these activists, the fate of eastern Ukraine and the Russian speakers there had been neglected by successive Russian presidents. With the annexation of Crimea and pursuit of the war in Ukraine, Putin was finally getting on board with what the activists wanted, and they were ready to lend the force of their arms both on the propaganda front, and on the actual front lines.

Indeed, many Russians still think Putin is not doing enough to assert Russia's views. When we spoke to Marina—even as she complained about the economy and fretted over the lack of political alternatives—her mind was on foreign policy. It was just a matter of weeks before Russia's team was due to head off to Pyongchang for the 2018 Winter Olympics, and Marina was concerned. International sporting authorities pursuing anti-doping allegations were threatening to bar large numbers of Russian athletes from competing, while requiring those who were allowed to go to South Korea to fly a neutral flag.

"We've lost our position, our authority," she said. "Every year they just keep pushing us down, down, humiliating us. It's offensive. From the point of view of an ordinary citizen, well, I just think we have the wrong foreign policy. I mean, in some areas we need to be more firm. Look at the Soviet Union, for example, which I remember, I'm of that age. Because they may have called us the Evil Empire or whatever, but when it came to our athletes, they were always protected and nobody would dare to say a word against them. It was simply unthinkable, even though, I'm sure, they were taking those drugs back then, too. So something's wrong with our foreign policy."

This is not to say that Russians were of one mind on the conflict in Ukraine, or that they are of one mind when it comes to the future direction of Russian policy. There clearly are different views on what represents the right path for Russia. While some favor a European path, others maintain that Russia should follow its own road. This is, of course, a longstanding difference of opinion among Russian political thinkers, dating back as far as the early days of the Muscovite principality. The differences of opinion on this question are even physically manifested in the buildings of the Kremlin itself, with Western-influenced, Italianate architecture sitting right alongside buildings constructed in the eastern Orthodox style. The very crenellations of the Kremlin walls are copied from the citadel of Milan.

A distinct path, of course, does not necessarily mean an anti-democratic path. Nor does the belief in a particular form of exceptionalism tell us much about the particulars of the path; after all, American, British and French politicians have all touted various forms of exceptionalism over the years. While many fear the consequences of such attitudes in those countries, the belief that a country has its own path and destiny is probably not incompatible with democracy. Nevertheless, the credit he gets for putting Russia back on its feet and standing up to the West is a key part of what makes Putin so popular and, consequently, so powerful.

The relationship between many Russians and Putin also seems to have changed qualitatively since the annexation of Crimea and the war in Ukraine. The crisis generated a sense of emotional engagement between many Russians and the regime that had been missing before. This emotional surge at the time of the annexation had profound effects on how Russians perceive politics and the world around them, creating a sense of well-being that extended to areas that were completely divorced from the actual politics of the moment. The crisis also elevated Putin's status to that of a charismatic national leader, who has been held above politics by millions of Russians.

Domestically, too, Putin's policies have also tapped into important forces within Russian society. A key building block in Putin's coalition are people with a conservative and/or authoritarian orientation. Although he may have begun his presidency as an economic liberal, Putin has constructed his current political powerbase as a conservative leader, promising to protect Russia from decadent Western values, as we documented in Chapter 2. People supported his anti-LGBT legislation and his laws against criticizing the Orthodox Church in part as a bulwark against expanding European influence—a threat powerfully projected by the Kremlin itself.

AUTHORITARIANISM FROM BELOW

Our argument, however, is not simply that the behavior of the Russian state is shaped by the preferences of important sections of Russian society. This is true, but our argument is larger. Our point is that much of the power of President Putin comes from Russian society—that power in Russia is co-constructed.

Co-construction happens in a number of different ways. At its most basic, some of Putin's power lies in the willingness of members of the state apparatus and ordinary citizens alike to follow instructions and anticipate his desires. This means other members of the elite, whether in politics, the security forces or big business circles, currying favor and seeking approval. More broadly, though, it means pensioners and low-level civil servants willing to attend "Putingi", or youth activists harassing foreign government officials, "guardians" trying to shape the public narrative online or activists volunteering to join up and fight in Ukraine, bikers riding to Crimea or assassins eliminating political opponents.

In the co-construction of authoritarianism, the whole is considerably greater than the sum of its parts. All of these individual actions give rise to a social consensus around the inevitability and righteousness of Putin's rule. As our interviews show, while there are plenty of convinced and intense supporters of the Russian president, there is no shortage of people with discontents and grumbles. And yet, these people vote for Putin, too. The social consensus makes it hard to think about alternatives. It also makes it costly to be critical. Supporting a presidential candidate other than Putin means more than bucking the Kremlin and the television. It means going against the supposed majority, contradicting friends, family, neighbors and colleagues. This is a step few are willing to take, and so the consensus goes unchallenged.

Most of the time, this consensus is broad but thin. As we showed in our pre-Crimea surveys, very few people considered the opposition to be a real alternative to the ruling regime, but that did not mean there was too much genuine love for the ruling United Russia party or even for Putin himself. In fact, many supporters were very passive in their orientation toward the president and his government. The events of history, however, can have unexpected consequences. The annexation of Crimea and the war in eastern Ukraine turned passive acquiescence into pride, hope and trust. Many Russians' views of the present, of the future, and even of the past, were transformed—not forever, of course, but on a mass scale and for months, if not years. The consensus spread to include even those who had been skeptical, and so the voices of opposition grew even more isolated.

All of this was based on shared lies and shared delusions—from the supposed righteousness of the annexation of Crimea, to the notion that Russia is under threat from domestic and foreign enemies. Social consensus, of course, is not some naturally occurring phenomenon, but is actively constructed in a variety of ways. The most obvious tool for building consensus is the media, and, in particular, television. As noted in previous chapters, the world as seen on Russian television looks quite different from the world most Westerners see on their screens. Consolidation of the media sphere in general and television in particular is in some ways the most significant "achievement" of the Putin years. In the 1999 parliamentary elections, Russian television channels presented sharply contrasting views of the world, as their competing owners battled to influence the succession to Boris Yeltsin. Once the Putin side had won, the next two decades saw the gradual elimination of distinctive points of view, and their replacement with a single Kremlin-approved message.[4] By 2018, only two of twenty-two television channels were not closely under the control of the Kremlin's information policy.[5] As a result, Russians who choose to get their news primarily from state television—and that's still around 70 percent of the population—are subjected to an almost constant campaign of patriotic and pro-Putin messages. Russia is presented as a besieged fortress, with Vladimir Putin as its savior on the ramparts.

In the aftermath of the conflict in Ukraine, the Soviet-born American satirical novelist Gary Shteyngart imprisoned himself in the Four Seasons Hotel in New York with nothing but four screens showing non-stop Russian television and a well-stocked minibar. For the author of books including *Absurdistan*, the idea was to experience first-hand the joys of brainwashing—and then write about it for *The New York Times*. What he got was a relentless barrage of propaganda, punctuated by aging singers crooning classic hits.[6]

"I came out of this experience feeling there was another reality," Shteyngart told us later. "I knew the reality was false, but it was so omnipresent that it was impossible to deny its existence and its power over many believers. It was almost like being exposed to another religion."[7]

Shteyngart's resistance was sorely tested, but for the tens of millions of Russians living outside of the comforts of the Four Seasons, this kind of propaganda was a key part of the creation of the emotional environment around the annexation of Crimea. As we discussed in Chapter 4, it is also a crucial element in normalizing support for Putin within the population and introducing them to the appropriate attitudes that upstanding citizens are expected to hold.

Fortunately, most people are condemned neither to watch state-controlled television, nor to believe it. Instead, people select media according to their tastes and political preferences, and they are guided by their social circles. We tend to watch things that we enjoy, that chime with our worldviews, and that keep us on the same wavelength with our friends. As a result, those who watch more state television are not only more likely to be fans of musical variety shows, they are also more likely to be supporters of the regime. Those who avoid state television and who use alternative online media are more likely to be regime opponents and to spend their time with other regime opponents (and perhaps have better taste in music, but that's another book). This means that the effect of "brainwashing" is not to convert the skeptical, but to further convince and radicalize the faithful, building their sense of identity and community and marginalizing and delegitimizing everyone else.[8] (Shteyngart, for what it's worth, was not converted.)

Furthermore, in Russia (as elsewhere) there is good evidence that people engage in what social scientists call "motivated reasoning" with regard to politics.[9] In other words, people are more likely to believe things that fit in with their preexisting worldview, and less likely to believe things that challenge that worldview. This partially limits the "brainwashing" effect, but it makes polarization worse. In the United States, where there is considerable choice in media sources and where "fake news" comes in many different flavors, the combined effects of media selection and motivated reasoning contribute to increasing division. People with different prior preferences start to experience different worlds and experience different realities. The US case is bad, of course: the dangers of sorting society into ideologically homogenous echo chambers are clear. But what happens when news and information are largely monopolized, as they are in Russia?

If the majority of citizens are willing to consume state-sponsored news—and if they are open to the messages that they receive—then the propaganda can create a consensus that is largely detached from reality, even without the existence of extensive censorship. And in Russia, this is clearly the case. Although a broad range of sources of information is potentially available to most Russians online, the reality is that the lion's share of people willingly consume state television news and are open to the messages it pushes. As a result, they are effectively cut off from reality as the rest of us understand it and left with a geopolitics largely created by the Kremlin.

To make matters worse, propaganda can work even on those in the fuzzy middle, who support neither the regime nor the opposition, mostly because they are not that interested in politics. In authoritarian regimes, only those with the clearest and most convinced anti-regime principles tend to be able to resist constant pro-regime messages over time.[10] In Russia specifically, there is experimental evidence that shows state-sponsored documentaries smearing the opposition can have an effect even on citizens who are opposed to the Putin administration.[11] The social science corroborates the stories we hear from opposition-oriented Russians, who report their formerly "normal" but mostly apolitical acquaintances being transformed into regime supporters following the annexation of Crimea.

This is dangerous. The impulse toward the collective creation of a fantasy world—more or less completely disconnected from reality—is precisely what Hannah Arendt warned us about in *The Origins of Totalitarianism*. People who are willing to believe what they are told, provided that it chimes vaguely with their own suspicions, and who are surrounded by people with similar tendencies can end up very far from reality indeed. For example, in a poll by the highly respected Levada Center in early March 2014—just after the revolution in Ukraine—more than 70 percent of Russians believed that ethnic Russians and other Russian speakers in Ukraine were under threat from the new government in Kyiv, even though there was little real reason to believe such a claim.

But the construction of consensus and unreality in Russia is not limited to television. In an interview in April 2018, Lev Gudkov, a leading Russian sociologist and director of the Levada Center, underlined the importance of the broader society in the manufacturing of consensus. Consensus, he noted, is created across a range of institutions—in the army, in churches and, increasingly, in schools. This is done precisely by presenting the Kremlin's view as society's consensus, weaving it into the fabric and ritual of daily life, in realms supposedly far removed from politics. In recent years, schools have been increasingly incorporating patriotic "moral" education alongside mandatory religious education, spreading the influence of the Kremlin-approved consensus well beyond the television screen itself.[12] Our own research provides solid data to back up Gudkov's intuitions. Television is critical in normalizing the regime and its policies, but so are other institutions in Russian society, including the Church.[13] The result, as we noted in Chapter 4, is what Hannah Arendt warned us about—the creation of "a lying world of consistency which is more adequate to the needs of the human mind than reality itself."[14]

Convincing large numbers of people to believe things that are without foundation in reality, is, of course, far from just a Russian problem. Despite a much broader range of available media, despite much stronger political institutions and despite decades of democratic experience, the power of so-called "fake news" has been on display across the world in the last decade. Some of the factors that make Russia vulnerable to the "lying world" are the same as those that make the West vulnerable. Economic dislocations resulting from the global financial crisis of 2008–09 and the inability of establishment political parties to formulate a coherent response have reshaped politics in many countries, detaching the debate from clearly articulated interests and policies. In the absence of a coherent policy response, fringe politicians appeal to values, to exclusionary notions of community, and to patriotism. The ability of such appeals to sway millions in the United States, the UK, France, Italy, Germany and elsewhere is clear. Nevertheless, in the absence of a diverse media environment and without competitive electoral politics and independent institutions, Russia's case of fake news fever has been far worse.

THE PEOPLE v. PUTIN

Of course, not all people are caught up in this process of consensus-building. As we have seen in repeated anti-corruption protests in Moscow and around the country, there is a slice of society, and of young people in particular, who reject the consensus around them. Often these people inhabit a largely different world from the mainstream, adopting ideas passed on by critical parents and peers.[15] For most of these citizens, news comes not from the national television channels at all, but from opposition-minded online news sources like Meduza and Republic, and from their friends on Facebook.[16]

In fact, there is a vigorous online public sphere in Russia, where everything from corruption at the highest level, to fraud in the presidential elections of 2018, to casualties among Russian contractors in Syria are discussed, analyzed and debated. At the time of writing, a video created by opposition leader Alexei Navalny's Anti-Corruption Foundation that presents evidence of vast corruption on the part of Prime Minister Dmitry Medvedev has had almost 28 million views. Certainly, many of these will be repeat views and many others are likely to be from people not living in Russia. But even so, millions of Russians are likely to have watched this extraordinary video.[17] Clearly, there are places in Russia in which discussion can take place and issues can be shaped. Nevertheless, the cumulative effects of control of the media and the artificially enforced and constructed consensus in the broader society means that room for maneuver is very narrow and constricted.[18] Equally crucially, the debate in this online public sphere and the official conversations often feel like two different worlds, each aware of the other only so as to despise it.

One of these spaces for free debate and discussion remains Dozhd, the online television station formerly run by Mikhail Zygar. Despite the corner into which his former station has been pushed, Zygar remains convinced that these divisions can be overcome. Hardcore believers on either side are difficult to shift, but the "soft middle" of Russian society, which is currently influenced by the pro-government media, could have their eyes opened by what Zygar calls "quality media"—by which he means media like Dozhd. He has in mind people like Galina, the market researcher from Yaroslavl, whom we met earlier. Neither of the Kremlin's two wedge issues—the law on religious sensibilities, and the LGBT "propaganda" law—registered on Galina's radar screen. When we asked about them in early 2018, she had heard about them only, as the Russians say, "by the edge of her ear." In both cases, though, she was opposed, despite the opinions of her patriotic boyfriend.

"Usually, I'm for strict laws," she said. "But in this case, probably not. Faith is a personal thing. Everyone has a right to say what they believe. . . . And I hadn't really heard about [the LGBT law], but I think that's also a personal thing."

For Zygar, hope lies in reaching people like Galina.

"Quality media are for those people who haven't yet formed their point of view," Zygar explained. "The sense here is that people who have a fully formed set of values aren't going to be remade. There is, so to say, one minority in society with liberal values, which is the core audience of quality media. And there is another minority with imperial values, which is the core audience of state TV. And there's this amorphous and indifferent majority, which, in fact, can watch both or either, depending on what's trending. Because they're not really interested in politics and prefer to be left alone, they keep their distance. And then there's the younger audience, which still hasn't formed their value system yet. Those are the audiences that everyone's competing for."

For the time being, though, the Kremlin is winning.

IT'S NOT HISTORY OR SOCIETY . . .

There is a saying in Russian, which holds that each of us understands the world through the lens of our own depravity. Without wishing to accuse our critics—or, really, any of our readers—of depravity (or to claim that we are not guilty of our own), it is a sentiment shared at one point or another by every author. At the end of the day, the meaning of what we write is generated less on these pages, than in the minds and interpretations of those who read them. Generally, this is an excellent thing; indeed, it is the miracle of literature. But it also has its pitfalls, among which is the virtual certainty of being misunderstood. With that in mind, it is probably worth taking some time to clarify what we are not arguing.

The first thing we are not arguing is that Russia—having no history of democratic governance—is doomed to eternal autocracy. This idea is so commonly asserted that it often passes for conventional wisdom. And like most pieces of conventional wisdom, it is not entirely without foundation. Russia has indeed been an autocracy for most of its history as an organized state, and history does do a lot to shape the paths countries are likely to take in the future. For example, it is true, as some point out, that after Communism fell in eastern and central Europe, the countries that transitioned most quickly and successfully to democratic politics were those that had had some previous experience of democracy, typically between the two world wars. It is also true that countries like the United Kingdom or the United States, which gradually evolved into what we recognize today as democracies, did so in part by building upon institutions, like parliament and limited suffrage, that existed in pre-democratic times.

However, the view that Russia has always been, is now and will always be an autocracy is mistaken in very important ways. First, all democracies that exist in the world today have a history of non-democratic, monarchical, oligarchic or exclusive politics. Democracy is a product of the modern era. Every country that is now a democracy used to be something different.

Skeptics might reply, of course, that recent history suggests that the prospects for transition to democracy in Russia are not very bright. And again, there is something to this argument. The dominant narrative on Russian history stresses an absence of strong institutions independent of the imperial throne, ruling out a British or US-style path (though a different telling of that history could point to many examples of such institutions at some times and in some places in Russia). Russia is also a state that depends heavily on the export of oil, gas and other natural resources for its revenue, and states like these (what political scientists call "rentier states") tend to have stable political systems. They are democratic if they were already democratic when they struck oil—think Norway—and they are durable autocracies if they were already autocratic when the natural resources came—here think Saudi Arabia. One other way in which democracy can come is through foreign pressure. The influence of the European Union, for example, has been powerful in pushing a pro-democratic agenda in many of the former Communist Bloc countries. But there is not much reason for optimism here either. Russia is large and more than capable of providing for itself economically and militarily, so it is only weakly affected by Western connections or foreign inducements to take a more democratic path. (It is also worth noting that some of the post-socialist countries most directly influenced by the West—including Hungary and Poland—have undone much of their democratic transition in recent years.)

Yet, there are also many factors associated with democratization that Russia does possess and that make Russia a very promising candidate for transition. Most importantly, perhaps, Russia is a very highly educated and reasonably wealthy country, traits that generally augur well for democracy. In 2016, the World Bank calculated income per capita in Russia at $9,720, making Russia what the Bank calls an "upper middle income" country. This placed Russia at number fifty-two in the world rankings of states by per capita income. Of the fifty-one states above Russia in the rankings at that time, only five—the United Arab Emirates, Kuwait, Brunei, Saudi Arabia and Turkey—were not democracies.

Moreover, Russia's wealth and high levels of education reflect deeper structures in society that are usually thought to be supportive of democracy. Even though Russia has become highly unequal since the end of Communism, the incidence of poverty has fallen considerably. By 2016, the proportion of the population living in what the World Bank defines as poverty was 13.4 percent, down from a massive 29 percent in 2000. This means that Russia possesses a large middle class—even if that middle class is much more tied to state employment than in most democratic countries—and a large middle class is seen by many scholars as a key driver of democratization. Relatedly, Russian civil society, which played an important role in sweeping away the Soviet system, has also continued to grow over the post-Soviet period. While challenges to civil society in the country are well documented, the intelligence, wit, creativity and bravery of Russia's active citizens are clear to anyone who spends time in the country.

Consequently, the basic structure of Russia's society and economy makes democracy neither impossible nor overwhelmingly likely. Russia could go either way, becoming much more democratic or remaining heavily autocratic. In the medium term—the next ten years or so—deep social, economic or historical factors will neither drive Russia into the democratic camp, nor preclude the development of democracy. It is politics that will determine the outcome.

. . . AND IT'S NOT CULTURE . . .

The second argument we are not making is that Russians themselves are somehow predisposed—culturally, psychologically, genetically or otherwise—to rule by a strong hand. As we discussed in Chapter 5, earlier generations of researchers sometimes argued that Russians (or Soviets) were collectively and individually anti-democratic in orientation on an immutable, fundamental level. To be clear, this is and always has been a myth, and the arguments and evidence in this book do not support such a claim. This is not to say that all Russians are keen democrats. In fact, as in most countries, attitudes to democracy vary from person to person and people express different opinions at different times, depending on the circumstances. But there is no reason to believe that Russians are fundamentally different in this respect from Americans, Western Europeans or anyone else.

There have been dozens of studies of Russian attitudes toward democracy over the decades, by both Russian and foreign scholars, and, as is often the case in academic research, there are almost as many opinions as there are studies. The research paints a complex picture, with more support for some aspects of democracy than others, and substantial differences between individual citizens. In other words, the extent to which one supports different elements of democracy is a political question in Russia— just as it is pretty much everywhere.

To illustrate this, consider one of the most interesting studies of attitudes toward democracy in Russia. In 1990, two (then) Soviet researchers—Maxim Boycko and Vladimir Korobov—began a collaboration with the American economist Robert Shiller (he of "irrational exuberance," the Case–Shiller index of house prices, and the Nobel Prize), to trace the evolution of views among Muscovites and New Yorkers across a quarter of a century. The idea was to dig into people's attitudes toward democracy as they actually experience it. This meant avoiding abstract questions—do you support democracy?—and focusing instead on concrete questions about things like a free press, how tolerant people are of minority political views and of political protests, and how they view trade-offs between order and freedom.

Boycko, Korobov and Shiller's findings are stunning. Despite all the turmoil and changes that have taken place over the last twenty-five years in Russia, attitudes have changed relatively little: support for freedom of speech, fair courts and a free press was high in Moscow in 1990 and it remains high today. Only 6 percent of Muscovites disagreed with the statement that "It is necessary that everyone, regardless of their views, can express themselves freely." In 2016, this number was little changed—8 percent—and was similar to the number of New Yorkers who disagreed in that same year (4 percent). On courts, 18 percent of Muscovites in 1990 thought it acceptable to imprison someone for a serious crime without a trial. By 2016, this number had fallen slightly to 15 percent and was very close to the figure for New Yorkers—19 percent. Where there was movement in the Moscow numbers was on attitudes to a free press. In 1990, only 2 percent of people in the Moscow sample did not think that the press should be protected by law from government persecution. This figure had ballooned to 20 percent in 2016. Yet, it was still well below the 27 percent of New Yorkers who opposed legal protections for the press.

This is not to say that all opinions are the same, however. Big differences between Muscovites and New Yorkers emerge when questions are framed in terms of an explicit trade-off between order and freedom. In 2016, fully three-quarters of the Moscow sample thought that "it is better to live in a society with strict order than to allow people so much freedom that they can bring destruction to the society." That was more than double the proportion of New Yorkers agreeing with the same statement. Back in 1990, Muscovites viewed the trade-off much less negatively. Similarly, nearly 60 percent of Muscovites in 2016 thought that radical groups should not be allowed to protest, because such events lead to disorder and destruction, up from 37 percent in 1990 and double the proportion of New Yorkers. Clearly, while support for the basic institutions of democracy remains high, the fear of disorder in Russia is higher now than it was in 1990—a shift created not by some innate feature of Russian culture, but by the politics of the past thirty years.

Similar conclusions can be found in other studies. Henry Hale of George Washington University, a leading Western scholar of Russian politics, argued in an influential essay that, while Russians differ greatly from one another in their attitudes to democracy, there is broad support for elections and political competition in general. However, support for the "liberal" elements of democracy is substantially lower. What matters to most Russians, according to Hale, is being able to elect leaders. What those leaders then do in office is a secondary matter. This basic structure of support for what political scientists call "delegative democracy" is different from the democratic ideal most Western scholars have in mind, but this combination of attitudes is actually pretty common around the world.

Indeed, three decades of political science and sociological research have given us no reason to believe that Russians are inherently anti-democratic. Moreover, researchers have long known that citizens tend to judge the importance of democracy by their own experience, looking at how well democracy performs in providing economic opportunities and security. In that sense, the 1990s, when Russians had something called democracy but suffered economic hardship and substantial social breakdown, were a setback for the country's democrats. Nevertheless, as our own surveys and interviews suggest, despite that experience most Russians still value the freedoms and rights that democracy represents.

That said, we should avoid phrases like "Russians think X." The survey data make it abundantly clear that not all Russians think alike. There are different camps within Russia on major issues and, as we have shown in the different chapters of this book, real evidence of political competition and polarization. Consequently, trying to identify a distinctively "Russian" style of politics is a fool's errand. Different Russians think different things, and the best way to understand politics in that country is not to seek to tap into some deeply mystical "Russian soul," but to do what we have attempted here: to use the concepts and tools of social science that are applied successfully around the world.

. . . IT'S POLITICS

In March 2018, Vasily, the 41-year-old St. Petersburg factory worker we met in Chapter 5, planned happily—even eagerly—to vote to reelect Vladimir Putin to another six years in office. But even as he declared his loyalty to the Kremlin, he seemed upset at the lack of a real opposition.

"I don't see anybody," he said. "Nobody at all. Not in the least. Regardless of everything, even if there is criticism, it is measured. The guy will immediately be shown his place. Yes, we have freedom of speech, everything is allowed. But all the same, at the right moment, you'll get a hint: take it too far, and you'll go to jail."

And what of Alexei Navalny?

"I have nothing to add," Vasily said. "I think he criticizes exactly as much as he's allowed to."

Navalny, of course, would reject the idea that he's muffled by the Kremlin. But in the end, of course, he wasn't allowed to contest the presidential election of 2018. In the months that followed, Navalny, Leonid Volkov and the team—when they weren't serving short prison sentences for involvement in one protest or another—worked to maintain the energy of their new network of volunteers. The goal, they told us, was to turn it into a dual-purpose structure: to be ready and able to contest formal elections when the opportunity arose, and to support local protest movements around the country in the interim.

"Regimes like Putin's aren't rare," Volkov philosophized. "There have been a lot of them, and they're all more or less the same. But human history has chewed through all of them. It chewed through and outlasted Pinochet and Suharto and Franco and so on. None of them were able to pass power on to the next generation. For a regime to be able to pass on power, its people need to be eating grass, like in North Korea. . . . So Alexei loses the election. We're not going anywhere. We haven't stopped being right, and they haven't stopped being wrong."

As history rolls forward, Volkov and his comrades—unsurprisingly—find the pace of change agonizingly slow. Corruption, Volkov likes to say, devours 12–15 trillion rubles a year. That's about $200 billion, and so each extra year of Putinism comes at a high cost.

"They're stealing our children's future," Volkov says, echoing every reformist politician to run for office in every country around the world. "That's why we want to win as quickly as possible."

But when Volkov talks about the challenges the opposition faces, Putin isn't among them.

"Our biggest enemy is the lack of belief that something can be changed," Volkov said. "That is undoubtedly our biggest problem. People have this really deep-seated sense that nothing at all can be changed. That is truly our biggest problem. Abstinence. A kind of self-isolation from everything political. . . . But that's also an opportunity. If we can wake these people up and explain to them that things depend on them, the situation can change very quickly. . . . Yes, on the one hand there's this idea that 'nothing can be changed,' but on the other hand there's 'we can't live like this any longer.' . . . We have been all over the country, and we have seen the people. There are people out there living in truly hopeless circumstances, earning 20,000 rubles with no prospects, no chances or hope for anything to improve. Absolutely desperate people, and there are a lot of them. And in this situation, yes, on the one hand, nothing can be changed, that's been beaten into people for twenty years. But on the other hand, something has to change. At some point, the latter will outweigh the former."

To a great extent, our findings support Volkov's analysis. Support for President Putin is interdependent: some people support him because of his policies and the direction in which he is taking the country, but many more support him because it is the socially acceptable thing to do, because the media they access is extremely propagandistic, and because, as a result, they see no alternatives. This equilibrium is politically constructed. It is strong because there are few incentives for people to switch from it unless other people start to defect from support. Yet, in this strength lies the source of Putin's weakness. The construction of the regime depends upon a social consensus that will one day unravel. And when it does, Russia's own experience suggests it will happen quickly.

The Kremlin understands this, and it has reason to worry. In the summer of 2018, just as the rest of the world was congratulating Russia on a well-hosted World Cup, alarm bells were going off in Kremlin offices. Despite the resounding success of the global showpiece that Russia had hosted—even the usually dismal Russian football team had exceeded expectations—domestic politics had its own logic. Perhaps hoping to use the cover of the World Cup to divert attention from unpopular policies, the government announced an increase in the pension age for both men and women in June 2018. Russians were furious, and the response was almost immediate: tens of thousands protested in dozens of cities across the country. Polls suggested that only about 9 percent of Russians supported the proposed reforms.[19]

The initial protests were followed after the World Cup with large rallies across Russia at which hundreds were arrested. The streets, though, were the least of the Kremlin's worries. In local elections that same month, the ruling United Russia party actually lost a string of gubernatorial and mayoral elections and was forced to concede that its victory in one strategically important part of the Russian Far East was generated by fraud. Worst of all, the difficulties created by pension reform were not limited to the ruling party and its candidates. President Putin himself saw a large and sudden fall in his popularity. The Levada Center reported a fall of fifteen points in Putin's approval rating between April and July 2018, and these falls were visible too in other polling agencies. In fact, the Kremlin's own favored pollster, the Public Opinion Foundation, reported that the proportion of people telling them that they would vote for Putin if an election were held dropped thirteen points to only 49 percent that same July.

The response was quick. In an extremely unusual step, President Putin made a thirty-minute televised address, explaining to Russians that pension reform was not just an economic policy question, but a matter of national security. Without pension reform, he said, Russia risked collapse. At the same time, Putin announced concessions, moderating the impact of the reforms on women in particular. Although it was too little and too late to save United Russia's fortunes at the ballot box, Putin's efforts seemed at press time to have staunched his own bleeding. At the end of September 2018, the Levada Center reported a twenty-point fall in the proportion of citizens saying they were ready to protest against the reforms—though about a third of respondents still said they would.[20] More importantly, Putin's popularity seemed to have at least stabilized at around 67 percent, according to Levada. As we write, it is too early to say how the pension reform will end. In fact, part of our argument is that making such predictions is inherently fraught. We will understand how Putin's popularity unraveled when it actually does, but predicting when that will happen is more guesswork than science.

BETRAYAL

The liberal opposition represented by Navalny, however, is only one of the Kremlin's headaches. There are the nationalists to think of too. Alexander Dugin, the nationalist ideologue who helped push Russia into war in Ukraine, is unhappy. Very unhappy. You might think that with Crimea annexed and large chunks of eastern Ukraine effectively under Russian control, he would be riding high, but he isn't.

"Now I see the results of my work, and I'm absolutely not satisfied," he told us. "I consider what is going on in modern Russia as a caricature of my ideas. Eurasianism is accepted, patriotism is accepted, anti-Western rhetoric is accepted, anti-liberalism is . . . Everything is almost how I wanted during the 90s, but at the same time I see I don't like it. It is a perversion, I would say. A caricature."

There was a time, Dugin said, when he would have blamed Vladislav Surkov, the *éminence grise* who ran the political block of Putin's presidential administration. Surkov, in Dugin's estimation, was a "trickster," playing the various factions of Russian politics off one another, seeking advantage always for himself, and sometimes for his employer. But then Surkov was fired, replaced first by Vyacheslav Volodin, then by Sergei Kirienko, and nothing changed. The problem, Dugin concluded, must be Putin himself.

Understanding Dugin's dissatisfaction with Putin—and, indeed, the dissatisfaction of Russian nationalists more broadly—is crucial. Many readers of this and other books about Russia are centrally concerned with Russian foreign policy and its direction, and here too our analysis has important implications. As highlighted in our argument, the narrative of "lifting Russia from its knees," whether it be in Georgia, Ukraine and Syria or in the rearming of the military has been a major component of the appeal Putin makes to Russians. This is unlikely to change while Putin remains president. Nor is it likely to change if someone else became president, especially if that president were to be democratically elected. The constituency supporting a strong, assertive Russia is simply too large and too important to be ignored. Put another way, no one is going to win a free and fair election by telling the vast majority of Russian voters that they've believed a lie.

Nevertheless, again it is important to be clear what this does and does not mean. One long-term goal of Russian policymakers has been to reassert Russia's status as a great power. This means having privileged influence over international affairs within what Russia considers its sphere of influence—essentially the former Soviet Union minus the Baltic states of Estonia, Latvia and Lithuania—and being consulted on broader issues of international concern. This is bad news for those Ukrainians who want to establish an independent pro-Western policy in their country. Russia will do what it can to make life difficult.

However, an assertive Russia does not mean we should expect open-ended, indiscriminate military confrontation with Russia's neighbors or the West. Russian capacity to challenge the West remains very limited, and so has to be used selectively. Moreover, the Crimea effect we analyze here is quite idiosyncratic. Neither northern Kazakhstan, nor eastern Estonia, nor anywhere else has the status of Crimea in Russian popular consciousness. As a result, we should not expect "Crimea syndrome" redux any time soon.

And this is where Dugin's irritation is important. From his point of view, Putin's confrontation with the West is situational and pragmatic, rather than ideological and profound. The nationalists' reading of the aftermath of Crimea and the Donbas is one of betrayal: what could, as Dugin told us, have been "the moment when Russian civilization should acquire its proper dimensions" turned into a quagmire precisely because Putin would not take it to its logical conclusion.

"Crimea was the culmination point, the last stop before changing absolutely the logic of the development of modern Russia," Dugin exclaimed. "But it didn't happen. I don't know why.... It was a betrayal. For the patriotic group, it was a betrayal by Putin of our awakening. And for liberals, it was a betrayal by Putin of globalist rules. So, Putin has betrayed both parties.... And it is the worst that could possibly happen, because we have committed half the crime, but paid the full price."

Dugin's geopolitical analysis aside, his political interpretation reflects that of an important constituency, both within the masses and the elite. His summary of the liberals' frustrations is also accurate: while they would not dare say so publicly, the leaders of Russia's banks, major corporations and even economics and finance ministries are clearly aghast at the road toward isolation from the world economy that Russia has taken. Putin cannot choose one side without alienating the other. As a result, he chooses neither—and risks alienating both. The only thing holding the ship together is his popularity.

THE END

We have tried to present in this book a different version of Russian politics than most people will have seen before. Our story is not about Putin's Russia—a country whose politics would be best understood by analyzing the actions of its seemingly eternal leader. Our story is instead a study of how a people and its politics interact with one another to create and sustain a system built around one highly popular, yet highly polarizing, personality—one who aggressively asserts conservative authoritarian politics at home and Russia's role in international affairs abroad. The two sides—the regime and the people—interact with each other, and it is on that interaction that anyone trying to understand where Russia is going must focus.

One way to think about the future of Russian politics is to recognize the transformation of Putin himself. He has gone from being a leader picked by the oligarchy as a tool to defend their interests, to being a "father of the nation," a president who is no longer a politician in the normal sense of the term but a national leader largely immune from the everyday problems that attach themselves to those below him. As we have argued in this book, this status was not achieved by fiat, or even by the considerable formal powers invested in the presidency by the Russian constitution. Instead, it was achieved through the support and emotional commitment of millions of Russians, who responded positively to the central axes of policy. This consensus around Putin and Putinism, in turn, is itself partly the product of aggressive propaganda on television and the ubiquitous reinforcement of the Putinist worldview across Russian society.

One conclusion from this analysis is that such a person is hard to replace. Even if, as seems likely, Vladimir Putin himself is a relatively ordinary person (albeit leading a rather extraordinary life), a person around whom such a following has been built cannot be succeeded quickly or easily. This is part of the reason why Putin has hung around so long, and why the decision was made to have him return to the presidency after the short dalliance with Dmitry Medvedev. If Russia were simply a KGB state or mafia state, or even a strong-man dictatorship, replacing Putin with someone else would potentially be much easier.

Take, for example, the late presidents of two other former Soviet states, Islam Karimov of Uzbekistan, and Saparmurat Niyazov of Turkmenistan, better known as "Turkmenbashi," or "Father of the Turkmen." Although both men had ruled their lands since even before the breakup of the USSR and were thought to be "indispensable," their deaths in fact brought remarkably little disruption. Both constructed highly repressive, highly personalized dictatorships and seemed completely essential to the systems they created. Both developed major personality cults—though Niyazov took the cake, installing a giant rotating golden statue of himself in the capital and renaming cities and even months of the calendar after himself and his mother. In both countries, there was tremendous anxiety about what would happen after the two great dictators departed the stage. And yet, when each man died, there was a highly orderly transition to an anointed successor, outside of the family of the former leader. In each case, the successor rather seamlessly took the reins of the existing machine and chose a new course of action, with little real change in the system of power. Nobody asked ordinary Turkmen and Uzbeks what they thought, of course. The key to the peaceful transition of power was elite consensus.

By contrast, in the model of Russian politics that we have described here, it would be hard to simply replace Putin with some less prominent figure from the existing elite, as happened in Uzbekistan and Turkmenistan. Doing so would require a period of political rebuilding that would be risky and costly. The godlike leaders in Central Asia were in fact replaceable because both Turkmenistan and Uzbekistan are hardcore autocratic regimes, in which the elites make the decisions and the citizenry are very far from being a factor. Russia is different. In Russia, public support is an important resource in politics, and the charisma of one leader cannot so seamlessly be passed on to another.

This factor helps to explain both Putin's longevity in office and his apparent freedom from threats from within the ruling elite. Factions can emerge around the president, but no one has the public standing to be a credible challenger.

Putin's perceived role as a national figure, above the grit and grime of day-to-day politics, is a bedrock both to himself and to those around him.

However, as we have noted throughout this book, Putin's position is not created simply by the rules or by elite consensus. Rather, it relies upon very active political work by the administration, by television and by the actions and interactions of Russian citizens and major social institutions, like schools and churches. Vladimir Putin does not own politics in Russia. Even he has to play to the gallery.

As we noted in Chapter 5, this sense of Putin's inevitability—and the importance of maintaining that sense—is a source of great strength, but it is also potentially a source of weakness. As Václav Havel pointed out decades ago, writing about "the power of the powerless" under Communism, maintaining the façade of unanimity requires many people to play their role. Once people begin to change their minds and refuse to act as expected, things can change extremely quickly.

This was indeed what happened with the fall of Communism both in Eastern Europe and in the USSR. In Eastern Europe, Communist countries like East Germany and Czechoslovakia, which had been quiet for years, suddenly fell to massive crowds. The sense of inevitability—of the impossibility of any other future—was shattered by the victory of Solidarity in Poland, and by Gorbachev's *Glasnost* and *Perestroika*. As the political scientist Timur Kuran famously argued, authoritarian rule depends very heavily on what citizens think others are likely to do.[21] Once citizens' expectations of how others are likely to behave change, whole regimes can crumble overnight. For decades, the smart greengrocer knew that it was best to cooperate with Communism. In the fall of 1989, it was smarter to rebel.

A similar phenomenon took place in Russia and the rest of the USSR once Gorbachev introduced competitive elections for political office. Ambitious politicians, public officials and even factory managers no longer had to look only to the Communist Party hierarchy for promotion. Their options multiplied, but there also arose a new necessity: looking below, to garner popular support. Previously loyal Communists from the Baltic states to Uzbekistan refashioned themselves as nationalist leaders. In a matter of a couple of short years, a superpower went from being unchallenged to being unsustainable. In the words of the American political scientist Mark Beissinger, "the impossible became the inevitable."[22] Or, as the Russian anthropologist Alexei Yurchak put it, the Soviet Union "was forever, until it was no more."[23]

The lessons for Russia's Putin are clear and ominous. When position and power depend heavily on the citizens— on their reading of their social surroundings, their sense of consensus, and the breadth of their imaginations—this support can disappear almost overnight. Putin's power will crumble when we least expect it. And yet, looking back, we will all have seen it coming.

DRAMATIS PERSONAE

Albats, Evgenia—Альбац Евгения Марковна, born September 5, 1958 in Moscow. Graduated from the journalism department of Moscow State University in 1980 and worked for the weekly news magazine *Nedelya* until joining the pathbreaking *Glasnost*-era *Moskovskie Novosti* in 1986. Later worked for the independent Ekho Moskvy radio station, while obtaining a PhD in political science from Harvard University and teaching Russian politics in the US and Moscow. In 2007, founded *The New Times*, an independent newsweekly (now online only) known for its investigative reporting.

Alekhina, Maria—Алехина Мария Владимировна, born June 6, 1988 in Moscow. Studied journalism and creative writing, writes poetry. In 2008, became active in environmental movements, including the Russian chapter of Greenpeace, and campaigns to protect Lake Baikal and the Khimki Forest. Later joined the feminist punk group Pussy Riot, which performed controversially in Moscow's Christ the Savior Cathedral in February 2012. In August of the same year, she and two other participants were sentenced to two years in prison;

she was released in a general amnesty in December 2013.

Dugin, Alexander—Дугин Александр Гельевич, born January 7, 1962 in Moscow. As a teenager, became involved in underground nationalist and fascist movements, including the Black Order of the SS and Pamyat, and eventually joined with Eduard Limonov to found the radical National Bolshevik Party. Despite not graduating from university, pursued and received a graduate degree in sociology, broke away from his previous affiliations and began to codify the ideology of "Eurasianism," envisioned as a metaphysical rejection of liberalism and Westernism. Although popular among some groups of Russian nationalists and with command of his own department at Moscow State University, remained politically marginalized until the outbreak of conflict in Ukraine in 2014, when Eurasianism became a popular framing for Russia's new foreign policy, although his visibility has faded since then. Serves as editor-in-chief of Tsargrad, a religious-themed television station owned by Konstantin Malofeev.

Girkin, Igor—Гиркин Игорь Всеволодович, born December 17, 1970 in Moscow. Studied history at university and became enamored with historical military reenactment, taking a particular liking to the anti-Bolshevik White Army during the Russian Civil War. After graduation in 1992, volunteered to fight on behalf of Russian-speaking separatists in the Transnistria region of Moldova, and from there went to Bosnia, where he fought on behalf of the breakaway Republika Srpska. Served in the regular Russian army 1993–94, and then in the FSB 1998–2005, including taking part in operations in the

Second Chechen War. In 2013, began running security for an investment fund owned by Konstantin Malofeev. In April 2014, under the *nom de guerre* of Igor Strelkov, crossed the border into Ukraine with fifty-two fighters and took part in the nascent conflict in Donbas. Eventually took command of the "Army of the People's Republic of Donetsk" and became minister of defense of the self-declared republic until returning to Moscow in late 2014.

Kadyrov, Ramzan—Кадыров Рамзан Ахматович, born October 5, 1976 in Tsentoroi, Chechnya. In 1994, two years after graduating from high school, he followed his father Akhmat Kadyrov into war, fighting for independence from Russia. After the First Chechen War ended in 1996, worked as an assistant and bodyguard to his father, who became Mufti of Chechnya. As the Second Chechen War began in 1999, Akhmat Kadyrov switched his allegiance to the Russian government, and Ramzan took command of his father's battalion, this time fighting against the separatists. After Moscow won the war, Akhmat Kadyrov became president of Chechnya, and Ramzan served in various posts in his father's administration, until the elder Kadyrov was killed in a bomb attack in 2004. A year later, Ramzan Kadyrov was appointed president of the republic, a post he continues to hold.

Kasparov, Garri—Каспаров Гарри Кимович, born April 13, 1963 in Baku, Azerbaijan (then part of the USSR). Began learning to play chess at the age of 5 and won his first USSR junior championship in 1976, at the age of 12. In 1980, at the age of 16, he became a Grand Master and won his first world junior championship. In 1985, at the age of 22, he won his first full world championship, defeating Anatoly Karpov. He would hold the title of world champion until losing to Vladimir Kramnik in 2000. During the 1990s, became involved in democratic politics in Russia, supporting Boris Yeltsin's favored Russia's Choice party. In 2001, began speaking out against Vladimir Putin's attacks on independent media and the war in Chechnya and became a prominent opposition figure, fleeing the country in fear of prosecution in 2013.

Khodorkovsky, Mikhail—Ходорковский Михаил Борисович, born June 26, 1963 in Moscow. Studied engineering but after graduating in the midst of Mikhail Gorbachev's economic *Perestroika* took advantage of new opportunities to open small private businesses under the aegis of the Communist Youth League. Earned money trading imported computers and other goods and launched a cooperative bank, Menatep, in 1989. After the fall of the USSR, Menatep flourished and took part in the privatization drive of the early 1990s, and its crown jewel became the oil company Yukos, Russia's largest. Yukos thrived until the early 2000s, when Khodorkovsky began to clash with Putin over tax and regulatory policy. In parallel, Khodorkovsky supported opposition parties in the Duma and funded civil society groups through his Open Russia foundation. In 2003, he was arrested on charges of tax fraud and Yukos was nationalized. Spent ten years in a Siberian labor camp, before being pardoned by Putin in December 2013 and moving to London. There, he reestablished Open Russia and funds a range of civil society and oppositional groups in Russia.

Kirienko, Sergei—Кириенко Сергей Владиленович, born July 26, 1962 in Sukhumi, Georgia (then part of the

USSR, now the capital of the breakaway republic of Abkhazia). Studied engineering in Nizhny Novgorod (then Gorky), working in shipbuilding until the end of the Soviet Union. Worked in finance in Nizhny Novogorod until Boris Nemtsov invited him to Moscow in 1997 to take up a job in the Ministry of Fuel and Energy, becoming minister shortly thereafter. Was appointed acting prime minister in March 1998, resigning after the August 1998 financial collapse. After his resignation, joined Nemtsov in creating the Union of Right Forces and served in the Duma until Putin appointed him presidential plenipotentiary to the Volga federal district in 2000. In 2005, was appointed CEO of the Russian nuclear holding company Rosatom, where he remained until 2016, when Putin appointed him head of the domestic politics division of the Presidential Administration, replacing Vyacheslav Volodin.

Kiselev, Dmitry—Киселев Дмитрий Константинович, born April 26, 1954 in Moscow. Studied Scandinavian languages at university before going to work for the Soviet state's Norwegian and Polish broadcast services, and later becoming a correspondent for Soviet state television. Worked for Boris Berezovsky's ORT TV in the 1990s, before going to work for Russian state television in 2003, where he gained a reputation for his highly polemical analysis. In 2013, when Vladimir Putin decreed the creation of a new overarching state media holding, with a mission to "promote Russia's interests at home and abroad," was appointed CEO.

Malofeev, Konstantin—Малофеев Константин Валерьевич, born July 3, 1974 in Pushchino, near

Moscow. Studied law at university where, in the early 1990s, he also became interested in Russian Orthodox Christianity. After graduation, went to work in a string of investment funds, becoming a successful corporate lawyer and investment manager. Developed close ties to the Russian Orthodox Church and founded the $40-million St. Basil the Great Foundation, which supports various Church-related causes and initiatives. Helped found and fund the Safe Internet League which, together with Duma deputy Elena Mizulina, pushed restrictive legislation after the 2011–12 protests.

Medvedev, Dmitry—Медведев Дмитрий Анатольевич, born September 14, 1965 in St. Petersburg (then Leningrad). Studied and taught law in St. Petersburg, joining the administration of Mayor Anatoly Sobchak in 1990, where he worked as an adviser to Vladimir Putin. Left the administration after Sobchak's death and went into business, where he invested in a number of regional industrial assets. In 1999, was invited by then-Prime Minister Putin to join the cabinet, moving into the presidential administration after Boris Yeltsin's resignation in 2000, and running Putin's election campaign that year. Remained in the presidential administration until being nominated to succeed Putin as president in 2008, during which time Putin became prime minister. After one term in office, Medvedev took the position of prime minister, while Putin returned to the presidency.

Milonov, Vitaly—Милонов Виталий Валентинович, born January 23, 1974 in St. Petersburg (then Leningrad). Went into politics immediately after graduating from university, joining the Free Democratic Party headed by human-rights activists Maria Salye and Lev Ponomarev, and serving as an aide to the noted human-rights defender Galina Starovoitova, until her murder in 1998. Over time, migrated into a string of Christian democratic parties and then conservative movements, eventually being elected to the St. Petersburg city council from United Russia in 2004. Gained notoriety for pushing restrictions on LGBT rights and other socially conservative policies—including attempts to ban concerts by Madonna—on the local level. Was elected to the Duma from United Russia in 2016.

Mizulina, Elena—Мизулина Елена Борисовна, born December 9, 1954 in Bui, near Kostroma. Studied history and law in Yaroslavl, before working as a legal consultant in regional courts and universities until the end of the Soviet Union. Was elected to the Federation Council (upper house of parliament) in 1993 from Boris Yeltsin's favored party, and then joined the reformist Yabloko party in 1995, from which she was elected to the Duma later that year. Left Yabloko to join Boris Nemtsov's Union of Right Forces in 2000, and in 2007 left that party to join the Kremlin-backed Just Russia party, which she continues to represent in the Duma. Is best known for promoting socially conservative legislation, including restrictions on abortion, LGBT rights and the internet.

Navalny, Alexei—Навальный Алексей Анатольевич, born June 4, 1976 in Butyn, near Moscow. Studied law and finance at university and graduate school. Worked in corporate and small-business law, developing a reputation as an activist shareholder, buying small stakes in state-controlled companies in order to gain access to shareholder meetings and financial information, about which he would

then write exposés. In 2000, joined the opposition party
Yabloko and rose to head its Moscow division, before being
pushed out of the party in 2007, allegedly for espousing
nationalist ideologies. Built his shareholder activism into a
series of campaigns for government transparency and
accountability, launching crowd-sourced websites and a
national movement, which evolved into the Foundation
for the Fight Against Corruption (FBK). Spearheaded the
2011–12 protest movements, together with Boris Nemtsov,
Sergei Udaltsov and others, and eventually emerged as the
most prominent face of the opposition. Found himself at
the center of two criminal investigations, on what his
supporters regard as trumped-up charges of embezzlement, and was sentenced to a string of short jail terms and
suspended sentences; has also repeatedly spent time in jail
for protest activities. Ran for mayor of Moscow in 2013,
losing to Sergei Sobyanin, with 27 percent of the vote.
Supported parliamentary and local government candidates
around the country, with some success, before trying—and
failing—to get on the presidential ballot in 2018.

Nemtsov, Boris—Немцов Борис Ефимович, born October
9, 1959 in Sochi, died February 27, 2015 in Moscow.
Studied physics at university and graduate school in
Nizhny Novgorod (then Gorky) and Moscow, before
taking a job as a researcher at the Soviet Academy of
Sciences. In the mid-1980s, became active in environmental movements and was a vocal opponent of nuclear
power after the Chernobyl disaster of 1986. Was elected
to the first freely elected Russian parliament in 1990,
where he first met Boris Yeltsin. Was appointed by Yeltsin
as acting governor of the Nizhny Novogorod region after

the 1991 coup and was elected to the same post in 1995. Was invited by Yeltsin to become deputy prime minister in 1997, with responsibility for economic and social reforms, but resigned after the August 1998 financial crisis and default. Helped found and lead the Union of Right Forces, a center-right political party that spearheaded the democratic opposition from 1998 through 2003, when the party failed to win seats in parliament. With no outright opposition in parliament, became a prominent leader of protest groups and critic of Vladimir Putin. Was murdered near Red Square in 2015.

Pavlovsky, Gleb—Павловский Глеб Олегович, born March 5, 1951 in Odessa, Ukraine (then part of the USSR). Studied history and taught in rural schools, before being arrested by the KGB in 1974 for distributing Alexander Solzhenitsyn's banned *The Gulag Archipelago*. After his release, worked odd blue-collar jobs in Moscow, where he became part of the dissident and *samizdat* movements, as a result of which he was again arrested in 1982. Went into opposition politics during Mikhail Gorbachev's *Glasnost* reforms, and later into journalism in the early 1990s. In 1995, he created a political consulting firm, the Foundation for Effective Politics, and became a consultant to the administration of President Boris Yeltsin. Together with the oligarch Boris Berezovsky, helped identify and promote Vladimir Putin as Yeltsin's successor, and served as Putin's chief domestic politics adviser throughout his first term in office, until he was eventually replaced by Vladislav Surkov. Cut formal ties with the Kremlin in 2011.

Poroshenko, Petro—Порошенко Петро Олексійович, born September 26, 1965 in Bolgrad, near Odessa in Ukraine (then part of the USSR). Studied and taught economics in Kyiv until 1992, when he started investing in chocolate factories, which he combined into Roshen, Ukraine's largest candy maker. He leveraged those investments into a major business empire, including automotive factories, a port and a television station; by 2014, he was estimated to have a net worth of $1.3 billion. Elected to the Ukrainian parliament, the Verkhovna Rada, in 1998 from the Social Democratic Party. In 2001, joined then-President Leonid Kuchma and Viktor Yanukovych in the Party of Regions, but eventually switched sides and supported Viktor Yushchenko during the Orange Revolution. Served as foreign minister under President Yushchenko and later as minister of economic development and trade under President Yanukovych. Supported the Euromaidan protest movement in 2013–14 and was elected president of Ukraine in May 2014.

Potupchik, Kristina—Потупчик Кристина Андреевна, born January 19, 1986 in Murom, near Vladimir. After graduating with a degree in linguistics, became an activist in the Kremlin-backed youth group Nashi, rising through the ranks to become press secretary, a position she would hold 2007–12. After leaving Nashi, she set up her own consulting business and began working for Timur Prokopenko, coordinating the Kremlin's online mobilization campaigns, until Prokopenko resigned in 2015.

Prilepin, Zakhar—Прилепин Евгений (Захар) Николаевич, born July 7, 1975 in the village of Ilyinka, near Ryazan, as Evgeny Prilepin. After two years of military service and a further three years in the riot police—during which time he served in the Second Chechen War—graduated from university with a degree in linguistics and began working as a journalist. Contributed to a range of mainstream, left-wing and nationalist publications, while publishing a string of increasingly successful novels and short-story collections. In 2014, became one of Russia's most celebrated writers, on the back of the success of his novel *Obitel*, and simultaneously left for Donbas, where he committed himself to the cause of the separatists.

Prokopenko, Timur—Прокопенко Тимур Валентинович, born May 27, 1980 in the town of Staraya Kupavna, near Moscow. Studied journalism and in 2003 went to work for ITAR-TASS as a wire reporter, eventually joining the press pool in the State Duma. In 2005, took the first of a number of positions as press secretary, to a string of Duma deputies and government agencies. In 2010, took the reins of the Young Guard, United Russia's youth wing, and a year later was himself elected to the Duma. Only three months after taking office, however, resigned and went to work for the Presidential Administration, in charge of youth and online politics. Resigned in March 2015 after hackers released a trove of his emails.

Putin, Vladimir—Путин Владимир Владимирович, born October 7, 1952 in St. Petersburg (then Leningrad). Graduated from law school in 1975 and was recruited into the KGB. Trained in counter-intelligence and in 1985 was assigned to Dresden, East Germany, where he would remain until 1990. Upon returning to the USSR, joined the St. Petersburg municipal government of Anatoly Sobchak, with responsibility for city property and international partnerships. After Sobchak's death in 1996, moved to Moscow, where he helped run the audit service in the Presidential Administration. In 1998, he was named director of the Federal Security Service (FSB), the successor to the KGB. In May 1999, an ailing Boris Yeltsin named him prime minister. Seven months later, Yeltsin resigned, making Putin acting president; three months after that, he won election to his first term in the Kremlin. The rest is history.

Samutsevich, Ekaterina—Самуцевич Екатерина Станиславовна, born August 9, 1982 in Moscow. Studied computer programming and worked on software for defense systems, including nuclear submarines, before joining the radical art group Voina in 2007. In 2011, joined the feminist punk group Pussy Riot, which performed controversially in Moscow's Christ the Savior Cathedral in February 2012. In August of the same year, she and two other participants were sentenced to two years in prison; her sentence was later commuted and she was released in a general amnesty in December 2013.

Simonyan, Margarita—Симонян Маргарита Симоновна, born April 6, 1980 in Krasnodar. Studied on an exchange program in New Hampshire, USA before coming home to study journalism at university. After graduation, worked for regional TV channels in Krasnodar and Rostov-on-Don before moving to Moscow in 2002 as a reporter on state television. In 2005, was appointed founding editor-in-chief of Russia Today, the Kremlin's English-language mouthpiece. As the result of the reorganization of the government's media assets in 2013, became editor-in-chief of the overarching state news agency Sputnik.

Sobchak, Ksenia—Собчак Ксения Анатольевна, born November 5, 1981 in St. Petersburg (then Leningrad) to Anatoly Sobchak, who was elected mayor of St. Petersburg in 1991. During her father's mayoralty, the family came to be close with one of his deputies, a former KGB agent named Vladimir Putin. After her father's death in 1996, she moved to Moscow and became involved in a range of media projects, hosting talk programs and reality shows on television, before moving eventually into more serious journalism. Played a prominent role in the 2011–12 election protests, alongside Alexei Navalny, Boris Nemtsov and Ilya Yashin, and has continued to be active in opposition circles ever since. In 2018, ran as an opposition candidate for the Russian presidency, in the absence of Navalny, but garnered only 1.7 percent of the vote.

Sobyanin, Sergei—Собянин Сергей Семенович, born June 21, 1958 in Naksimvol, a village in Russia's Siberian far north, some 700 km from the nearest regional capital. Studied engineering in Kostroma, before moving to Chelyabinsk to work in a pipe factory. In 1984, was sent by the Communist Youth League back to his home region to do political work in the village of Kogalym, where he quickly became deputy chair of the village council. In 1988, moved up to regional government, with responsibility for housing and utilities, shuffling back and forth between increasingly high-ranking positions in municipal and regional government until joining the Federation Council (upper house of parliament) in 1996. In 2001, elected governor of the Tyumen region, an oil-rich part of western Siberia, a post he held until joining the Presidential Administration in 2005. In 2010, was appointed mayor of Moscow by then-president Dmitry Medvedev. He won election to the same position in

September 2013, after President Vladimir Putin reinstated direct gubernatorial and mayoral elections.

Strelkov, Igor—see Girkin, Igor

Surkov, Vladislav—Сурков Владислав Юрьевич, born
September 21, 1964 in Solntsevo, near Lipetsk, but spent
his early years in Chechnya. In the late *Perestroika* years,
took an interest in marketing, advertising and public
relations, creating one of the country's first marketing
agencies, Metapress, and becoming president of the
Russian Association of Advertisers in 1992. At the same
time, became an executive in Menatep bank, owned by
Mikhail Khodorkovsky, and a PR adviser to the government. Joined the Presidential Administration in 1999,
where he helped create the Unity Party, which would
win the 1999 parliamentary elections and soon thereafter became United Russia. Rose through the ranks of
the Presidential Administration, with responsibility for
"special projects," gradually replacing Gleb Pavlovsky as
Putin's *éminence grise*, until assuming oversight of internal
politics in 2008. Widely credited with authoring most of
Putin's ideological approaches during the 2000s and
early 2010s, including the term "Sovereign Democracy."
After failing to head off the protests of 2011–12, and
amid falling approval ratings for the president, was
demoted by Putin in 2013 to the role of adviser. In 2014,
took responsibility for managing affairs in Ukraine.

Tolokonnikova, Nadezhda—Толоконникова Надежда
Андреевна, born November 7, 1989 in Norilsk. Studied
art and philosophy and joined the radical art group
Voina, taking part in a number of provocative public
performances. In 2011, joined the feminist punk group

Pussy Riot, which performed controversially in Moscow's Christ the Savior Cathedral in February 2012. In August of the same year, she and two other participants were sentenced to two years in prison; she was released in a general amnesty in December 2013.

Udaltsov, Sergei—Удальцов Сергей Станиславович, born February 16, 1977 in Moscow. While studying law in 1998 organized the Red Youth Avantgarde, a radical protest arm of Russia's struggling political left wing. In 2005, helped create the Left Front and led it into collaboration with centrist and right-wing opposition groups, including those led by Garri Kasparov, Boris Nemtsov and eventually Alexei Navalny. In 2014, he was sentenced to four and a half years in prison for his role in organizing the May 6, 2012 protest, which ended in violence not far from the Kremlin.

Varlamov, Ilya—Варламов Илья Александрович, born January 7, 1984 in Moscow. A programmer and designer who rose to be Russia's most successful blogger. Was prominent in the 2011–12 electoral protests in Russia, with his blogs and social media feeds providing an important source of information to participants and supporters, a role he reprised during the events of 2013–14 in Ukraine.

Volkov, Leonid—Волков Леонид Михайлович, born November 10, 1980 in Ekaterinburg (then Sverdlovsk). A computer programmer and entrepreneur, Volkov became active in opposition groups in Ekaterinburg beginning in 2009, before volunteering to work with Alexei Navalny's anti-corruption campaigns. In 2013, fled to Luxembourg, to avoid politically motivated prosecution, but returned to Moscow in 2014 to head up Navalny's eventual bid for the Russian presidency.

Volodin, Vyacheslav—Володин Вячеслав Викторович, born February 4, 1964 in Alekseevka, near Saratov. Worked as an engineer and then a lecturer until going into local and regional government in 1992, rising to be vice governor of the Saratov region in 1996, before moving to Moscow to go into business and join the ranks of the Fatherland Party, from which he was elected to the Duma in 1999. After the party merged with others to become United Russia (Putin's ruling party), Volodin rose through the ranks to become party secretary in 2007. In 2011, became deputy director of the Presidential Administration, in charge of managing domestic politics, a post he held until he returned to the Duma as speaker in 2016.

Yanukovych, Viktor—Янукович Віктор Федорович, born July 9, 1950 in Enakievo, Ukraine (then part of the USSR). Worked in heavy industry in and around Donetsk before going into regional government in 1996 and eventually rising to lead the Donetsk-based Party of Regions. Served as prime minister of Ukraine under President Leonid Kuchma until a fraudulent presidential election that would have made him president in 2004 was undone by the wave of protests that came to be known as the Orange Revolution. Later served as prime minister under his Orange Revolution opponent Viktor Yushchenko, 2006–7, before being elected to the presidency in 2010. Fled to Russia in February 2014, during the wave of protests that came to be known as the Euromaidan. Currently lives in semi-hiding in Rostov-on-Don, Russia.

Yashin, Ilya—Яшин Илья Валерьевич, born June 29, 1983 in Moscow. Involved in opposition politics from the age of 23, through a variety of political parties and protest movements. A close ally of Boris Nemtsov and sometime ally of Alexei Navalni and Ksenia Sobchak.

Yeltsin, Boris—Ельцин Борис Николаевич, born February 1, 1931 in the village of Butka in the Ural Mountains, died April 23, 2007 in Moscow. Worked in heavy industry in and around Ekaterinburg (then Sverdlovsk), before joining the ranks of the Communist Party and moving his way into local and regional government. Elected to the Supreme Soviet of the USSR in 1978, becoming a member of the Central Committee of the Communist Party in 1981—a position from which he resigned in 1990, when he was elected to lead the Russian Soviet Federative Socialist Republic (within the USSR). In that position, he regularly challenged Soviet President Mikhail Gorbachev. Led the resistance against Communist hard-liners during the August 1991 coup against Gorbachev and subsequently negotiated the breakup of the USSR with the leaders of the Ukrainian and Belarusian Soviet Socialist Republics. Served as president of the Russian Federation until January 1, 2000, at which point he handed power to then-prime minister Vladimir Putin as acting president.

Zakharchenko, Alexander—Захарченко Александр Владимирович, born June 26, 1976, died August 31, 2018, both in Donetsk, Ukraine (part of the USSR when he was born, partially occupied by Russia when he died). Began his career as a coal mine mechanic before getting involved in the retail business, helping to found and run a number of companies. In April 2014, took up arms to occupy the Donetsk municipal administration and rapidly rose through the ranks of the nascent Donetsk People's Republic, becoming prime minister in November 2014, a position he held until he was killed in a bomb attack in August 2018.

Zaldostanov, Alexander—Залдостанов Александр «Хирург» Сергеевич, born January 19, 1963 in Kirovgrad, Ukraine (then part of the USSR). Studied medicine (gaining the nickname "Surgeon," though not the degree) before getting involved in motorcycles in the mid-1980s. Formed the Night Wolves motorcycle club in 1989. The club, known for its nationalist leanings, has led rallies to Crimea (prior to the annexation), to Berlin and elsewhere, often with the support of Vladimir Putin. Spearheaded the Anti-Maidan rallies in Moscow and elsewhere in 2015.

Zhirinovsky, Vladimir—Жириновский Владимир Вольфович, born April 25, 1946 in Almaty, Kazakhstan (then part of the USSR). Founded the Liberal Democratic Party of Russia and led it to a resounding electoral success in the parliamentary vote of 1993 on a platform of anti-Semitism and anti-Western nationalism. Has held a seat in the Duma ever since and continues to lead the party, which won 5.65 percent of the national vote in 2018.

Zygar, Mikhail—Зыгарь Михаил Викторович, born January 31, 1981 in Moscow. Grew up in Angola before studying journalism in Moscow and Cairo. In 2010, helped found the independent TV station Dozhd, of which he served as editor-in-chief until the end of 2015, a period covering the election protests of 2011–12, the occupation and annexation of Crimea, and Russia's launch of a separatist war in eastern Ukraine.

ENDNOTES

1. THE PEOPLE AND VLADIMIR PUTIN

1. Natalya is not her real name. Throughout this book, we present quotes and insights from interviews conducted with ordinary Russian citizens in Moscow, St. Petersburg and Yaroslavl in early 2018. To protect the interviewees, we have given them pseudonyms. To help ensure that these interviews were open and honest, the interviews were conducted on our behalf and using our questions by native Russian sociologists, as many Russians might feel uncomfortable talking about their political views with an American and a Scot.

2. Freedom House. (2018, January 16). "Democracy in Crisis: Freedom House Releases Freedom in the World 2018." Retrieved October 10, 2018, from https://freedomhouse.org/article/democracy-crisis-freedom-house-releases-freedom-world-2018

2. THE KREMLIN UNDER FIRE

1. In his official campaign biography for the 2000 presidential election, the now famously athletic Putin blames beer for his flabby appearance in shirtless photographs taken during the Dresden days. See Kolesnikov, A., Gevorkyan, N. P., and Timakova, N. (2000). *Ot pervogo litsa. Razgovory s Vladimirom Putinym*. Vagrius. Retrieved from https://www.litmir.me/bd/?b=132894&p=1

2. *"Мы здесь власть!"*

3. Navalny was an anti-corruption blogger turned protest leader, Udaltsov was a radical left-wing politician and Nemtsov, a former deputy prime minister turned oppositionist. Radio Svoboda. (2012, May 7). "'Marsh millionov'. Naval'nyy, Nemtsov, Udal'tsov zaderzhany." Retrieved October 10, 2018, from https://www.svoboda.org/a/24571375.html; TV Rain. (2012, May 7). "'Marsh millionov'. Informatsionnyy vypusk, final'naya chast." Retrieved October 10, 2018, from https://tvrain.ru/lite/teleshow/experiment/marsh_millionov_informatsionnyy_vypusk_finalnaya_chast-246014/

4. Ekho Moskvy. (2012, May 7). "Sotni chelovek zaderzhany, desyatki postradali v khode vcherashnikh aktsiy protesta i stolknoveniy s politsiey v

Moskve." Retrieved October 10, 2018, from https://echo.msk.ru/news/885899-echo.html; Lenta.ru. (2012, May 7). "Na pyatachke: Grazhdane i omonovtsy vervye poprobovali drug druga na prochnost'." Retrieved October 10, 2018, from https://lenta.ru/articles/2012/05/07/shestoyemaya/

5. Vikalyuk, A. (2013, June 4). "Biznesmen Kozlov vyshel iz kolonii 'svobodnym chelovekom'." RIA Novosti. Retrieved October 10, 2018, from https://ria.ru/incidents/20130604/941164092.html

6. BBC News. (2012, March 6). "Obvinyaemye v 'pank-molebne' v KhKhS arestovany do 24 aprelya." Retrieved October 10, 2018, from https://www.bbc.com/russian/russia/2012/03/120306_pussy_riot_arrest.shtml

7. Bocharova, S., Zheleznova, M., Kornya, A., and Glikin, M. (2013, May 30). "Ekspertov privlekli k delu YuKOSa." Vedomosti. Retrieved October 10, 2018, from https://www.vedomosti.ru/politics/articles/2013/05/30/delo_yukosa_mozhet_pojti_na_tretij_srok; Chelishcheva, V. (2013, May 29). "Mest' otvyazavsheysya pushki." Novaya Gazeta. Retrieved October 10, 2018, from https://www.novayagazeta.ru/articles/2013/05/29/54911-mest-otvyazavsheysya-pushki

8. RBK. (2012, August 17). "Uchastnits Pussy Riot prigovorili k dvum godam kolonii." Retrieved October 10, 2018, from http://top.rbc.ru/society/17/08/2012/665147.shtml; RBK. (2012, October 10). "Delo Pussy Riot: E.Samutsevich otpustili, ee podrug otpravyat v koloniyu." Retrieved October 10, 2018, from http://top.rbc.ru/society/10/10/2012/673669.shtml

9. On November 9, 2012, Maksim Luzianin was the first to be sentenced, receiving four and a half years in prison. On April 23, 2013, Konstantin Lebedev was sentenced to two and a half years. On October 8, 2013, Mikhail Kosenko was given an indefinite sentence in a psychiatric hospital. On February 24, 2014, Andrei Barabanov, Iaroslav Belousov, Denis Lutskevich, Aleksei Polikhovich, Stepan Zimin, Sergei Krivov and Artem Savelov were sentenced to terms of two and a half to four years, while Aleksandra Dukhanina was given a suspended sentence. On August 18 of the same year, Aleksei Gaskarov, Il'ia Gushchin and Aleksandr Margolin were given prison terms of two and a half to three and a half years, while Elena Kokhtareva received a suspended sentence, and on October 10 Dmitrii Ishevskii was sentenced to three years and two months in prison. The final sentence, of two and a half years, was handed down to Ivan Nepomniashchikh on December 22, 2015, after he had spent almost a year under house arrest. See Gazeta.ru. (2012, November 9). "Sud vynes pervyy prigovor po 'bolotnomu delu': Maksim Luzyanin poluchil 4,5 goda lisheniya svobody." Retrieved October 10, 2018, from https://www.gazeta.ru/politics/news/2012/11/09/n_2609281.shtml; Shainyan, K. (2013, April 25). "Opyat' dvoyka: oglashen prigovor Lebedevu." Radio Svoboda. Retrieved October 10, 2018, from https://www.svoboda.org/a/24968001.html; Kommersant. (2014, February 24). "Semero figurantov 'bolotnogo dela' budut sidet'." Retrieved October 10, 2018, from https://www.kommersant.ru/doc/2415425; Newsru. (2014, August 18). "Chetyre figuranta 'bolotnogo dela' prigovoreny k nakazaniyu ot uslovnogo do 3,5 let kolonii." Retrieved October 10, 2018, from https://www.newsru.com/russia/18aug2014/4bolot.html; Ishevskiy, D. (2014,

December 1). Retrieved October 10, 2018, from https://grani-ru-org. appspot.com/people/2203/; Dzhanpoladova, N. (2015, December 22). "Chekisty vzyalis' za pravnuka." Radio Svoboda. Retrieved October 10, 2018, from https://www.svoboda.org/a/27443336.html

10. Interfax. (2012, October 11). "Udal'tsov rasskazal pro poisk deneg." Retrieved October 10, 2018, from https://www.interfax.ru/russia/270303

11. Dzhanpoladova, N. (2013, June 21). "Udal'tsov i Razvozzhaev nachinayut znakomit'sya s delom." Radio Svoboda. Retrieved October 10, 2018, from https://www.svoboda.org/a/25024150.html

12. BBC News. (2014, July 24). "Udal'tsov i Razvozzhaev prigovoreny k 4,5 godam kolonii." Retrieved October 10, 2018, from https://www.bbc.com/russian/russia/2014/07/140724_udaltsov_sentence_verdict.shtml

13. Lenta.ru. (2014, March 12). "Konstantin Lebedev rasskazal o rossiyskom 'mikromaydane'." Retrieved October 10, 2018, from https://lenta.ru/news/2014/03/12/lebedev/

14. RT na russkom. (2012). "Putin v Luzhnikakh: Vystuplenie na mitinge 23 fevralya." Retrieved from https://www.youtube.com/watch?v=mWUxcGCfdiI

15. *Не будоражить народ.*

16. Skovoroda, E. (2012, October 22). "Gaz bez antidota." *The New Times*. Retrieved October 10, 2018, from https://www.webcitation.org/6DfA3H4CN

17. Sokolov, M. (2008, December 16). "Boris Nemtsov ob itogakh s"ezda vserossiyskogo dvizheniya 'Solidarnost'." Radio Svoboda. Retrieved October 10, 2018, from https://www.svoboda.org/a/477229.html

18. Author interview with Gleb Pavlovsky, 27 October 2016. Moscow.

19. Hillygus, D. S., and Shields, T. G. (2016). *The Persuadable Voter: Wedge Issues in Presidential Campaigns*. Princeton University Press.

20. Matveeva, G. (2012). "Pank-moleben 'Bogoroditsa, Putina progoni' Pussy Riot v Khrame." Retrieved from https://www.youtube.com/watch?v=GCasuaAczKY. The original video was taken down as supposedly violating YouTube's policy on "hate speech." An alternative posted later can be viewed at https://www.youtube.com/watch?v=eHxBKK6fw_4, retrieved November 16, 2018.

21. RBK. (2012, October 10). "Delo Pussy Riot: E.Samutsevich otpustili, ee podrug otpravyat v koloniyu." Retrieved October 10, 2018, from http://top.rbc.ru/society/10/10/2012/673669.shtml

22. Mel'nikov, A. (2012, February 27). "Proshcheniia ne budet." *Nezavisimaia Gazeta*.

23. Samokhina, S., and Korchenkova, N. (2013, June 11). "Gosduma prinyala zakon ob oskorblenii chuvstv veruyushchikh." Kommersant. Retrieved from https://www.kommersant.ru/doc/2209841

24. Legoyda, V. (2013, May 14). "Materialy SMI: 'Kart-blansh. Chuvstva veruyushchikh i neveruyushchikh, ili pochemu ne stoit khodit' so svoim ustavom v chuzhoy monastyr'." Interfax. Retrieved October 10, 2018, from http://www.interfax-religion.ru/?act=news&div=51159

25. Svetova, Z. (2012, June 11). "Umalili dukhovnuiu osnovu gosudarstva." *The New Times*.

26. *Vedomosti*. (2013, April 11). "Ot redaktsii: Pochti bez chuvstv."

27. Davydov, I. (2015, August 24). "Ia znaiu apostolov antikhrista po imenam." *The New Times*.

28. Gazeta.ru. (2012, February 8). "Avtor skandal'nogo zakona o geyakh predlagaet formirovat' otryady politsii nravov iz kazakov." Retrieved October 10, 2018, from https://www.gazeta.ru/news/lenta/2012/02/08/n_2196741.shtml; Interfax. (2013, September 23). "10 samyh izvestnyh iniciativ deputata Milonova." Retrieved October 10, 2018, from https://www.interfax.ru/russia/330435

29. ITAR-TASS. (2012, February 29). "V Peterburge prinyat zakon o shtrafakh za propagandu pedofilii i gomoseksualizma." Retrieved November 22, 2018, from https://tass.ru/obschestvo/573556

30. Petrovskaya, I. (2012, April 7). "'Serdtsa geev nado szhigat' i zakapyvat' v zemlyu'. Chadolyubivyy televedushchiy predlozhil retsept dlya spaseniya detey." *Novaya Gazeta*. Retrieved October 10, 2018, from https://www.novayagazeta.ru/articles/2012/04/07/49123-171-serdtsa-geev-nado-szhigat-i-zakapyvat-v-zemlyu-187-chadolyubivyy-televeduschiy-predlozhil-retsept-dlya-spaseniya-detey

31. Rabochy put'. (2013, June 6). "Smolensk: V krestovyy pokhod za semeynye tsennosti!" Retrieved October 10, 2018, from http://www.rabochy-put.ru/society/43259-smolensk-v-krestovyjj-pokhod-za-semejjnye-cennosti.html

32. Grani.ru. (2013, May 11). "V Volgograde soversheno zverskoe ubiystvo na pochve gomofobii." Retrieved October 10, 2018, from https://graniru.org/Society/Neuro/m.214558.html

33. Eysmont, M. (2013, May 20). "Mariya Eysmont: Gei i my." *Vedomosti*. Retrieved October 10, 2018, from https://www.vedomosti.ru/opinion/articles/2013/05/20/solidarnost_s_geyami

34. Ivashkina, D. (2014, January 7). "Ivan Okhlobystin poprosil vernut' stat'yu za 'muzhelozhestvo'." *Komsomol'skaya Pravda*. Retrieved October 10, 2018, from https://www.kp.ru/online/news/1627527/

35. Kondakov, A. (2017). "Prestupleniya na pochve nenavisti protiv LGBT v Rossii. Tsentr nezavisimykh sotsiologicheskikh issledovaniy." CISR.ru. Retrieved from http://cisr.ru/publications/hate-crime-against-lgbt-in-russia/

36. The sample included Russian citizens living in cities of 1 million or more inhabitants, with at least some university education, at least a middle-level income and between the ages of 16 and 65. As we hoped, the sample over-represented those who opposed the Kremlin: 48.2 percent of respondents somewhat or fully approved of Putin's activities as president, and only 39.3 percent reported voting for him in the 2012 election.

37. Respondents who reported voting for Putin were about 12 percentage points more likely to fully support the religious sentiment law and 20 percentage points more likely to fully support the anti-LGBT law than respondents who reported voting for an opposition candidate. It is notable that opponents of the religious sentiment law were much more numerous (nearly 70 percent of the opposition) than opponents of the anti-LBGT law (only about 30 percent of supporters of the political opposition—and the majority of these expressed lukewarm opposition).

38. Respondents who rarely or never watched TV news were some 25 percentage points more likely than regular TV watchers to fully oppose the LGBT law, and some 40 percentage points more likely to oppose the religious sentiment law.

39. Boytsova, M. (2013, June 14). "Deputat pod krovat'yu." Rosbalt. Retrieved October 11, 2018, from http://www.rosbalt.ru/piter/2013/06/14/1140900. html

40. Golitsyna, A. (2012, July 9). "Gosduma odobrila fil'tratsiyu runeta." *Vedomosti.* Retrieved October 11, 2018, from https://www.vedomosti.ru/technology/articles/2012/07/09/proshel_bez_filtra

41. Newsru. (2014, March 13). "Roskomnadzor zablokiroval dostup k portalam 'Grani.ru', 'Kasparov.ru', 'Ezhednevnomu zhurnalu' i ZhZh Naval'nogo." Retrieved October 11, 2018, from https://www.newsru.com/russia/13mar2014/block.html

42. Krasnikov, E., and Naberezhnov, G. (2014, April 21). "Pavel Durov uvolen s posta gendirektora 'VKontakte'." RBK. Retrieved October 11, 2018, from http://top.rbc.ru/economics/21/04/2014/919473.shtml

43. RBK. (2013, December 9). "S.Mironyuk – kollektivu RIA 'Novosti': S nami postupili nespravedlivo." Retrieved October 11, 2018, from http://top.rbc.ru/society/09/12/2013/893728.shtml; Lenta.ru. (2013, December 19). "Putin ob"yasnil naznachenie Kiseleva glavoy 'Rossii segodnya'." Retrieved October 11, 2018, from https://lenta.ru/news/2013/12/19/patriotic/

44. Andreeva, N. (2012, February 12). "Rassredotochilsya. Soratniki novogo zamglavy administratsii prezidenta Volodina zanimayut krupnye posty." *Novaya Gazeta.* Retrieved October 11, 2018, from https://www.novayagazeta.ru/articles/2012/02/12/48190-rassredotochilsya-soratniki-novogo-zamglavy-administratsii-prezidenta-volodina-zanimayut-krupnye-posty

45. Meduza. (2014, December 26). "'Shaltay-Boltay' ulichil Kristinu Potupchik v maskirovke pod byvshego press-sekretarya Naval'nogo." Retrieved October 11, 2018, from https://meduza.io/news/2014/12/26/shaltay-boltay-ulichil-kristinu-potupchik-v-maskirovke-pod-byvshego-press-sekretarya-navalnogo

46. The term translates literally to "defenders" but could also be translated as "conservators."

47. Gamson, W. A. (1992). *Talking Politics.* Cambridge University Press; Goffman, E. (1986). *Frame Analysis: An Essay on the Organization of Experience.* Northeastern University Press.

48. Polletta, F., and Jasper, J. M. (2001). "Collective Identity and Social Movements." *Annual Review of Sociology,* 27(1), 283–305. https://doi.org/10.1146/annurev.soc.27.1.283

49. Some 97 percent of her reports mention Putin; 96 percent of the reports talked about war; 98 percent mention the opposition; 96.5 percent mention Navalny; 52 percent mention Nemtsov; 27 percent mention Mikhail Khodorkovsky; 86 percent mention Ukraine; 60 percent mention Europe; 57 percent mention the United States; 56 percent mention Crimea; 54 percent mention sanctions; 33 percent mention Donbas; and 31 percent mention Novorossia.

50. Amos, H. (2014, December 15). "Russian Ruble Crashes to World's Worst-Performing Currency." *The Moscow Times.* Retrieved October 11, 2018, from http://themoscowtimes.com/articles/russian-ruble-crashes-to-worlds-worst-performing-currency-42275

3. THE RUSSIAN SPRING

1. Kchetverg.ru. (2014, April 23). "Zhitel' Lesnogo pomogal 'otvoevyvat" Krym. Eksklyuzivnoe interv'yu opolchentsa." Retrieved October 11, 2018, from http://www.kchetverg.ru/2014/04/23/zhitel-lesnogo-pomogal-otvoevyvat-krym-eksklyuzivnoe-intervyu-opolchenca/

2. Lenta.ru. (2014, February 20). "Medvedev poprosil Yanukovicha ne byt' tryapkoy." Retrieved October 11, 2018, from https://lenta.ru/news/2014/02/20/medvedev/

3. Euronews. (2014, February 20). "Dozens killed in Kyiv as Ukraine 'truce' shattered." Retrieved October 11, 2018, from https://www.euronews.com/2014/02/20/ukraine-death-toll-rises-as-protesters-retake-maida

4. BBC News. (2014, February 26). "V Simferopole proizoshli stolknoveniya pered Radoy." Retrieved October 11, 2018, from https://www.bbc.com/russian/international/2014/02/140226_ukraine_crimea_tensions

5. Bigmir.net. (2014, February 28). "Zakhvat Rady Kryma i novyy Kabmin. Khronika 27 fevralya." Retrieved October 11, 2018, from http://news.bigmir.net/ukraine/796985-Zahvat-Rady-Kryma-i-novyj-Kabmin--Hronika-27-fevralja; NTV. (2014, February 27). "Vooruzhennye lyudi zakhvatili zdaniya parlamenta i pravitel'stva Kryma." Retrieved October 11, 2018, from https://www.ntv.ru/novosti/848321/?fb

6. NTV. (2014, February 28). "Vooruzhennye lyudi v voennoy forme zablokirovali aeroport Simferopolya." Retrieved October 11, 2018, from https://www.ntv.ru/novosti/848838/?fb

7. Blokpost Sevastopol'. (n.d.). Retrieved October 11, 2018, from https://www.blokpostsevastopol.ru/

8. Nightwolves. (2014, March 31). "Khirurg: 'My gotovili' k zatyazhnoy voyne s banderovtsami, gotovilis' k osade'." Retrieved October 11, 2018, from http://www.nightwolves.ru/rm/news/1639/

9. Author interview with Roland Oliphant, 6 October 2017.

10. Varlamov, I. (2014, March 4). "Situatsiya v Krymu, chast' 1 – Varlamov.ru." Retrieved October 11, 2018, from https://varlamov.ru/1017094.html

11. ZN.ua. (2014, March 4). "Putin zayavil, chto v Krymu deystvuyut ne rossiyskie voyska, a mestnye sily samooborony." Retrieved October 11, 2018, from https://zn.ua/POLITICS/putin-zayavil-chto-v-krymu-deystvuyut-ne-rossiyskie-voyska-a-mestnye-sily-samooborony-140331_.html

12. Shevchenko, V. (2014, March 11). "'Little green men' or 'Russian invaders'?" BBC News. Retrieved from https://www.bbc.com/news/world-europe-26532154

13. Oliphant, R. (2014, March 16). "Crimeans Vote Peacefully in Referendum, But Have Little Choice." *The Telegraph*. Retrieved from https://www.telegraph.co.uk/news/worldnews/europe/ukraine/10701676/Crimeans-vote-peacefully-in-referendum-but-have-little-choice.html

14. BBC News. (2005, April 25). "Putin deplores collapse of USSR." Retrieved from http://news.bbc.co.uk/2/hi/4480745.stm; Putin, V. (2007, February 10). Speech and the Following Discussion at the Munich Conference on Security Policy. Retrieved October 11, 2018, from http://en.kremlin.ru/events/president/transcripts/24034

15. Rodina's key figures were, however, coopted by the Kremlin itself. Dmitrii Rogozin was appointed ambassador to the EU and NATO, before being

made deputy prime minister in charge of the military–industrial complex. Sergei Glaz'ev spent a number of years in the political wilderness but was made an economic adviser to Putin after his reelection in 2012, pushing a *dirigiste* agenda.

16. Other nationalist leaders arrested at the time included Dmitrii Rumiantsev, Sergei Korotkikh and Nikita Tikhonov.
17. Verkhovskiy, A. (2015, December). "Natsional-radikaly ot prezidenstva Medvedeva do voyny v Donbasse." *Kontrapunkt.* Retrieved October 26, 2018, from http://www.counter-point.org/wp-content/uploads/2015/12/verkhovsky_counterpoint2.pdf
18. Prokopenko, P., Davidyak, S., and Shtykaleva, V. (2013, October 17). "Politsiya i sotrudniki FMS provodyat v Moskve reydy po vyyavleniyu nezakonnykh migrantov."TVC. Retrieved October 11, 2018, from http://www.tvc.ru/news/show/id/19253
19. The one exception was the Communist Party candidate Ivan Mel'nikov.
20. Polit.ru. (2013, August 24). "Naval'nyy zapretit v stolitse lezginku i razreshit gey-parady." Retrieved October 11, 2018, from http://polit.ru/news/2013/08/24/navalny/
21. Putin, V. (2014, March 18). "Obrashchenie Prezidenta Rossiyskoy Federatsii." Retrieved October 11, 2018, from http://kremlin.ru/events/president/news/20603
22. Some of it was being heard by professional historians for the first time, too, and Putin has been accused of taking liberties with the historical record.
23. In July 2013, Ukraine was mentioned in some 35 percent of posts, up from only 3 percent in June.
24. Mentions of Ukraine grew from 44 percent of posts in November 2013 to 67 percent in January 2014. Attention to Europe and the US also spiked in early 2014, to peaks of 62 percent and 39 percent, respectively. It was Ukraine, however, that was the key focus of attention.
25. At the same time that attention to Ukraine spiked, so did discussion of gays (37 percent of posts), 'liberal values' (18 percent of posts) and fascism (41 percent of posts).
26. Kchetverg.ru. (2014, April 23). "Zhitel' Lesnogo pomogal 'otvoevyvat'" Krym. Eksklyuzivnoe interv'yu opolchentsa." Retrieved October 11, 2018, from http://www.kchetverg.ru/2014/04/23/zhitel-lesnogo-pomogal-otvoevyvat-krym-eksklyuzivnoe-intervyu-opolchenca/
27. May, Yu. (2014, April 10). "Turchinov poobeshchal ne arestovyvat' zakhvatchikov SBU v Luganske." Vesti. Retrieved October 11, 2018, from https://vesti-ukr.com/donbass/46797-turchinov-poobewal-ne-arestovyvat-zahvatchikov-sbu-v-luganske
28. Fakty. (2014, April 18). "Rossiyskie spetsnazovtsy rasstrelivali nas iz avtomatov prakticheski v upor." Retrieved October 11, 2018, from https://fakty.ua/180361-rossijskie-specnazovcy-rasstrelivali-nas-iz-avtomatov-kalashnikova-prakticheski-v-upor; Vesti. (2014, April 13). "V Slavyanske nachalas' Antiterroristicheskaya operatsiya." Retrieved October 11, 2018, from https://vesti-ukr.com/donbass/47186-v-slavjanske-nachalas-antiterroristicheskaja-operacija
29. "'Vezhlivye lyudi'v Luganske boyatsya fotokamer i ne znayut, chego khotyat." (n.d.). Retrieved October 11, 2018, from http://blognews/307982-vezhlivye-lyudi-v-luganske-boyatsya-fotokamer-i-ne-znayut-chego-hotyat.html

30. TASS. (2014, April 16). "Zdanie Donetskogo gorsoveta zakhvatili aktivisty khar'kovskoy organizatsii 'Oplot'." Retrieved October 11, 2018, from https://tass.ru/mezhdunarodnaya-panorama/1125050

31. Novikova, G. (2014, April 17). "Vezhlivye lyudi prishli v Donetskiy aeroport." *Komsomol'skaya Pravda v Ukraine*. Retrieved October 11, 2018, from https://kp.ua/politics/448909-vezhlyvye-luidy-pryshly-v-donetskyi-aeroport

32. Balinskiy, V., Vesilyk, Yu., Gerasimova, T., Dibrov, S., Zaporozhets, V., Ivashkina, V., ... Shtekel', L. (2014, June 26). "Khronologiya sobytiy v Odesse 2 maya 2014-go goda (chast' 1)." Taimer. Retrieved October 11, 2018, from http://timer-odessa.net/statji/hronologiya_sobitiy_v_odesse_2_maya_214_go_goda_chast_1_219.html

33. Radio Svoboda. (2014, April 17). "Putin: v Krymu deystvovali rossiyskie voennye." Retrieved October 11, 2018, from https://www.svoboda.org/a/25352506.html

34. Putin, V. (2015, December 17). "Bol'shaya press-konferentsiya Vladimira Putina." Retrieved October 11, 2018, from http://kremlin.ru/events/president/news/50971; Khomami, N., and Walker, S. (2015, December 17). "Vladimir Putin Press Conference: 'Russian military personnel were in Ukraine'—as it happened." *The Guardian*. Retrieved from https://www.theguardian.com/world/live/2015/dec/17/vladimir-putins-annual-press-conference-live

35. Kireev, Yu. (2014, June 4). "Komanduyushchiy Soprotivleniem Donetskoy narodnoy respubliki Igor' Strelkov." *Moskovskii Komsomolets*. Retrieved October 11, 2018, from https://www.mk.ru/editions/daily/2014/06/04/komanduyushhiy-soprotivleniem-doneckoy-narodnoy-respubliki-igor-strelkov.html; Vinogradov, D. (2014, June 5). "Boevye zaslugi: kto nauchil voevat' Igorya Strelkova." SVPressa. Retrieved October 11, 2018, from http://svpressa.ru/society/article/89194/

36. Ponomarev, A. (2014, May 14). "Mylovary, emememshchiki, pevtsy. Kto vozglavil opolchentsev yugo-vostoka Ukrainy?" Slon.ru. Retrieved October 11, 2018, from http://slon.ru/world/kto_vse_eti_dyudi_spisok_novykh_upravlentsev_ukrainy-1097871.xhtml

37. Glavred. (2014, May 17). "Stsenarii dlya Kryma i Donbassa gotovila odna komanda – 'prem'er' separatistov." Retrieved October 11, 2018, from https://glavred.info/politics/279802-scenarii-dlya-kryma-i-donbassa-gotovila-odna-komanda-premer-separatistov.html

38. RIA Novosti. (2014, May 16). "'Vezhlivye lyudi' kak novyy obraz Rossiyskoy armii." Retrieved October 11, 2018, from https://ria.ru/defense_safety/20140516/1007988002.html

39. *Pravda*. "Boroday: Na Donbasse povoevali ot 30 do 50 tysyach rossiyan." (2015, August 27). Retrieved October 11, 2018, from http://www.pravda.com.ua/rus/news/2015/08/27/7079232/

40. Walker, S., and Grytsenko, O. (2015, January 21). "Ukraine Forces Admit Loss of Donetsk Airport to Rebels." *The Guardian*. Retrieved from https://www.theguardian.com/world/2015/jan/21/russia-ukraine-war-fighting-east

41. Petrovskaya, I. (2014, July 17). "TV, ledenyashchee dushu." *Novaya Gazeta*. Retrieved October 11, 2018, from https://www.novayagazeta.ru/articles/2014/07/17/60385-tv-ledenyaschee-dushu; Ponomarev, A. (2014,

July 14). "Zhurnalisty ne nashli podtverzhdenie syuzhetu 'Pervogo kanala' o raspyatom v Slavyanske rebenke." Slon.ru. Retrieved October 11, 2018, from http://slon.ru/fast/russia/zhurnalisty-ne-nashli-podtverzhdeniya-syuzhetu-pervogo-kanala-o-raspyatom-v-slavyanske-rebenke-1126851.xhtml

42. Pervyy kanal. (2014, December 21). "Zhurnalisty Pervogo otvechayut na obvineniya vo lzhi v svyazi s syuzhetom pro ubiystvo rebenka v Slavyanske." Retrieved October 11, 2018, from https://www.1tv.ru/news/2014-12-21/31502-zhurnalisty_pervogo_otvechayut_na_obvineniya_vo_lzhi_v_svyazi_s_syuzhetom_pro_ubiystvo_rebenka_v_slavyanske

43. Bigmir.net. (2014, November 27). "Chetvert' rossiyan uvereny, chto v Ukraine est' voyska RF – opros." Retrieved October 11, 2018, from http://news.bigmir.net/ukraine/861538-Chetvert-rossiyan-yvereni-chto-v-Ykraine-est-voiska-RF--opros

44. 5.ua. (2015, May 20). "Tsar'ov ofitsiyno viznav krakh 'proektu Novorosiya'." Retrieved October 11, 2018, from https://www.5.ua/ato-na-shodi/tsarov-ofitsiino-vyznav-krakh-proektu-novorosiia-81024.html

45. To try to gauge the effect that the Ukraine crisis was having on the coherence of the nationalist community, we ran a linguistic analysis of all of the posts across the sixteen community pages in our dataset and measured the mathematical divergence in terms of the words used. This divergence can range from 0 (no divergence, i.e., everyone writing about the same thing using the same words) to 1 (total divergence, with no overlap in vocabulary whatsoever). When we first "meet" our groups in December 2011, the level of divergence is high (0.79). It remains relatively high (fluctuating from 0.44 to 0.76) until about May 2013, the same time that the nationalists begin worrying in earnest about the prospect of Ukraine's association agreement with the EU. After that, the online nationalist discussion becomes more and more homogenous, falling to a divergence of 0.26 in August 2013, and to a divergence of below 0.1 by June 2014. It remains at that remarkably low level until May 2015, when Tsarev drops his bomb and divergence spikes to 0.51. Divergence falls again, but then begins an inexorable upward climb.

46. Regnum. (2016, April 6). "MGB DNR provodit 'zachistku' vysshego rukovodstva Donetska." Retrieved October 11, 2018, from https://regnum.ru/news/polit/2112967.html; Segodnya. (2016, April 20). "Rukovoditeley 'DNR' i 'LNR' zhdet zachistka – Gritsak." Retrieved October 11, 2018, from https://www.segodnya.ua/regions/donetsk/rukovoditeley-dnr-i-lnr-zhdet-zachistka-gricak-709425.html; Snegirev, D. (2015, January 3). "Chistki u separatistov: kto i pochemu 'ubiraet' glavarey boevikov?" Gordon. Retrieved October 11, 2018, from https://gordonua.com/day_question/pochemu-ubili-betmena.html

47. Vashchenko, V. (2017, July 5). "Organizator 'Russkikh marshey' zaderzhan FSB." Gazeta.ru. Retrieved October 11, 2018, from https://www.gazeta.ru/social/2017/07/05/10774934.shtml; Meduza. (2017, September 23). "Lider 'Khristianskogo gosudarstva' Aleksandr Kalinin arestovan." Retrieved October 11, 2018, from https://meduza.io/news/2017/09/23/lider-hristianskogo-gosudarstva-aleksandr-kalinin-arestovan

48. Eysmont, M. (2015, March 5). "Sindrom opolchentsa." Snob. Retrieved October 11, 2018, from https://snob.ru/selected/entry/89001. Reproduced with permission of the International Media Project "Snob" (snob.ru).

49. "Grebtsov Igor Aleksandrovich." (n.d.). Retrieved October 11, 2018, from http://gruz200.net/?n=38941

4. THE GATHERER OF LANDS

1. When Yanukovych fled to Russia, Ukrainian citizens opened his palatial presidential compound to the public, exposing the preposterous luxury in which the president of a relatively poor country lived. For some pictures taken onsite see: *The Telegraph*. "In Pictures: Inside the Palace Yanukovych Didn't Want Ukraine to See." (2014, February 27). Retrieved from https://www.telegraph.co.uk/news/worldnews/europe/ukraine/10656023/In-pictures-Inside-the-palace-Yanukovych-didnt-want-Ukraine-to-see.html

2. Hutchings, S., and Szostek, J. (2016). "Dominant Narratives in Russian Political and Media Discourse During the Ukraine Crisis." In Pikulicka-Wilczewska, A., and Sakwa, R. (2016). "Ukraine and Russia: People, Politics, Propaganda and Perspectives." E-International Relations. Retrieved from http://www.e-ir.info/wp-content/uploads/2015/03/Ukraine-and-Russia-E-IR.pdf; Teper, Y. (2015). "Official Russian Identity Discourse in Light of the Annexation of Crimea: National or Imperial?" *Post-Soviet Affairs*, 32(4), 378–396; Hansen, F. S. (2014). "Framing Yourself into a Corner: Russia, Crimea, and the Minimal Action Space." *European Security*, 24(1), 141–158.

3. Medvedev, S. (2014). "Russkiy resentiment." Retrieved October 12, 2018, from http://www.strana-oz.ru/2014/6/russkiy-resentiment

4. Borodina, A. (2014, July 3). "Televizor Olimpiady i Ukrainy: rekordy propagandy." Forbes. Retrieved October 12, 2018, from http://www.forbes.ru/mneniya-opinion/konkurentsiya/261539-televizor-olimpiady-i-ukrainy-rekordy-propagandy

5. Sobolev, S. (2014, November 20). "TNS zafiksirovala istoricheskiy rekord interesa k telenovostyam." RBK. Retrieved October 12, 2018, from http://top.rbc.ru/technology_and_media/20/11/2014/546dff7bcbb20f48e98df5fa

6. Cottiero, C., Kucharski, K., Olimpieva, E., and Orttung, R. W. (2015). "War of Words: The Impact of Russian State Television on the Russian Internet." *Nationalities Papers*, 43(4), 533–555.

7. Rogov, K. (2015). "'Krymskiy sindrom': mekhanizmy avtoritarnoy mobilizatsii." *Kontrapunkt*. Retrieved October 12, 2018, from http://www.counter-point.org/%D0%BA%D1%80%D1%8B%D0%BC%D1%81%D0%BA%D0%B8%D0%B9-%D1%81%D0%B8%D0%BD%D0%B4%D1%80%D0%BE%D0%BC/

8. Verkhovskiy, A. (2015, December). "Natsional-radikaly ot prezidenstva Medvedeva do voyny v Donbasse." *Kontrapunkt*. Retrieved October 26, 2018; from http://www.counter-point.org/wp-content/uploads/2015/12/verkhovsky_counterpoint2.pdf

9. Solnick, S. L. (1998). *Stealing the State: Control and Collapse in Soviet Institutions*. Harvard University Press.

10. See for example: Groenendyk, E. (2011). "Current Emotion Research in Political Science: How Emotions Help Democracy Overcome its Collective Action Problem." *Emotion Review*, 3(4), 455–463; Neuman, W.

R., Marcus, G. E., Crigler, A. N., and MacKuen, M. (eds). (2007). *The Affect Effect: Dynamics of Emotion in Political Thinking and Behavior.* University of Chicago Press; Mercer, J. (2010). *Reputation and International Politics.* Cornell University Press; Petersen, R. D. (2002). *Understanding Ethnic Violence: Fear, Hatred, and Resentment in Twentieth-Century Eastern Europe.* Cambridge University Press; Pearlman, W. (2013). "Emotions and the Microfoundations of the Arab Uprisings." *Perspectives on Politics,* 11(2), 387–409.

11. Jasper, J. M. (2011). "Emotions and Social Movements: Twenty Years of Theory and Research." *Annual Review of Sociology,* 37, 285–303; Conover, P. J., and Feldman, S. (1986). "Emotional Reactions to the Economy: I'm mad as hell and I'm not going to take it anymore." *American Journal of Political Science,* 30(1), 50–78.

12. See Zajonc, R. B. (1980). "Feeling and Thinking: Preferences Need No Inferences." *American Psychologist,* 35(2), 151.

13. Cassino, D., and Lodge, M. (2007). "The Primacy of Affect in Political Evaluations." In Neuman, Marcus, Crigler, and MacKuen, (eds). (2007). *The Affect Effect.* University of Chicago Press. 101–123.

14. Lodge, M., McGraw, K. M., and Stroh, P. (1989). "An Impression-driven Model of Candidate Evaluation." *American Political Science Review,* 83(2), 399–419; McGraw, K. M., Lodge, M., and Stroh, P. (1990). "On-line Processing in Candidate Evaluation: The Effects of Issue Order, Issue Importance, and Sophistication." *Political Behavior,* 12(1), 41–58.

15. See Ibid. This is what political scientists and psychologists call the "online processing model."

16. Zajonc (1980). "Feeling and Thinking."

17. MacKuen, M., Marcus, G. E., Neuman, W. R., and Keele, L. (2007). "The Third Way: The Theory of Affective Intelligence and American Democracy." In Neuman, Marcus, Crigler, and MacKuen, (eds). (2007). *The Affect Effect.* University of Chicago Press. 124–151.

18. There is some very careful political science research demonstrating this. See for example Young, L. E. (2016). "The Psychology of Repression and Dissent in Autocracy." Columbia University. https://doi.org/10.7916/D86110HB

19. Rubenstein, J. (2016). *The Last Days of Stalin.* Yale University Press. Chapter 4.

20. Alexievich, S. (2016). *Secondhand Time: The Last of the Soviets.* Random House Publishing Group.

21. Arendt, H. (1973). *The Origins of Totalitarianism.* Houghton Mifflin Harcourt, Preface to the Third Edition. Cited in Baehr, P. (2007). "The 'Masses' in Hannah Arendt's Theory of Totalitarianism." *The Good Society,* 16(2), 12–18.

22. Arendt (1973). *The Origins of Totalitarianism.* 353. Cited in Canovan, M. (1994). *Hannah Arendt: A Reinterpretation of Her Political Thought.* Cambridge University Press. 55.

23. Canovan. (1994). *Hannah Arendt.* 56. Arendt's account, of course, is more theoretical than empirical. Though she does rely heavily on eyewitnesses and first-person accounts, often collected at the Nuremberg Trials, much

of her account is at odds with empirical work conducted since on voting patterns and support for the Nazis. Rather than appealing to an undifferentiated mass, support for the NSDAP was in fact highly structured with clear variation across social classes, religion and regions, though patterns of support did vary over time. See: Childers, T. (1976). "The Social Bases of the National Socialist Vote." *Journal of Contemporary History*, 11 (4), 17–42.

24. For details, see: Greene, S. A., and Robertson, G. B. (2018). "The Co-Construction of Authoritarianism: Emotional Engagement and Politics in Russia after Crimea." Available at SSRN: https://papers.ssrn.com/sol3/papers.cfm?abstract_id=3289134

25. Volkov, D., and Goncharov, S. (2014). "Rossiiskii media-landshaft: Televidenie, pressa, internet." Levada-Center.

26. In each round 43 percent said Russian ethnicity was a very important part of their personal identity. Orthodox Christianity was very important to 25 percent before Crimea and 27 percent after—proportions that are statistically indistinguishable given the survey margin of error.

27. Formally in sociology this field is known as interaction ritual theory. See Collins, R. (2004). *Interaction Ritual Chains*. Princeton University Press.

28. A good modern translation is Durkheim, É., and Swain, J. W. (2008). *The Elementary Forms of Religious Life: A Study in Religious Sociology*. Scholar's Choice.

29. Durkheim, É. (1965). *The Elementary Forms of Religious Life*. Free Press. 213.

30. Wiltermuth, S. S., and Heath, C. (2009). "Synchrony and Cooperation." *Psychological Science*, 20(1), 1–5.

31. Bonilla, Y., and Rosa, J. (2015). "# Ferguson: Digital Protest, Hashtag Ethnography, and the Racial Politics of Social Media in the United States." *American Ethnologist*, 42(1), 4–17; see also González-Bailón, S., Borge-Holthoefer, J., and Moreno, Y. (2013). "Broadcasters and Hidden Influentials in Online Protest Diffusion." *American Behavioral Scientist*, 57(7), 943–965.

32. Ipsos MORI Political Monitor. (n.d.). Untitled. Retrieved from https://www.ipsos.com/sites/default/files/migrations/en-uk/files/Assets/Docs/Polls/margaret-thatcher-poll-rating-trends.pdf

33. Gallup Inc. (n.d.). Presidential Approval Ratings—George W. Bush. Retrieved October 12, 2018, from https://news.gallup.com/poll/116500/Presidential-Approval-Ratings-George-Bush.aspx

34. Levada-Tsentr. (n.d.). Retrieved October 12, 2018, from http://www.levada.ru/

35. Tharoor, I. (2014, March 19). "It's Not Just Putin: Russia's Obsession With Crimea Is Centuries-Old." *Time*. Retrieved October 12, 2018, from http://time.com/29651/putin-crimea-russia-annexation/

36. Tharoor, I. (2014, December 4). "Why Putin says Crimea is Russia's 'Temple Mount'." *The Washington Post*. Retrieved October 12, 2018, from https://www.washingtonpost.com/news/worldviews/wp/2014/12/04/why-putin-says-crimea-is-russias-temple-mount/

37. Hermanowicz, J. C., and Morgan, H. P. (1999). "Ritualizing the Routine: Collective Identity Affirmation." *Sociological Forum*, 14(2), 197–214.

38. See Madsen, D., and Snow, P. G. (1991). *The Charismatic Bond: Political Behavior in Time of Crisis*. Harvard University Press. Chapter 1.

5. PUTIN'S GREENGROCERS

1. Havel Václav. (2018). "The Power of the Powerless." East European Politics and Societies, 32(2), 353–408.
2. Mandler, P. (2013). *Return from the Natives: How Margaret Mead Won the Second World War and Lost the Cold War*. Yale University Press. xii.
3. Ibid. 45–46; Mead, M., and Métraux, R. (eds). (2000). *The Study of Culture at a Distance* (Vol. 1). Berghahn Books.
4. Mead, M., Gorer, G., and Rickman, J. (2001). *Russian Culture* (Vol. 3). Berghahn Books. 138.
5. Mandler. (2013). *Return from the Natives*. Chapter 4.
6. Ibid. 232.
7. Mead, Gorer, and Rickman. (2001). *Russian Culture*. 144.
8. Ibid. 148.
9. Christal, R. E. (1992). "Author's Note on 'Recurrent Personality Factors Based on Trait Ratings'." *Journal of Personality*, 60(2), 221–224.
10. The terms used in the original Tupes and Christal were Culture, Dependability, Extraversion, Agreeableness and Emotional Stability, though each of the contemporary terms was included in their description of the traits. See Tupes, E. C., and Christal, R. E. (1961). "'Recurrent Personality Factors Based on Trait Ratings', Technical Report ASD-TR-61-97." Personnel Laboratory, Aeronautical Systems Division (AFSC).
11. Goldberg, L. R. (1981). "Language and Individual Differences: The Search for Universals in Personality Lexicons." *Review of Personality and Social Psychology*, 2(1), 141–165.
12. Bouchard, T. J. (1994). "Genes, Environment, and Personality." *Science-AAAS-Weekly Paper Edition*, 264(5166), 1700–1701.
13. DeYoung, C. G. (2010). "Personality Neuroscience and the Biology of Traits." *Social and Personality Psychology Compass*, 4(12), 1165–1180.
14. Friedman, H. S., Tucker, J. S., Tomlinson-Keasey, C., Schwartz, J. E., Wingard, D. L., and Criqui, M. H. (1993). "Does Childhood Personality Predict Longevity?" *Journal of Personality and Social Psychology*, 65(1), 176–185. Cited in Roberts, B. W., Kuncel, N. R., Shiner, R., Caspi, A., and Goldberg, L. R. (2007). "The Power of Personality: The Comparative Validity of Personality Traits, Socioeconomic Status, and Cognitive Ability for Predicting Important Life Outcomes." *Perspectives on Psychological Science*, 2(4), 313–345.
15. Weiss, A., and Costa Jr, P. T. (2005). "Domain and Facet Personality Predictors of All-cause Mortality Among Medicare Patients Aged 65 to 100." *Psychosomatic Medicine*, 67(5), 724–733. Cited in Roberts et al. (2007). "The Power of Personality."
16. Bogg, T., and Roberts, B. W. (2004). "Conscientiousness and Health-related Behaviors: A Meta-analysis of the Leading Behavioral Contributors to Mortality." *Psychological Bulletin*, 130(6), 887; Hampson, S. E., Andrews, J. A., Barckley, M., Lichtenstein, E., and Lee, M. E. (2000). "Conscientiousness, Perceived Risk, and Risk-reduction Behaviors: A Preliminary Study." *Health Psychology*, 19(5), 496. Cited in Ozer, D. J.,

and Benet-Martinez, V. (2006). "Personality and the Prediction of Consequential Outcomes." *Annual Review of Psychology*, 57, 401–421.

17. Caspi, A., Roberts, B. W., Pervin, L. A., and John, O. P. (1990). "Personality Continuity and Change Across the Life Course." In Pervin, L. A. (1990). *Handbook of Personality: Theory and Research*. Vol. 2. Guilford Publications. 300–326; McCrae, R. R., and Costa, P. T. (1984). *Emerging Lives, Enduring Dispositions: Personality in Adulthood*. Little, Brown and Company; Roberts, B. W., and Mroczek, D. (2008). "Personality Trait Change in Adulthood." *Current Directions in Psychological Science*, 17(1), 31–35.

18. Danner, D. D., Snowdon, D. A., and Friesen, W. V. (2001). "Positive Emotions in Early Life and Longevity: Findings from the Nun Study." *Journal of Personality and Social Psychology*, 80(5), 804. Cited in Roberts et al. (2007). "The Power of Personality."

19. Roberts et al. (2007). "The Power of Personality." 322.

20. Scollon, C. N., and Diener, E. (2006). "Love, Work, and Changes in Extraversion and Neuroticism Over Time." *Journal of Personality and Social Psychology*, 91(6), 1152–1165.

21. Roberts et al. (2007). "The Power of Personality."

22. Robins, R. W., Caspi, A., and Moffitt, T. E. (2002). "It's Not Just Who You're With, It's Who You Are: Personality and Relationship Experiences Across Multiple Relationships." *Journal of Personality*, 70(6), 925–964. https://doi.org/10.1111/1467-6494.05028. Cited in Roberts et al. (2007). "The Power of Personality."

23. Ozer and Benet-Martinez. (2006). "Personality and the Prediction of Consequential Outcomes."

24. For a seminal article on the importance of framing see Druckman, J. N. (2004). "Political Preference Formation: Competition, Deliberation, and the (Ir)relevance of Framing Effects." *American Political Science Review*, 98(4), 671–686. https://doi.org/10.1017/S0003055404041413

25. See Iyengar, S., and Hahn, K. S. (2009). "Red Media, Blue Media: Evidence of Ideological Selectivity in Media Use." *Journal of Communication*, 59(1), 19–39. https://doi.org/10.1111/j.1460-2466.2008.01402.x and Hopkins, D. J., and Ladd, J. M. (2014). "The Consequences of Broader Media Choice: Evidence from the Expansion of Fox News." *Quarterly Journal of Political Science*, 9(1), 115–135. https://doi.org/10.1561/100.00012099

26. For more technical details of the survey and how we measured personality traits and other items see Greene, S., and Robertson, G. (2017). "Agreeable Authoritarians: Personality and Politics in Contemporary Russia." *Comparative Political Studies*, 50(13), 1802–1834. https://doi.org/10.1177/0010414016688005

27. https://www.levada.ru/

28. 31 percent of educated urbanites thought that minority protections were important for society, while 38 percent said minority protections didn't matter.

29. While 42 percent of our survey takers supported the legislation, fully 51 percent opposed it.

30. Only 10 percent said their Russian nationality was not that important to them, and 46 percent said it was a very important part of their identity. Being a citizen of the Russian state was very important to the self-conception of 40 percent, and was not that important only to 10 percent.

31. Attitudes to other foreign countries were much more moderate. Only 7 percent considered China to be an enemy of Russia (though 35 percent thought it a rival); a mere 4 percent thought Germany an enemy and only 16 percent considered it a rival.

32. Since we were running an online survey and people taking online surveys—as we all know—have short attention spans, we measured personality traits using an extremely short list of ten questions. The personality test we used is called the Ten Item Personality Inventory (TIPI) and was pioneered by Gosling, Rentfrow and Swan. See Gosling, S. D., Rentfrow, P. J., and Swann, W. B. (2003). "A Very Brief Measure of the Big-Five Personality Domains." *Journal of Research in Personality*, 37(6), 504–528. https://doi. org/10.1016/S0092-6566(03)00046-1. Though it is short, research suggests that the TIPI performs as well as longer, more sophisticated instruments and it has been extensively used in political science applications where a host of other issues in addition to personality data are examined. To the extent that using such a short personality inventory is a problem from a scientific perspective, it ought to underestimate the size of the personality effects. See Carney, D. R., Jost, J. T., Gosling, S. D., and Potter, J. (2008). "The Secret Lives of Liberals and Conservatives: Personality Profiles, Interaction Styles, and the Things They Leave Behind." *Political Psychology*, 29(6), 807–840. https://doi.org/10.1111/j.1467-9221.2008.00668.x and Credé, M., Harms, P., Niehorster, S., and Gaye-Valentine, A. (2012). "An Evaluation of the Consequences of Using Short Measures of the Big Five Personality Traits." *Journal of Personality and Social Psychology*, 102(4), 874–888. https://doi.org/10.1037/a0027403. The questions are set up so that agreeing to the description means opposite things in each case, reducing errors in the case of people who just like to agree or disagree with everything.

33. Here we define a high score as being one standard deviation above the mean and a low score as being one standard deviation below the mean.

34. Ormel, J., Riese, H., and Rosmalen, J. G. M. (2012). "Interpreting Neuroticism Scores Across the Adult Life Course: Immutable or Experience-Dependent Set Points of Negative Affect?" *Clinical Psychology Review*, 32(1), 71–79. https://doi.org/10.1016/j.cpr.2011.10.004

35. For more details on the peripheral nature of agreeableness to politics in the existing research see Greene and Robertson. (2017). "Agreeable Authoritarians."

36. Meduza. (2018, March 15). "Ideal'naya Rossiya glazami chitateley 'Meduzy'. V odnoy kartinke." Retrieved October 12, 2018, from https:// meduza.io/short/2018/03/15/idealnaya-rossiya-glazami-chitateley-meduzy-v-odnoy-kartinke

37. For more details see Hale, H. E. (2005). *Why Not Parties in Russia? Democracy, Federalism, and the State.* Cambridge University Press; Hanson, S. E. (2010). *Post-Imperial Democracies: Ideology and Party Formation in Third Republic France, Weimar Germany, and Post-Soviet Russia.* Cambridge University Press; and Gel'man, V. (2015). *Authoritarian Russia: Analyzing Post-Soviet Regime Changes.* University of Pittsburgh Press.

38. Dubin B. V. (2011). *Rossiya nulevykh: politicheskaya kul'tura — istoricheskaya pamyat' — povsednevnaya zhizn'.* Rosspen. Retrieved from http://ru.b-ok. org/book/2381358/10d9b2

39. Mickiewicz, E. P. (2014). *No Illusions: The Voices of Russia's Future Leaders.* Oxford University Press. 88–89.
40. Mondak, J. J. (2010). *Personality and the Foundations of Political Behavior.* Cambridge University Press. 58.
41. Kieras, J. E., Tobin, R. M., Graziano, W. G., and Rothbart, M. K. (2005). "You Can't Always Get What You Want: Effortful Control and Children's Responses to Undesirable Gifts." *Psychological Science,* 16(5), 391–396. https://doi.org/10.1111/j.0956-7976.2005.01546.x
42. Graziano, W. G., Bruce, J., Sheese, B. E., and Tobin, R. M. (2007). "Attraction, Personality, and Prejudice: Liking None of the People Most of the Time." *Journal of Personality and Social Psychology,* 93(4), 565–582. https://doi.org/10.1037/0022-3514.93.4.565

6. RUSSIA AT WAR

1. *Novaya Gazeta.* (2014, March 15). "V Moskve zavershilsya 'Marsh mira' (KhRONIKA)." Retrieved October 12, 2018, from https://www.novaya-gazeta.ru/news/2014/03/15/97994-v-moskve-zavershilsya-171-marsh-mira-187-hronika
2. Rustamova, F., and Volkova, D. (2014, September 11). "Meriya Moskvy soglasovala oppozitsionnyy 'Marsh mira'." RBK. Retrieved October 12, 2018, from http://top.rbc.ru/politics/11/09/2014/948321.shtml
3. Rustamova, F. (2014, September 11). "'Marsh mira' v Moskve proydet pod lozungami v podderzhku Ukrainy." RBK. Retrieved October 12, 2018, from http://top.rbc.ru/politics/11/09/2014/948493.shtml
4. Kataev, D. (2014, September 20). "Boris Nemtsov o predstoyashchem 'Marshe mira': soglasovali bystro – meriya otlichno znaet, chto eto pervaya aktsiya za mnogo-mnogo mesyatsev." TV Rain. Retrieved October 12, 2018, from https://tvrain.ru/teleshow/here_and_now/boris_nemtsov_o_predstojaschem_marshe_mira_soglasovali_bystro_merija_otlichno_znaet_chto_eto_pervaja_aktsija_za_mnogo_mnogo_mesjatsev-375588/
5. BBC News. (2014, September 21). "Desyatki tysyach lyudey proshli po Moskve 'Marshem mira'." Retrieved October 12, 2018, from https://www.bbc.com/russian/russia/2014/09/140921_moscow_peace_demo.shtml
6. Kanashevich, S., and Rustamova, F. (2014, September 21). "V Moskve proydet 'Marsh mira' protiv voyny na Ukraine." RBK. Retrieved October 12, 2018, from http://top.rbc.ru/politics/21/09/2014/950310.shtml
7. Nemtsov, B., Larina, K., and Dymarskiy, V. (2015, February 27). "Vesennee vozrozhdenie: vernetsya li oppozitsiya v politicheskoe pole?" Ekho Moskvy. Retrieved October 12, 2018, from https://echo.msk.ru/programs/year2015/1500184-echo/
8. *The New Times.* (2015, March 1). "Boris Nemtsov." Retrieved October 12, 2018, from https://newtimes.ru/articles/detail/95244
9. http://vesna.today/
10. Among the highlights have been: a July 2012 law authorizing Roskomnadzor to censor internet sites; a July 2012 law requiring NGOs engaging in "political activity" and receiving foreign funding to declare themselves publicly as "foreign agents"; June 2013 laws criminalizing "propaganda of non-traditional sexual relations" and "offending the feelings of religious believers"; a June 2014 law requiring all Russians holding

dual citizenship or foreign residence permits to register; and a May 2015 law mandating a list of "undesirable organizations," work on behalf of whom in Russia would be a criminal offense.

11. Greene, S. A. (2014). "Beyond Bolotnaia: Bridging Old and New in Russia's Election Protest Movement." *Problems of Post-Communism*, 60(2), 40–52. https://doi.org/10.2753/PPC1075-8216600204

12. Some of the older, "legacy" organizations included:

   • Golos, whose name translates to "Voice" or "Vote," Russia's largest and oldest election-monitoring organization;

   • Memorial, one of Russia's oldest and largest human-rights organizations, with a particular focus on chronicling Soviet-era political repressions and human-rights violations;

   • Imprisoned Rus, a movement created by journalist Olga Romanova and other volunteers to defend the rights of wrongly accused and imprisoned citizens, including Romanova's own husband, Alexei Kozlov;

   • Parnas, the People's Freedom Party, chaired (until his death) by Nemtsov, alongside former prime minister Mikhail Kasianov, Vladimir Milov and Vladimir Ryzhkov.

   Among the newer groups were:

   • We were on Bolotnaya and will come again, a group modeled after the Zucotti Park movement that launched Occupy Wall Street, the largest online movement organization created during the 2011–12 protest wave;

   • The League of Voters, one of two Bolotnaya-era organizations created to focus specifically on the (then) upcoming March 2012 presidential elections;

   • White Ribbon of Protest, a broad online movement, whose name refers to the white ribbons that came to symbolize the Bolotnaya-era movement;

   • Citizen Observer, the second of the two organizations created to focus on the March 2012 presidential elections, with a particular emphasis on mobilizing and coordinating independent election observation volunteers.

13. Activity fell from some 1,100 interactions per day in March 2012 (the month of Putin's re-re-election) to fewer than 100 in December 2013.

14. Activity in the opposition network spiked to more than 5,300 interactions a day in early March 2014, frequently peaking above 600 interactions a day through the summer, and remaining above 200 through September, before declining again as time wore on—again, showing the "abeyance" pattern we would expect from a protest movement.

15. The number of individual users in our network grew from about 20,000 to more than 35,000 over the course of March 2014, and climbed to nearly 45,000 by the summer of 2015.

16. Participation grew still further into the fall, and some 8,200 individuals were active in the network during the September 21, 2014, Peace March, which brought 50,000 people out onto the streets of Moscow and around half as many in St. Petersburg.

17. In our (admittedly limited) dataset, 98.8 percent of those recruited in July 2014 were new, and 75.7 percent of those active in September of that year were also brand new to the broader movement.

18. Mineeva, Y. (2015, August 18). "Na severe Moskvy zhiteli blokirovali vyrubku Parka Druzhby." *Novaya Gazeta*. Retrieved October 12, 2018, from https://www.novayagazeta.ru/news/2015/08/18/114353-na-severe-moskvy-zhiteli-blokirovali-vyrubku-parka-druzhby

19. For details on the evolution of the movement, as well as current updates, see the protesters' two Facebook pages: https://www.facebook.com/groups/OboronaLevobereg and https://www.facebook.com/parkdrug

20. Mishina, V. (2016, May 19). "Po 'Druzhbe' so sluzhby." Kommersant, 4. Retrieved 28 October, 2018, from http://www.kommersant.ru/doc/2990190

21. https://www.facebook.com/ZAPARK1/

22. https://www.facebook.com/events/1685759934987983/

23. Antonova, E., Galaktionova, A., and Makutina, M. (2015, November 19). "Bunt dal'noboyshchikov: vtoruyu volnu protesta podderzhali v 24 regionakh." RBK. Retrieved October 12, 2018, from http://www.rbc.ru/politics/19/11/2015/564dd7a09a79471bb0b58dcd

24. Azar, I. (2015, February 21). "Rasserzhennye patrioty: 'Antimaydan' proshel marshem po Moskve." Meduza. Retrieved October 12, 2018, from https://meduza.io/feature/2015/02/21/rasserzhennye-patrioty

25. Greene. (2014). "Beyond Bolotnaia."

26. Meleshenko, A. (2017, May 15). "Bolee 35 tysyach moskvichey prinyali uchastie v mitingakh v podderzhku renovatsii." *Rossiiskaya Gazeta*. Retrieved October 12, 2018, from https://rg.ru/2017/05/15/reg-cfo/bolee-35-tysiach-moskvichej-priniali-uchastie-v-mitingah-v-podderzhku-renovacii.html

27. Mos.ru. (2017, June 17). "Podvedeny itogi golosovaniya po proektu renovatsii v 'Aktivnom grazhdanine' i tsentrakh gosuslug." Retrieved October 12, 2018, from https://www.mos.ru/news/item/25633073/

28. Naval'nyy, A. (2016a). "Mer i ego taynye kvartiry v Mayami." Retrieved from https://www.youtube.com/watch?v=q8GvCG0t7Fo

29. Chayka. (n.d.). Retrieved October 12, 2018, from https://chaika.navalny.com/

30. Naval'nyy, A. (2016b). "Sobaki vitse-prem'era Shuvalova letayut na chastnom samolete." Retrieved from https://www.youtube.com/watch?v=tx8ZqZtjyT4

31. Dimon.navalny. "On vam ne Dimon. Taynaya imperiya Dmitriya Medvedeva." (n.d.). Retrieved October 12, 2018, from https://dimon.navalny.com/#intro

32. Reilhac, G., Soldatkin, V., and Solovyov, D. (2017, October 17). "Russian Opposition Leader's Fraud Conviction Arbitrary, Europe's Top Rights Court Says." Reuters. Retrieved from https://uk.reuters.com/article/uk-russia-navalny-echr/russian-opposition-leaders-fraud-conviction-arbitrary-europes-top-rights-court-says-idUKKBN1CM1EY

33. https://2018.navalny.com/news/

34. Meduza. (2017, March 26). "Mitingi v rossiyskikh regionakh. Video: Aktsii protesta proshli v desyatkakh gorodov po vsey strane." Retrieved October 12, 2018, from https://meduza.io/feature/2017/03/26/mitingi-v-rossiyskih-regionah-video

35. Meduza. (2017, March 26). "V Moskve zaderzhany bolee 900 chelovek." Retrieved October 12, 2018, from https://meduza.io/news/2017/03/26/v-moskve-zaderzhany-bolee-500-chelovek; Lyaskin, N. (2017, March 26). "Glava moskovskogo otdeleniya Partii progressa popal v bol'nitsu posle zaderzhaniya." Meduza. Retrieved October 12, 2018, from https://meduza.io/news/2017/03/26/glava-moskovskogo-otdeleniya-partii-progressa-popal-v-bolnitsu-posle-zaderzhaniya

36. OVDinfo. Delo 26 marta. (n.d.). Retrieved October 12, 2018, from https://ovdinfo.org/story/delo-26-marta

37. cf Robertson, G. B. (2011). *The Politics of Protest in Hybrid Regimes: Managing Dissent in Post-Communist Russia.* Cambridge University Press.

38. In 2017, the network was averaging 62,529 communicative interactions (i.e., posts and comments, but not likes, of which there were many times the number) per month, compared to 4,255 interactions per month in 2012–15.

39. At least 9 percent of its online participants had been in Bolotnaya-era groups like the League of Voters or Citizen Observer in 2012–15, 5.7 percent had been in the anti-war movement, and another 2.6 percent had been connected with Team Navalny during that time. Given the nature of the data and the fact that it will not capture all participants, these numbers probably actually underestimate the degree of overlap.

40. Navalny's network recruited only 18.9 percent of its participants from earlier protest waves (in proportions similar to those for the anti-demolition movement).

41. Some 10.7 percent of anti-demolition members were active in the Navalny network, and some 3.5 percent of Navalny activists were also present in the anti-demolition groups.

42. Some 38 percent of those who engaged with Khodorkovsky's #Nadoel rallies in April on Twitter had previously engaged with Navalny's "Dimon" protest in March, as did 11 percent of the anti-demolition protesters and 21 percent of the Russia Day protesters in June. Whether those who engaged on Twitter actually came out into the street is another question, which we cannot answer.

43. The measure in question is what network analysts call "weighted degree."

44. The measure in question is what network analysts call "average path length."

45. These are what network analysts call the "clustering coefficient," or the gravity that each individual exerts on those around them, as well as a "triadic census" characterizing the links between all individuals, and the relative size of the largest "component" of the network.

46. On Facebook the Navalny and anti-demolition communities "clustered" around the same vocabularies with an 87 percent and 86 percent probability, respectively. We found similar results for the truckers' protests.

47. Meduza. (2017, April 28). "Vokrug shum: Naval'nogo prodolzhayut oblivat' zelenkoy." Retrieved October 12, 2018, from https://meduza.io/shapito/2017/04/28/vokrug-shum-navalnogo-prodolzhayut-oblivat-zelenkoy

48. Meduza. (2017, March 18). " 'To est' patriotov v vashem klasse net?': Direktor shkoly iz Bryanskoy oblasti beseduet s uchenikami o Naval'nom,

Putine i geopolitike. Rasshifrovka." Retrieved October 12, 2018, from https://meduza.io/feature/2017/03/18/to-est-patriotov-v-vashem-klasse-net

49. Meduza. (2015, February 21). "Politsiya otsenila chislennost' aktsii 'Antimaydana' v 35 tysyach chelovek." Retrieved October 12, 2018, from https://meduza.io/news/2015/02/21/politsiya-otsenila-chislennost-aktsii-antimaydana-v-35-tysyach-chelovek

50. Varlamov, I. (2015, February 21). "Antimaydan v Moskve." Retrieved October 12, 2018, from https://varlamov.ru/1281822.html

51. Lenta.ru. (2015, August 14). "Enteo s pravoslavnymi aktivistami razgromili vystavku v 'Manezhe'." Retrieved October 12, 2018, from https://lenta.ru/news/2015/08/14/enteomanege/

52. Interfax. "'Antimaydan' sobralsya prepyatstvovat' provedeniyu v Moskve aktsii Naval'nogo." (2017, March 22). Retrieved October 12, 2018, from https://www.interfax.ru/moscow/554749; Berg, E. (2017, May 2). "Aktivisty dvizheniya SERB — predpolagaemye napadavshie na Alekseya Naval'nogo. Kto oni takie?" Meduza. Retrieved October 12, 2018, from https://meduza.io/feature/2017/05/02/aktivisty-dvizheniya-serb-predpolagaemye-napadavshie-na-alekseya-navalnogo-kto-oni-takie

53. RIA Novosti. "Bozh'ya volya" raskololas' iz-za druzhby Enteo s uchastnitsey Pussy Riot." (2017, October 3). Retrieved October 12, 2018, from https://ria.ru/religion/20171003/1506117881.html; Abrikosovo, T. (2017, October 3). "V 'Bozh'ey vole' zayavili, chto Enteo izgnan za svyatotatstvo." Life.ru. Retrieved October 12, 2018, from https://life.ru/t/%D0%BD%D0%BE%D0%B2%D0%BE%D1%81%D1%82%D0%B8/1048791/v_bozhiei_volie_zaiavili_chto_entieo_izghnan_za_sviatotatstvo

54. VK.com. Wall posts. (2017, June 9). Retrieved October 12, 2018, from https://vk.com/wall-55284725_470527

55. Naval'nyy, A. (2017, June 11). "Mitingi 12 iyunya: ob"yasnyayu na utochkakh." Retrieved October 12, 2018, from https://navalny.com/p/5425/

7. RUSSIA'S PUTIN

1. Gereykhanova, A. (2017, January 9). "Pered Oktyabr'skoy revolyutsiey Nikolay II nabiraet podpischikov." URA. Retrieved October 12, 2018, from https://ura.news/articles/1036269937

2. Anderson, J. (2006). "The Chekist Takeover of the Russian State." *International Journal of Intelligence and CounterIntelligence*, 19(2), 237–288. https://doi.org/10.1080/08850600500483699; *The Economist*. (2007, August 23). "The Making of a Neo-KGB State." Retrieved from https://www.economist.com/briefing/2007/08/23/the-making-of-a-neo-kgb-state; Bandow, D. (2014, December 26). "Lubyanka Runs the New Russia, Much Like the Old Soviet Union." *The Huffington Post*. Retrieved October 12, 2018, from https://www.huffingtonpost.com/doug-bandow/lubyanka-runs-the-new-rus_b_6383554.html

3. Gerber, T. P. (2014). "Beyond Putin? Nationalism and Xenophobia in Russian Public Opinion." *The Washington Quarterly*, 37(3), 113–134. https://doi.org/10.1080/0163660X.2014.978439

4. Ostrovsky, A. (2016). *The Invention of Russia: The Rise of Putin and the Age of Fake News*. Penguin; Gehlbach, S., and Sonin, K. (2014). "Government

Control of the Media." *Journal of Public Economics*, 118, 163–171. https://doi.org/10.1016/j.jpubeco.2014.06.004

5. Gudkov, L. (2018, April 27). "Lev Gudkov, 'Levada-tsentr': 'Propaganda chrezvychayno effektivna'." RTVi. Retrieved October 12, 2018, from https://rtvi.com/broadcast/lev-gudkov-levada-tsentr-propaganda-chrezvychayno-effektivna-/

6. Shteyngart, G. (2015, February 18). "Out of My Mouth Comes Unimpeachable Manly Truth." *The New York Times*. Retrieved from https://www.nytimes.com/2015/02/22/magazine/out-of-my-mouth-comes-unimpeachable-manly-truth.html

7. Authors' email correspondence with Gary Shteyngart, 15 October 2018.

8. There is interesting research on media consumption in the United States that shows precisely this effect. For a survey see Prior, M. (2013). "Media and Political Polarization." *Annual Review of Political Science*, 16(1), 101–127. https://doi.org/10.1146/annurev-polisci-100711-135242

9. Robertson, G. (2017). "Political Orientation, Information and Perceptions of Election Fraud: Evidence from Russia." *British Journal of Political Science*, 47(3), 589–608. https://doi.org/10.1017/S0007123415000356

10. Geddes, B., and Zaller, J. (1989). "Sources of Popular Support for Authoritarian Regimes." *American Journal of Political Science*, 33(2), 319–347. https://doi.org/10.2307/2111150

11. Robertson. (2017). "Political Orientation, Information and Perceptions of Election Fraud."

12. Parents can choose to have their children take Orthodoxy, Islam, Judaism or Buddhism, or "Fundamentals of Religious Culture and Secular Ethics."

13. Greene, S., and Robertson, G. (2017). "Agreeable Authoritarians: Personality and Politics in Contemporary Russia." *Comparative Political Studies*, 50(13), 1802–1834. https://doi.org/10.1177/0010414016688005

14. Arendt, H. (1973). *The Origins of Totalitarianism*. Houghton Mifflin Harcourt. 353. Cited in Canovan, M. (1994). *Hannah Arendt: A Reinterpretation of Her Political Thought*. Cambridge University Press. 55.

15. In the interview cited above, Gudkov estimates this group to constitute a mere 3 or 4 percent of the population.

16. https://meduza.io/; https://republic.ru/

17. Naval'nyy, A. (n.d.). "On vam ne Dimon." Retrieved from https://www.youtube.com/watch?v=qrwlk7_GF9g&t=909s

18. See by contrast, *The New Yorker*. (2018). "David Remnick Interviews Masha Gessen about Putin, Russia, and Trump." Retrieved from https://www.youtube.com/watch?v=3J98qByki7o

19. Radio Svoboda. (2018, June 5). "Opros FOM: povyshenie pensionnogo vozrasta odobryayut 9% rossiyan." Retrieved October 12, 2018, from https://www.svoboda.org/a/29272009.html

20. Levada.ru. (2018, September 27). "Chislo zhelayushchikh protestovat' protiv pensionnoy reformy rezko snizilos'." Retrieved October 12, 2018, from https://www.levada.ru/2018/09/27/chislo-zhelayushhih-protestovat-protiv-pensionnoj-reformy-rezko-snizilos/

21. Kuran, T. (1991). "Now Out of Never: The Element of Surprise in the East European Revolution of 1989." *World Politics*, 44(1), 7–48. https://doi.org/10.2307/2010422
22. Beissinger, M. R. (2002). *Nationalist Mobilization and the Collapse of the Soviet State*. Cambridge University Press.
23. Yurchak, A. (2013). *Everything Was Forever, Until It Was No More: The Last Soviet Generation*. Princeton University Press.

INDEX

INDEX